CLASSROOMS
AND
CORRIDORS

CLASSROOMS AND CORRIDORS

The Crisis of Authority in Desegregated Secondary Schools

MARY HAYWOOD METZ

UNIVERSITY OF CALIFORNIA PRESS   *Berkeley · Los Angeles · London*

In memory of my father,
RICHARD MANSFIELD HAYWOOD

University of California Press
Berkeley and Los Angeles, California

University of California Press, Ltd.
London, England

ISBN 0-520-03396-5
Library of Congress Catalog Card Number: 76-55566
Printed in the United States of America

1 2 3 4 5 6 7 8 9

Contents

PREFACE   ix

PART I: PERSPECTIVES

1. THE SCHOOLS OF CANTON   3

The Two Schools
The Canton Community
Research Design

2. ORGANIZATIONAL TENSIONS AND AUTHORITY
IN PUBLIC SCHOOLS   15

Goals
Technology
Structure
Environment
Authority

PART II: CLASSROOMS

3. TEACHERS' DEFINITIONS OF CLASSROOM
RELATIONSHIPS   35

Incorporative and Developmental Education

Proto-Authority and Non-Directive Guidance
Abdication from Teaching
A Typology of Teaching Philosophies
The Limits of Variety in Canton's Teaching
    Philosophies

4. STUDENTS' DEFINITIONS OF CLASSROOM
    RELATIONSHIPS   69

Characteristics of the Tracks
High Track Students' Definitions of
    Classroom Relationships
Low Track Students' Definitions of
    Classroom Relationships
Quiet Students' Definitions of the
    Classroom Situation

5. CLASSROOM INTERACTION: THE TEACHERS
    ADJUST TO THE STUDENTS   91

Students' Challenges
Teachers' Resources for Control
The Effect of Track Level on Teachers'
    Activities
The Matching of Teachers' Styles with
    Distinctive Student Bodies

6. CLASSROOM INTERACTION: PRINCIPLED
    CONFLICT   121

Rejection of the Teacher's Capacity to Play
    the Superordinate Role
Rejection of the Teacher's Definition of
    the Student Role

Rejection of a Teacher's Claim to Serve His
    Proclaimed Educational Goals
Conclusion

PART III: CORRIDORS

7. THE PROBLEM OF ORDER IN THE SCHOOL
    AT LARGE   147

The Difficulty of Maintaining Order in
    the School at Large
Arrangements for Maintaining Order
Two Classic Methods of Obtaining Order
The Effect of Changes in the Canton School
    District
Levels of Disorder in Canton's Schools
The Developmental Approach to Order

8. FACULTY CULTURE AND STUDENT ORDER   168

Differences in Order at Hamilton and
    Chauncey
The Plant and the History of Hamilton
    and Chauncey
Faculty Culture
The Effect of Faculty Culture on
    Student Order
The Effect of Student Order on
    Faculty Culture

9. THE PRINCIPALS' IMPACT ON THE SCHOOLS   188

Chauncey: Mr. Brandt's Administration
Hamilton: Mr. Henley's Administration

An Informative Issue: The Pledge of Allegiance
Overall Staff Treatment of Students at the
    Two Schools

10. DIFFERENCES IN STUDENT CULTURE AT
    CHAUNCEY AND HAMILTON   219

    Student Social Structure
    Student Culture
    The Schools Respond to Crisis
    Conclusion

PART IV: CONCLUSION

11. BEYOND CANTON   243

    The Paradox of the Schools' Mission
    Authority in Education

    APPENDIX: SOURCES OF DATA   255

    Interview Samples and Settings
    Participant Observation

    BIBLIOGRAPHY   263

    INDEX   269

Preface

IN THE UNITED STATES there is much civic discussion of what the public schools ought to be doing, but much less discussion of what they *are* doing. Yet in a society convinced of the value of the scientific method, it does not seem necessary to argue that description should precede prescription. We need to know what the schools do, why they do it, and with what consequences before we prescribe what they should do differently. The primary task of this book is such detailed description of life in the classrooms and corridors of two desegregated urban junior high schools.

The book is based on my field work in the schools (and one other used for a pilot study) over a period of more than a year. I observed classes, studied documents, and interviewed persons ranging from rebellious lower track students to the principals. I accumulated roughly three thousand pages of interview transcripts and over a thousand pages of typed field notes.

The guiding questions throughout the book concern the ways that staff members and students, and the schools as whole organizations, addressed the twin tasks of pursuing education and maintaining civility, safety, and order. The two schools described here are far from typical. At the same time, they provide an unusually informative context for understanding the relationship between the pursuit of education and the pursuit of order, because both ends were especially difficult to achieve.

The schools were recently desegregated and still adjusting to changes in their student populations. They contained children of an age particularly unlikely to be readily cooperative and civil with their teachers or with one another. And they were dominated by working-class black children at a time of rising black consciousness and by upper middle class white children at a time when restlessness among this group was close to its height. Because it was difficult to persuade the children to cooperate with activities designed to further either education or order, the conditions needed for each were unusually visible. The details of life in these schools do not reflect the specific patterns of life in schools with more ordinary children in more ordinary times. But the processes which stood revealed under special circumstances do affect practice in more settled contexts—where they are no less important for being less visible.

I am a sociologist and I therefore address the reality I saw in these schools with a sociologist's questions. I use as tools for analysis theoretical propositions about the functioning of formal organizations in general and a systematic conceptualization of authority. Still, because this book is intended not only for other sociologists but for students and for teachers, administrators, and the parents to whom they must be responsive, I have tried to minimize the use of technical terms and to avoid as much as possible breaking up the story with purely theoretical observations.

Like all authors I have incurred staggering debts in the course of creating this book. I am grateful for much financial support, without which research of this depth and detail would have been simply impossible. The Danforth Foundation supported my living expenses as a Kent Fellow during the field work and the writing of my dissertation, in which the study was first reported. Two small grants given through the University of California from National Science Foundation Cost of Education funds and National Defense Education Act Cost of Education funds helped to defray the cost of typing transcripts of tape recorded interviews.

The writing of the present report of the research was supported by part of a grant from the National Institute of Education, Department of Health, Education, and Welfare—which bears no responsibility for its content.

Several persons have contributed useful criticism at various stages of the research and writing. I am indebted on this score to Martin Trow, Philip Selznick, Todd LaPorte, Michael Otten, Steven Bossert, Robert Ubbelohde, and Maya Anyas. Of course I received the greatest assistance of all from the Canton School District and the many individuals within it who gave generously of their time and of themselves as they helped me to understand the operation of the schools. The district was willing to open its doors to research with a broad focus which probed most aspects of the schools' daily activity. Individuals in the schools not only supported a scientific study but were courteous to an inquisitive stranger in their midst. I wish that I could thank them more directly and individually than the use of pseudonyms allows.

Authors' husbands must endure all the preoccupation and bad temper which authors' wives are frequently thanked for accepting, yet they receive fewer plaudits for their selflessness. My husband, Don, has borne these burdens with grace, humor, and a sense for giving support when and where it was most needed.

As I transformed a dissertation into a book, Marie Phinney's good care for our two preschool sons gave me not just the hours but the peace of mind necessary to work on the project. After a family move, Nancy Torphy capably took over their care while I was taking the manuscript through the last stages of preparation for publication.

Finally, I am grateful to Carolyn Caldie, Joy Hussey, Joyce Jackson, Rosemary Wesler, and Phyllis Wilson who performed the difficult tasks of typing transcripts of interviews and drafts of the manuscript.

Part I: PERSPECTIVES

CHAPTER 1

The Schools of Canton

AMERICANS HAVE unrealistic expectations of public schools. The accomplishments they expect are dazzling in ambition and variety. Public schools should give every child a sound grasp of the three Rs, foster creativity, impart a thorough knowledge of our world history, literature and art, train minds in the scientific method of inquiry, offer vocational training, develop problem-solving ability, foster imagination, develop independence, impart skills of social interaction with adults and peers, and support good moral character. My list is not exhaustive.

Not only are the accomplishments expected of the schools too many, they also require contradictory approaches. In practice real teachers and students in real schools and classrooms must develop priorities among such goals and pursue some with vigor while relegating others to oblivion or pious rhetoric.

The public as well as school staffs emphasizes some dimensions of education over others. And the emphases change through time. It seems that one important factor causing that change is the demographic composition of the schools. Each level of education—elementary, secondary, and finally higher education—has experienced a change in goals with a change in the number and character of its students. Each has dealt initially with a small, relatively homogeneous group of students destined for leading positions within a society which was perceived as stable. Goals have stressed the passing on of an unquestioned tradition and the production of young recruits who would share the elite's values, its traditions, its knowledge and its skills as they took responsible positions in their communities. But with the arrival of large numbers of new students unfamiliar with past traditions, lacking skills and attitudes facilitating traditional education, and expecting quite different future lives, the schools had to change. One way in which they changed was by concentrating upon the individual learner, rather than the body of knowledge, upon the "child" rather than the "subject." The focus on the child helped the teachers, and educators in general, to learn what these new children could and would learn, and to develop some new techniques for getting them to learn it. [1]

In the late nineteenth century the first "progressive" impetus was felt in elementary education. It sprang up independently from many sources. In the time right after World War II, progressive education reached the high schools in guises as various as vocational education and the "life adjustment" movement. And in the 1960s the same emphasis upon the individual and his private learning needs entered importantly into educational debate in higher education. Each of these levels of education at these periods was coping with large increases in student numbers and consequent changes in the kind of student to be educated.

In each historical period these new students throw into question not only the pedagogical methods of a school system but its very assumptions about the nature of young people and the character of education. These issues concern the staff as they pursue their primary task of education. But such new students also disrupt the orderly routines of the school. They are likely to be restless as they pursue learning tasks not designed for them and follow procedures which restrain their activities for uncertain

1. Informative treatments of the relationship between the introduction of a new population of students and debate over pedagogical ends and means are to be found in Lawrence Cremin, *The Transformation of the School,* pp. 58–89, and Martin Trow, "The Second Transformation of American Secondary Education."

benefits. From the point of view of teachers and administrators, just as the educative process is growing more difficult, order also becomes problematic. "Discipline" or school routine and rules may be preoccupying. Changes in routine are likely to accompany pedagogical changes.

In the late sixties a new form of this familiar phenomenon occurred at both the elementary and secondary levels. Universal and nearly universal attendance had already been reached and accepted, so there were no new students in a physical sense. But in a social sense there were. Racial and social consciousness in the whole society, but especially among the poor and non-white groups, changed with great speed. Children from experienced families walked through the schoolhouse door with new expectations, while their parents watched with new eyes. The government, with its anti-poverty funds and concern with de facto segregation, supported those expectations in scattered but concrete ways. At the same time, secondary school students at the other end of the social spectrum were watching and identifying with the rebellion of college and university students. They too brought to the school expectations and demands which had been foreign to their older brothers and sisters.

Many school systems in both the inner city and the suburbs floundered and experimented as they attempted to respond to these new expectations and demands. And there was once more an outpouring of narrative, hortatory, and analytical writing suggesting that educational goals should be partially defined by the students and pedagogical strategy adjusted to the particular requirements of individuals and groups.

In the seventies, as militancy among minorities becomes less volatile and as the children of the affluent become more acquiescent in facing a stagnant economy rather than a controversial foreign war, the students seem less new, less in need of tailormade treatment. The inevitable excesses of any adjustment come to light and the pendulum of educational theory and practice starts to swing from open classrooms and "learner-centered approaches" to tradition, "fundamentals," and good discipline.

At the same time, the gradual spread of court ordered desegregation brings together students who formerly attended separate schools, differently run. Teachers accustomed to working only with children from one kind of social background must now handle widely diverse classes and student bodies. Pedagogical philosophy and strategy and the maintenance of order require fresh approaches once again.

In judging the benefits of each wave of pedagogical insight, we need to know more about factors which modify the translation of educational theory into daily practice and about outcomes that result from different approaches with various kinds of students under specific conditions.

The pages that follow address such questions. They tell in some detail of life in the classrooms and corridors of two desegregated junior high schools. They describe the differing ideas of educational purpose held by teachers and by students and analyze the conflicts and accommodations which occurred as teachers and their classes worked out a common existence inside the confines of a classroom. They explore the conditions affecting order in the corridors and the school at large. They describe the collective perspectives and strategies for both education and order developed by the adults at the two schools, the processes which gave rise to differences in the two staffs' approaches, and the consequences of these choices for the life of the student body and of the school considered as a whole.

THE TWO SCHOOLS

The two schools were endowed with unusually good resources and subjected to unusually great strain. Both were located in "Canton,"[2] a city of over 100,000 which is part of a large metropolitan area and includes a large university. The Canton school district was well financed. Its teachers and administrators were, as a group, academically well prepared and honestly dedicated to the learning of the students.

2. All proper names in this study are pseudonyms.

The student bodies of the schools had been matched so that both schools mirrored the racial and social composition of the whole city. Each school had a large cadre of children from upper middle class, often professional, homes who brought to school developed cognitive skills and active intellectual interests. The poorer children of the city—almost all black—experienced many of the difficulties in school common to children of the urban black ghetto, but their homes and their community were less poverty stricken and socially isolated than those in the core of many large—and small—northern cities.

At both schools educational goals could not be taken for granted. The faculties of each, while dedicated to students' learning, disagreed about the kinds of learning that were important and diverged in their methods for teaching and otherwise interacting with students. The student body of each school was diverse and required a complex response. And a large proportion of the students were challenging the school's values and practices in a radical fashion. The surrounding community and the surrounding society were making demands upon the schools which required contradictory actions.

The year was 1967—68. Protest over the Vietnam War was reaching the crescendo which drove Lyndon Johnson from office. University students across the country, and in Canton's own university, were dramatically expressing their doubt of the wisdom of the leaders of society and of its educational institutions alike. The upper middle class white students identified with the university students, read news magazines, and tested the nearest representatives of the adult world, their teachers, to the limit.

Black self-consciousness was rising across the country and especially so in the larger urban area around Canton which was home to an active, visible, and rising militant black group. Martin Luther King and Robert Kennedy were assassinated. This context intensified explicit and implicit conflict between Canton's black students and the schools.

The schools of Canton in 1967—68 were thus unusual in their social composition and temporal setting. But the strains which made them far from typical nevertheless make them informative cases from which to learn about public secondary schools in general. Because of the fact that they were under strain, processes and latent structures could be relatively clearly seen in their life which would be far less visible in a more smoothly functioning system.

Strain and crisis are particularly revealing of processes of control, and these are a major concern of this study. More generally, the subject of the study is a search for the social structures and processes which shape behavior—often without the full realization of the participants—as adults and children in school translate desires and duties into daily action in their quest for education and a tolerable context in which to pursue it.

Canton's plan for desegregation unintentionally constructed a scientific research design without the constraints of a laboratory. The careful racial and social matching of the student bodies in the junior high schools made it possible to distinguish the effects on students' behavior of the policies and beliefs of their staffs from the effects of students' origins, which were the same in the two settings.

The district also established a policy that every teacher should work with both high and low track classes, and this policy was followed with few exceptions. Consequently, it was possible to see classes of widely different social characteristics, who would formerly have attended separate schools, interacting with a single teacher. One could separate the effects of students' characteristics from those of the teacher's personality.

Because students were tracked in some subjects (English, social studies, mathematics, and foreign language), they were in practice resegregated at both ends of the academic continuum. In an attempt to compensate for this effect, the district established a policy encouraging teachers to move successful children out of lower track classes during the course of the year. As a consequence, the middle track was well integrated, but the bottom tracks were deprived of intellectual leaders and positive exemplars. Thus students remaining in the lower track classes were those most at odds with the school, who can not be taken as representative of the areas from which they came or as typical of the majority of children with their social characteristics. They are rather representative of that portion of children from poor minority backgrounds who are most unable, or unwilling, to cooperate with the schools' agenda. As such, they are an instructive group to study.

THE CANTON COMMUNITY

Canton has some distinctive characteristics which have had a significant impact on its junior high schools. The most important of these are a demographic character and political history which brought a coalition of blacks and professional whites to power in school (and city) affairs at the beginning of the 1960s. The policies of this group led to desegregation of the junior high schools in 1964. The plan turned Lincoln, the junior high school which had been working class and predominantly black, into Darwin, a school to serve all the ninth graders of the city. The other two junior high schools, Chauncey and Hamilton, were turned into seventh—eighth grade schools with their boundary lines drawn to produce student bodies with similar racial and social characteristics. This book is based on a case study of Chauncey and Hamilton in the fourth year of desegregation.

Canton was originally a separate community but is now part of an urban belt with eastern and western boundaries which are nothing but lines on a map. To the north it is separated from "the City" by "the River." To the south it is bounded by rising ground which marks the edge of a scattered suburban ring. The city is well west of the Alleghenies, and its cultural style has none of the tradition of the East or South. In fact the community is self-consciously progressive, open to change. And public education, including the state university, is an acceptable course for children of the elite as well as for others.

In these respects Canton is like many other cities. It is demographically distinctive in three crucial respects. First, it has for a century been home to a university which since World War II has grown in size and in its economic, cultural, and political

importance in city life. With more than a local reputation, the
university has provided a magnet attracting professionals and
other highly educated persons to live in Canton even though they
work in other parts of the urban area.

Second, its black population is in some ways distinctive. In
1940 the black population was four percent. In 1966 it was
twenty-five percent. (The black population in the schools was
forty-one percent.) This growth is common, but the blacks who
were oldtimers were heavily composed of educated and established persons who were long-time residents. This group along
with some newcomers provided a strong locally oriented leadership who had the capacity and tenacity to bring about changes in
the schools and to monitor their implementation. Further, the
non-white population,[3] though employed in only slightly higher
status occupations than the national average for non-whites, had
considerably higher education as a group. They thus had the
background not to be awed by the schools, but perhaps to be
frustrated over the benefits of schooling.[4]

Third, Canton's population is bimodal. It has more than its
share of college graduates and persons in professional or managerial positions, according to the census, but it approximates
the national urban average in its proportion of persons in bottom
educational, economic, and occupational categories. Canton
lacks a significant white working or lower class. It lacks visible
white ethnic enclaves. It consequently has fewer than its share of
persons who fiercely defend the educational status quo at school

3. The non-white population was six percent non-black in 1960, mostly
Oriental. The Oriental group in the city is socially and geographically dis-
persed. Generally better educated and more prosperous than the blacks, the
Orientals mingle more with the whites. Neither the parents nor the children
had a collective impact upon school affairs, where the children were eight
percent of the total school population. Individual children generally made
themselves inconspicuous. While this strategy of invisibility makes the group
interesting for the study of minorities, it meant that the Oriental children had
little impact as a group in the schools. Consequently, they will not be systematically treated as a separate group in the following analysis.

4. Their income was also somewhat higher than the national average for
urban non-whites, but this figure may in part reflect the high incomes of the
state and urban area as a whole. These figures are drawn from the 1960 census.

board meetings and accept the schools' ways in the classroom and corridor.

All three of these factors made desegregation and some pedagogical innovation in Canton possible, if not easy. All three also produced a student body which was dominated by students who challenge the schools rather than accept them.[5]

More will be said of the distinctive character of Canton and its school policies and population as these matters are relevant to various aspects of the case study.

RESEARCH DESIGN

The data for the study of Canton's schools were gathered at all three of its junior high schools. In the spring of 1967 I spent two months at Darwin—the all-ninth grade school—which had been Lincoln, the working and lower class junior high school. This work was a pilot study to which I make only occasional reference in the case materials. I spent the whole of the school year 1967—68 gathering data at Chauncey and Hamilton, the two seventh—eighth grade schools. I concentrated on the eighth grade.

My procedures for gathering data were the same at each of the two schools. I obtained the principal's permission to do the study, then was introduced to the faculty at a regular faculty meeting. (Principals did not sponsor my activities after their initial introduction.) I then followed each of four children through a whole school day. After that, I followed fifteen teachers through a day and interviewed them afterward. I interviewed twenty eighth grade children distributed by sex, track level, and

5. In order to explore the impact upon the findings here of the special political character of the Canton community and of the lack of lower status whites in the schools, I later studied two junior high schools in a small, conservative, industrial and farming center. The school population was less than ten percent black. The different environment created a different overall pattern and the processes discovered in Canton were less visible without the strains on the system existent in Canton. But the study confirmed rather than questioned their importance even though they were less readily evident. (See Mary Haywood Metz, "The Exercise of Control in Two Midwestern Junior High Schools.")

disciplinary record. I interviewed counselors, deans, vice-principals and principals. I also made a systematic census of all the sheets recording the "referral" of an eighth grade child sent out of class to the dean for disciplinary reasons from the opening of school through January 15 at each school. Throughout the study I collected and analyzed bulletins for teachers and students, handbooks, yearbooks, special announcements, etc. Throughout, I attended assemblies, all faculty meetings, and some committee meetings. I engaged in participant observation in the corridors and other public spaces of the school, in the teachers' lounge, and among the adults in the cafeteria.

My purpose in this study is not to survey practices in the Canton schools—to discover the frequency of various patterns—but to identify the character and connections of crucial social variables which shape the life of all public schools. In technical terms, my aims are analytic, not descriptive. I therefore did not attempt to draw random samples of persons, settings, or interactions. Instead I looked for situations and incidents which would be especially telling, particularly for my primary interest in authority and control in general. For these purposes I paid special attention to the actions of both formal and informal leaders and less to the rank and file. And I sought out situations of tension, conflict and crisis, whether trivial or all-encompassing. It is in conflict that the assumptions and sanctions which support smoothly operating control relationships are made visible.

This strategy affected my observation and recording of classes. After I became thoroughly familiar with routine events in various kinds of classes in a given school, I might summarize fifteen minutes of a class in a brief paragraph of field notes, but write a page or more of notes about everything surrounding one thirty second exchange. Parts of my field notes on several incidents and crises in the classroom and in the whole schools are included in the text.

Similarly, I made my interviews open-ended and allowed respondents to expand at length on topics they found crucial, even though I occasionally had to cover other questions hastily. I analyzed interview materials as much for use of language, striking omissions and assumptions, or depth of interest in a given matter as for their manifest information.

Clearly, research such as this, which relies heavily upon diffuse qualitative data and purposive sampling, is open to highly subjective interpretation. I have taken a number of precautions to minimize subjectivity. First, I tried throughout the field work to be aware of my own pedagogical prejudices and personal likes and dislikes and to lean over backwards to see what they would tempt me to deny. More formally, I made a rule not to accept even small conclusions without data from several sources and preferably data of several different varieties. For example, I checked statements made in interviews not only against those in other interviews but against classroom and other observation and against documents. In reporting my conclusions here, I do not use information obtained from just one or even just two or three informants without giving the reader specific warning of the slim data base.

Since I did not draw random samples of either events or persons, I cannot generalize from the frequency of any event or characteristic in my sample to its frequency in the school. I therefore make all my quantitative statements in vague terms which would be inappropriate in a descriptive report. I intentionally use such phrases as "few teachers said this" or "most students did that." I do this with the purpose of reminding the reader that I am not giving precise descriptions of these schools. If I were to report that "three out of fifteen teachers" or "forty-five out of fifty classes" behaved in such and such a way, I would imply that these proportions reflected patterns in the whole school. My sample does not allow me to make such inferences. My quantitative statements are only broad approximations of the situation in these schools.

I make this argument at length because so much research in education is heavily preoccupied with sampling technique and statistical accuracy. These are indeed important for some kinds of questions. But the dearth of systematic yet broad analyses of schools reflects a hesitance to ask important questions where these techniques cannot be applied. The questions should set the methods, not the other way around.

The reader who is concerned with further methodological details will find a description of the methods for choosing samples of teachers and students in the Appendix. It also contains a brief discussion of my strategies as an observer.

CHAPTER 2

Organizational Tensions and Authority in Public Schools

SCHOOLS ARE formal organizations. So are ITT, the local laundromat, prisons, churches, and the Republican Party. One can learn a good deal by analyzing schools' characteristics and conflicts in terms sociologists have developed in the study of other kinds of organizations. These have been but scantily applied in the study of schools.[1]

This chapter introduces the major elements of organizations which sociologists have found to be useful in explaining their form and their activities. It describes the distinctive character of these elements in schools. While I arrived at this formulation as a

---

1. In the mid-sixties an article on the school as an organization in a landmark compilation of theoretical and empirical knowledge about organizations emphasized the scanty body of knowledge to review. (See Charles Bidwell, "The School as a Formal Organization," p. 972.) A decade later, in a book summarizing our knowledge of "educational organizations," Ronald Corwin reviewed a significantly larger corpus of research but one still slim compared with that on a variety of other kinds of organizations. (See Ronald Corwin, *Education in Crisis,* especially Chapter 1.)

product of the study of Canton's schools, for the reader it provides an orientation at the outset. The analysis which follows in the rest of the book uses the theory of formal organizations as the dominant framework for explanation. This relatively focused theoretical approach is used in preference to the eclectic one which is more common in the sociological study of schools for the sake of analytical coherence.

GOALS

Formal organizations exist for the accomplishment of formally stated goals. People enter an organization with an obligation to contribute to those goals; those who fail to do so may be disciplined. Outside groups which support an organization may punish it as an entity for failure to meet its announced goals. Thus production and profit for business, the glorification of God and fostering of Christian community for churches, and the winning of elections and responsible governing of the country for parties are the touchstone by which thousands of daily activities and decisions are—or are supposed to be—measured.

But many, if not most, organizations have goals which upon close inspection are varied or diffuse and difficult to measure. When this happens the different goals or different aspects of a diffuse goal will be in competition for scarce resources. They may contradict one another directly, or means which are most appropriate for reaching one may tend to subvert another.

In one sense there is remarkable clarity about the goals for which public schools are established. Each is created to educate the children of a given geographic area. But as soon as one asks what it means to educate the young, unanimity turns to debate. Educational goals are endless in their variety and subtle in their complexity. Most have a kind of halo which makes them hard to reject outright, even though any two of them may require conflicting attitudes and activities. For example, it is important to have children master a good deal of specific information and to teach children to follow instructions, but it is also important to stimulate their curiosity and teach them to follow out their own lines of questioning. In a given course or a given class these goals will frequently conflict. Consequently, in simply "educating" the children the public schools are usually seeking multiple and pragmatically contradictory ends.

Furthermore, every organization has to seek other goals besides the formal goals which provide its reason for being. If it is to remain an instrument capable of performing its formal goals, it has to insure its own healthy functioning and its own survival in the face of threats from without. It therefore has an array of instrumental goals which are as important as the formal goals to the accomplishment of its official task. These goals attract little notice when they are satisfactorily met, but when their attainment becomes difficult they can absorb more energy than the original purpose of the organization. Arrangements for meeting them can change or subvert the formal goals which an organization actually pursues. The overt or covert sacrifice of an organization's declared purposes for the sake of its survival or smooth functioning has been repeatedly documented in settings as diverse as government agencies, junior colleges, churches, prisons, and mental hospitals.[2]

For schools the most difficult instrumental goal is the maintenance of order among a student body which is only half socialized, comes and remains by legal compulsion, and frequently includes persons with radically different educational and social expectations.

Almost as difficult is the task of maintaining freedom from attack, let alone obtaining support or assistance, from the surrounding community. This community has a license to run the affairs of the schools with fairly close fiscal and policy supervision through local school taxes and elected local school boards. Yet parents and other interested members of the community may have a knowledge of the complexities of pedagogy and the practical necessities of running a school based primarily on

2. For examples in these categories see the following studies: Philip Selznick, *TVA and the Grassroots*; Burton R. Clark, *The Open Door College*; Donald L. Metz, *New Congregations*; Gresham Sykes, *The Society of Captives*; Charles Perrow, "Hospitals, Technology, Structure, and Goals."

memories of their childhood participation in schools. Their educational goals and social outlook may vary enormously as they bring their influence to bear on a single school or set of schools.

In Canton the schools' problem of conflicting goals was clearly visible. The teachers espoused a considerable variety of educational priorities, and many were passionate both in supporting their own and in criticizing others'. The problem of maintaining order among a diverse and skeptical set of students was preoccupying in one form or another for the staff at all the schools. And the community exerted unremitting pressures on the schools.

Schools in general, and in Canton dramatically so, are forced to make choices among their formal goals or to exist with managed or unmanaged conflict. And they must reconcile the requirements of these formal goals with the requirements of maintaining order among the students and support from the community, a task which Part III will suggest often requires sacrifices of the formal goals.

TECHNOLOGY

The study of formal organizations more generally directs us to look for other conflicts in schools. It teaches that the character of the technology, the work process,[3] which an organization uses to accomplish its primary tasks tends to be a fundamental characteristic of the organization to which other characteristics must conform.[4] Whether or not there exists a technological process

3. The goals of an organization can be perceived as end states of a raw material which the organization exists to transform. This raw material need not be inanimate matter changed in physical or chemical ways; it may be a person or even a symbol. Technology is the process which transforms it. Technology in this sense need include no physical hardware. Salesmanship and non-directive psychotherapy are technologies. So is teaching.

4. Recent studies which treat the effect of technology upon organizational structure are: Joan Woodward, *Industrial Organization*; James Thompson, *Organizations in Action*; Charles Perrow, "A Framework for the Comparative Analysis of Organizations"; and Stanley Udy, *Organization of Work*. My treatment here follows Perrow most closely, but it also draws directly upon Udy.

which reliably accomplishes one or another of the organization's goals affects the practical, if not the rhetorical, priorities among those goals.[5]

In the school, the question of technology is of central importance. The raw material of the school's work process, the students, is variable. Differences in cultural background, social position, and individual emotional and cognitive characteristics have an enormous impact on the educational process appropriate to a given child. Yet the process of learning in general, let alone in a given case, is poorly understood.[6]

A considerable range of technological approaches has been and is being used in schools without any incontrovertible demonstration that one is much superior to another, even with a given group of children.[7] It is rarely even claimed that a given approach is reliably appropriate with all students in the way that a chemical manufacturing process may be successful with all properly processed batches of ingredients.

Further, it is almost impossible to know when the school's technology has been successful and when it has not. Teachers

5. For a cogent argument along these lines in the case of the mental hospital see Perrow, "Hospitals, Technology, Structure, and Goals."

6. In a review article, Boocock concludes that we do not know "what the effective teacher is or does." (See Sarane Boocock, "The School as a Social Environment for Learning," p. 44.) Jackson also makes this point in an empirically based discussion of teachers' strategies for inducing learning and for assessing their success in this effort. (See Philip Jackson, *Life in Classrooms,* pp. 159—63.)

7. There are of course many reports of dramatic improvements in given situations with a change of methods, but one has to remain skeptical, wondering about the probability of a "Hawthorne effect." Writers such as Herbert Kohl, Sylvia Ashton-Warner, and A. S. Neill, who report great improvements with their methods, may create their effects less through their actual techniques than through their own belief in the efficacy of the method and their expectation that their children will learn though others expect them to fail. (See Herbert Kohl, *Thirty-Six Children*; Sylvia Ashton-Warner, *Teacher*; and A. S. Neill, *Summerhill.*) Indeed, one of the most effective tools at a teacher's disposal may be an expectation that his pupils will do well, regardless of the reason for his expectation. (See Robert Rosenthal and Lenore Jackson, *Pygmalion in the Classroom.*) Brophy and Good summarize the recent literature stimulated by the controversy over this study on the effects of teachers' expectations on pupils. (See Jere E. Brophy and Thomas L. Good, *Teacher—Student Relationships.*)

have no way of checking on their students' memory of material even a year later, much less when they come to need it in the vicissitudes of adult life. Much learning is intended not as an end in itself but as a basis for developing broad capacities. It is expected that one develops a more logical mind from learning algebra or gains creativity from writing free-form poetry. But how can one assess such capacities reliably, let alone trace their origins? If education is supposed to impart strength of character or richness of personality, the problem of measurement defies description.

Technology, then, is a major problem for the public schools. They are faced with the task of creating changes in diverse raw material through processes which are poorly understood, in the absence of any universally effective means, and without any trustworthy way of measuring the success or failure of whatever methods they finally apply. These technological problems combine with the vague and conflicting goals of education to create a perfect setting for endless controversy. People can disagree forever about the accomplishment of vaguely stated purposes through inadequate means which create results that cannot be satisfactorily measured.[8]

The character of the school's technology thus compounds the tendency to conflict over diverse educational goals. It also makes it easy for a school to sacrifice elusive instructional goals to pressing ones for the maintenance of order. This is especially the case in those schools where students are hard to teach and given to resistance to adults and interference with one another. Thus the weakness of the school's technology makes educational goals most vulnerable where they are most needed.[9]

---

8. Or they may become ritualistic, asking no questions about the benefits of their daily efforts but mechanically following local practice and then disclaiming responsibility for the results. For a detailed description of the bases of this adjustment see Gertrude H. McPherson, *Small Town Teacher*.

9. Compulsory education, requiring all students to attend school and the public school to accept all comers, compounds the technological problems of the school by recruiting diverse and partially resistant raw material. At the same time—as Carlson points out—compulsory education ensures the public school at least minimal public support whether or not it is as effective or

In Canton disagreements about teaching goals were often intertwined with disagreements about technological effectiveness. Everyone wanted the children "to learn." But teachers' (and students') differing beliefs about the relative importance of different kinds of learning were inextricably mixed with their ideas about the nature and progression of the learning process.[10] And since it was very difficult to measure learning under different systems which were also different in their goals, the arguments had no solid external reference point. In such a situation, conflict cannot be objectively resolved and tensions can mount very high indeed, as they did at one of the schools.

STRUCTURE

Technology shapes an organization not only in its interaction with multiple goals but in its impact on social structure. If the major technological processes of an organization are well understood and routine so that they can be broken into small standardized operations, the organization can be centralized and hierarchical with decisions made at the top and carried out by a large work force of persons with little skill. But when, as in the case of the school, the technology is not well understood and the variable character of the material prevents standardized operations, then the organization is most appropriately decentralized and "flat." The persons who perform the actual work of the organization need to be given relatively large and diffuse tasks with the right to make important decisions independently as they use their intuition to adjust their methods to the requirements of each specific instance.[11]

---

efficient as it could potentially be. (See Richard O. Carlson, "Environmental Constraints and Organizational Consequences.")

10. Lortie describes in detail the way that the technological conditions of teaching, along with the structure of the school and the reward system for teachers, interact with processes of recruitment and training of teachers to create prevalent occupational attitudes and behaviors. (See Dan C. Lortie, *Schoolteacher*.)

11. Stanley Udy, "The Comparative Analysis of Organizations," pp. 690–691.

The spatial and temporal structure of the average American public secondary school is in many ways constructed for the pursuit of a non-routine technology. A single teacher works alone with a group of children for a whole school year. He works out of the sight and hearing of other adults and needs to co-ordinate his efforts with those of other teachers only in minimal ways. Each teacher has a comprehensive task in teaching the whole of a given subject to a constant group of children for a year and he is free to use his intuition and his personality as he goes about it.

In some school systems this isolation is accompanied by a larger autonomy. Teachers are given significant prerogatives in deciding both the content and the style of their teaching without fundamental questioning from colleagues or administrators. Such a situation can also alleviate strains arising from the school's multiple goals. Differences within a faculty need not be carried to the point of open debate leading to victory or defeat, but rather each teacher quietly follows his own ideas in his own classroom.

A model like this is followed—roughly at least—at the university level. But anyone familiar with a range of public schools knows that it is not typical. Teachers' autonomy is limited. In some districts, it is almost non-existent, as standardized curriculum guides prescribe not only the content but much of the method for each class. Two-way intercoms or directives to leave doors open may vitiate the physical isolation of the classroom, as they allow intrusions without warning. There may even be exact rules for teachers' treatment of a large range of classroom situations. These measures are extremes, but their existence underscores the fact that teachers' autonomy is a variable and not a constant factor in public schools. Constraints upon teachers' autonomy reflect fundamental organizational pressures which work upon school structure in direct contradiction to the pressures of the technological requirements of teaching.

ENVIRONMENT

The most important of these pressures come from the students' attacks upon order and from the unfriendly intrusion of parents or community into the school's daily activities. Comparative studies of organizations have found that they cope most easily with environments likely to attack their practices if their structure is centralized and hierarchical and their technological procedures routinized and unambiguous.[12] This strategy is dramatically clear in the response of organizations with subordinates most prone to disorder: prisons.[13] Thus, the most pressing instrumental goals of the school, those of coping with a hostile environment of students or of parents (or other influential community members), suggest a social structure and a technological style diametrically opposed to that most suitable for furthering educational goals.

Typical public school structure reflects these contradictory pressures. The physical, temporal, and social separation of each class with the teacher is contradicted by the formal social structure of the school. Most are formally hierarchical bureaucracies, with the teachers directly responsible to a principal who is in turn responsible and accountable to superiors in the school district administration. The structure of the school is thus ambivalent.[14]

Districts vary in the way that practice shapes the actual operation of the organization. The teachers' independence with their classes may be both proclaimed and generally practiced, or the chain of command may be firmly emphasized. These variations will in each case be the result of a multitude of pressures

12. Ibid.

13. For a discussion of relevant organizational processes and conflicts, see for example: Donald Cressey, "Prison Organizations"; Richard McCleery, *Policy Change in Prison Management*; and Sykes, *Society of Captives*. Erving Goffman documents similar processes in a variety of "total institutions" which process large "batches" of people, prone to resist the desires of the organization. Such institutions vary from public mental hospitals to conscript armies. See his *Asylums*, especially Part I.

14. Most of the available analysis of schools which calls systematically upon the study of organizations deals with contradictions between schools' bureaucratic structures and teachers' need for autonomy in dealing with their technological problems. See James Anderson, *Bureaucracy in Education* for an extended discussion of these problems along with a review of the relevant educational and organizational literature. The book also reports a study of the effects of differential use of bureaucratic rules upon the staffs of ten junior high schools.

coming from dominant conceptions of educational goals, from the technological requirements of teaching given kinds of students, and from pressures in the environment.[15] Still, each particular pattern constitutes a way of coping with a set of contradictory organizational imperatives, not a way of exorcising them. The potentiality for strain can be expected to remain, even though compromises blunt the effects of inherent tensions.

The severity of the conflict will vary considerably from district to district depending on the character of the students and community and the strategy of the school. Some student bodies offer only relatively mild problems of disorder, others severe ones. Parents vary in their interest in the schools and in their predisposition to be aggressive or cooperative in addressing what they perceive to be problems. School staffs vary in the diversity and the kind of educational goals which they seriously pursue. Some goals require more technological flexibility than others. Some student bodies respond to standardized techniques while others require the teachers to experiment and explore to the maximum as they go about the pedagogical process.

These differences in student body, community and staffs will appear in a plethora of particular constellations which will affect the daily life of the schools as total configurations. To say that it is necessary to look at the interplay of educational goals, technology, structure, and environmental pressures in order to understand events in the schools is thus to make only the barest beginning toward an analysis of any one school.

In Canton the contradictory pressures described here were especially severe. Both the lower class black children and the affluent white children resisted cooperation with the schools' routines. Order was chronically problematic. Furthermore, the black parents and the professional white parents watched the schools closely to maintain their children's rights and integrity in

15. The expectations, or demands, of staff members for one kind of structure over another are an important element in this equation as will be evident in Part III. Formally, personal preferences of particular staff members as whole persons—rather than as role players—are conceptualized as part of the organization's environment by students of organizations.

the face of school discipline. Both were ready to mount a vigorous attack on any practices they considered inappropriate. These pressures encouraged the schools to use protective measures and structures.

At the same time, both sets of parents insisted that the schools pursue effective academic education with their fullest energies. They monitored the schools' performance in this context as best they could. The character of the children at both ends of the academic scale was such as to present a technological challenge in accomplishing such education. To succeed the teachers often needed imaginative, unconventional, and flexible methods. These pressures encouraged the schools to allow teachers and students freedom to work out their methods together in a variety of ways. Flexible structures were required.

Canton's schools thus needed opposed methods and structures in pursuing instrumental and formal goals where both were especially difficult to achieve. They suffered from strain as a consequence.

At the level of formal policy, the school board and district administration stressed educational goals before all else. Following the expectations of the parents and the temper of the times, they encouraged varied and flexible technological approaches and established a decentralized structure which gave principals and classroom teachers a very large measure of autonomy in choosing their means and ends within the context of general policy. They therefore made a set of consistent choices for one set of goals and supporting organizational arrangements.

However, when problems of order or parental attacks did occur, the board and the district staff expected the staffs of the schools to be expeditious in dealing with them. The tensions arising from the contradictions the district faced thus were passed on to the individual schools. It was there that they were felt in strains upon daily activity and acted out in a variety of conflicts. Part III, Corridors, is primarily concerned with the contrasting ways in which these organizational problems were experienced and handled at Chauncey and at Hamilton.

At both schools, district policy granting the teacher curricular flexibility and autonomy in the conduct of the class made the classroom a unit with significant independence from the wider school. Part II, Classrooms, deals with the adjustments of teachers and students within the classroom, taking both schools together. To understand the interaction of teachers and students as they went about defining their common purpose and procedures in the classroom, it is necessary to understand one more element of organizational life.

AUTHORITY

In a formal organization authority provides the major means for carrying goals, technology, and structure from ideals into action. Especially in the classroom context, it is in closely studying relationships of authority that we will see the tensions of the school expressed in daily action. Principals and teachers fulfill their goals by directing others to participate in activities designed to accomplish them. Since principals and teachers have the formal responsibility for carrying out the school's goals and the right to see that others do their part, they possess authority.

Authority is distinguished from other relationships of command and obedience by the superordinate's *right* to command and the subordinate's *duty* to obey. This right and duty stem from the crucial fact that the interacting persons share a relationship which exists for the service of a *moral order to which both owe allegiance.* This moral order may be as diffuse as the way of life of a traditional society or as specific as the pragmatic goals of a manufacturing organization. But in any case, all participants have a duty to help realize the moral order through their actions. This duty may arise from emotional or moral attachment to the order itself, but may be as unsentimental as the manual worker's obligation to give a fair day's work in exchange for a fair day's pay.[16]

16. There is no acknowledgment of moral responsibility at all from subordinates in many organizations. Inmates in prisons are the most extreme examples. Many students in public schools also do not make such an acknowledgement of duty to educational ends. But it is my argument that failing such attachment, a genuine relationship of authority does not exist. See Chapters Three and Four for a fuller discussion of this issue.

Authority exists to further the moral order. It exists because a person in a given position is more able than others to perceive the kinds of actions which will serve the interests of the moral order. On the basis of this capacity he has the right to issue commands which others have the duty to obey. For the sake of generality it is helpful to call persons who give commands superordinates and those who receive them subordinates. The same individual may be simultaneously a superordinate and a subordinate as he acts out different aspects of a single role. Teachers are superordinates in interacting with students but subordinates in interacting with their principal.

Authority is a formal and continuing relationship, an institutionalized one. Strictly speaking it is a relationship of roles, not of persons. The superordinate's right to command rests both upon his occupancy of a role and his presumed ability to translate the needs of the moral order into specific activities which will support it. This ability may stem from several kinds of sources, ranging from the mystic endowments which let a Pope speak infallibly ex cathedra to the pragmatic knowledge of an executive who receives reports from several divisions of a company. The subordinate's duty to obey the superordinate rests upon the superordinate's claim to be acting for the moral order. If this claim is valid, then obedience to the superordinate is obedience to the needs of the moral order.

These characteristics of authority can be summarized in a formal definition. *Authority is the right of a person in a specified role to give commands to which a person in another specified role has a duty to render obedience. This right and duty rest upon the superordinate's recognized status as the legitimate representative of a moral order to which both superordinate and subordinate owe allegiance.*

Authority can thus be graphically represented by a triangle as in Figure 1. This model makes it clear that in every instance of authority one must consider not only the roles of superordinate and subordinate and their relationship but also the moral order and the relationship of both superordinate and subordinate to it. Any one of these elements or relationships affects the shape of every other.

Despite the crucial importance of the moral order as the basis

FIGURE 1
The Elements of Authority

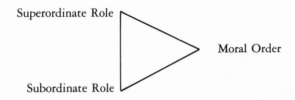

Superordinate Role

Moral Order

Subordinate Role

of the relationship of superordinate and subordinate, they may not make reference to it in most of their transactions. Under ordinary circumstances, the subordinate *trusts* the superordinate's competence and good faith in the service of the moral order sufficiently to assume that the superordinate's specific commands further its requirements. The fact that the superordinate has given the command is sufficient guaranty of its validity. The act of obedience discharges the subordinate's obligation to the moral order.

In the give-and-take of daily contact, then, the position of the superordinate comes to be the immediate source of his right to command. And indeed the man in the street, even the semi-professional subordinate,[17] commonly comes to identify authority with the person of the superordinate. So long as events go along smoothly this model suffices. But when trouble arises, when the superordinate has to make unconventional or heavy demands, or when the subordinate grows restive, then both will tend to call upon the moral order directly to sustain—or object to—a command.

Social scientists have also concentrated upon the role of the superordinate in their investigations of variations in authority

17. For example, Robert Peabody asked employees in a police department, a social work agency, and an elementary school for a definition of authority. At least one-fourth of each group responded by naming their superior. And a majority of those giving other defining qualities responded in some variation of the general phraseology, "authority is a person who. . . ." However, supervisors were less likely than subordinates to define authority in personal terms. (See Robert Peabody, *Organizational Authority*, pp. 87–90.)

and the complexities which attend its practice. But also relevant are other questions asked less often by either social scientists or laymen. These revolve around the role of the subordinate, and around *his understanding* of his relationship with his superordinate and of his relationship with the moral order, and indeed around his understanding of the very nature of the moral order.[18]

These questions are less often addressed in considerations of authority, because the answers to them are frequently taken for granted. Much of the time authority works because subordinates never seriously analyze the character of their own role or its relationship to any of the other elements of authority. They accept the definitions of these matters supplied to them by superordinates. They usually do this because they are subordinates as a result of ascriptive positions which they have always held. They are of a race, social class, sex, or age which has traditionally held subordinate status and accepted commands from above in participating in the society's institutions. Alternatively, and often at the same time, they do not question these matters because they have no significant stake in most of them. In organizations, people who work at routine jobs are generally not very interested in their contribution to the organization's overall goals—so long as the company can meet its payroll.

Schools deal with the young, whose experience has traditionally been designed to re-enforce their assumption that they should trust all their elders by virtue of a difference in age.

18. The analysis of authority I am using here combines the approaches of Max Weber and Chester I. Barnard. Weber's classic analysis and his three types of authority—charismatic, traditional, and rational legal—stress the moral order, the role of the superordinate, and the relationship between these two. Weber gives relatively minor attention to the role of the subordinate and its relationship to the other elements of authority. (See Max Weber, *From Max Weber,* pp. 96–252.) Barnard, on the other hand, defines authority as the acceptance of a command by the subordinate. He argues that a subordinate gives such acceptance if the command is in accordance with the needs of a shared moral order as *the subordinate understands* those needs. (See Chester I. Barnard, *The Functions of the Executive,* pp. 163–74.) In the context of the school, where compliance depends heavily on students' intrinsic rewards, Barnard's insights are especially relevant. For a fuller discussion of the derivation and details of the model of authority used here see Mary Haywood Metz, "Authority in the Junior High School," Chapter One.

Children belong to an ascriptively subordinate group. However, the assumption of elders' wisdom and good will was radically undermined during the sixties for large numbers of upper middle class children. Poor black children, often already skeptical of these qualities in the school staff, became much more openly challenging. While many of the children of all the races attending Chauncey and Hamilton still accepted adults' trustworthiness, a large minority did not. They were therefore primed to ask pointed questions about justifications for commands given to them in relationships of authority.

One can in any case generally expect more close scrutiny of the moral order and its relationship to specific commands from subordinates in schools than in many other kinds of organizations. Diffuse goals and a non-routine technology require subordinates independently to understand and apply the principles inherent in a moral order. The more a school emphasizes these qualities in its goals and technology, the more subordinates will routinely make independent reference to the school's moral order.

Further, the distinctive, though not unique, place of students in schools encourages them to be independently attached to a moral order. First, students are themselves the material to be transformed. Even more than professional workers, they have every reason to feel intimately interested in both the overall character of the organization's product and the processes used to transform it.[19]

Secondly, students receive no pay for compliant participation. Other extrinsic rewards are meager. A high school diploma is valuable for almost anyone. But this is a distant and abstract reward for an eighth grader, and one he is likely to think will be his whether he is cooperative or not. Ambitious students for whom good grades and a good record will be useful in gaining access to higher education and other selective postsecondary

19. Indeed the best analogy for students in schools is in many respects not that of other organizational subordinates but that of clients interacting with free professionals. However, this relationship is altered by the necessity to regulate their activities for the sake of organizational routine as well as education. For an exploration in detail of the differences between professional—client relations and those of students and schools see Charles Bidwell, "Students and Schools."

options receive some extrinsic rewards for cooperation. But these too are relatively abstract. And if high grades are to have meaning for some students, others must receive low grades.[20] There will necessarily be a large number of students who do not expect much return for their work. Thus since students receive little extrinsic reward for their cooperation, the intrinsic rewards must be heightened proportionately if they are to have reason to be voluntarily cooperative with the school's program.

The school's task is infinitely complicated in this context by the existence of compulsory attendance. Students must go to school whether they want to or not, by compulsion of law. In most cases they must go to a particular school and even sit in the class of a particular teacher without any possibility of choice in the matter.

In such a context, students who reflect upon their situation are likely to move in one of two opposite directions. They may become intensely involved in the intrinsic character of their education, taking it for its own reward and thus caring about its nature. Or they may become thoroughly alienated from a context which compels participation but offers neither extrinsic nor intrinsic rewards which are of value to them.[21]

In Canton a sizable group went to each extreme. The most able students from professional families were not under pressure to obtain outstanding grades because most would enter the highly respected state university rather than more selective private colleges. They looked to the intrinsic character of their education for reward. The least able or least conforming of the black students found the school to offer neither intrinsic rewards nor practical assistance. They withdrew from commitment to its moral order.

In this perspective, it is not surprising that the staffs of many schools try to prevent their students from reflecting upon their situation. They try instead to present them with a consistent

20. Dreeben analyzes the process by which teachers in the elementary grades teach children to value grades as inherent rewards. (See Robert Dreeben, *On What is Learned in School,* pp. 37−39.)

21. For a somewhat different perspective on the same set of problems see William Spady, "The Authority System of the School and Student Unrest."

pattern of expectations which is so widely taken for granted that students do not think to ask what rewards they are receiving. But in such schools the potential for the kinds of questioning of authority which occurred in Canton is still always present.

Part II analyzes the ways in which Canton's teachers and students defined their relationships of authority in the intimate context of the classroom—along with the practical adjustments they made to one another. Part III returns to the contradictory imperatives of goals, technology, and environment as these affected the way each school functioned as a unit.

Part II: CLASSROOMS

CHAPTER 3

Teachers' Definitions of Classroom Relationships

CANTON'S TEACHERS entered their classrooms with diverse ideas of the educational goals they should pursue there. These goals, which constitute the moral order justifying their relationship of authority with students, were associated with diverse ideas of the appropriate roles which both students and teachers should play in a classroom. Teachers' ideas about these matters formed more or less coherent patterns, so that it is possible to identify several types of approach to the educational task and to classroom relationships which portray the variety evident in Canton.

The positions to be discussed are ideal types, which catch the essence of a group of teachers' understandings even though individuals held the positions with special variations. These types are used here as an analytical device to give sharp focus to the discussion. However, when teachers in a school become self-conscious about their differences they tend to formulate more systematic philosophies than their practice might suggest and to do battle with more clear-cut and consistent opposing philosophies than their flesh-and-blood opponents actually hold. The idealized philosophical positions given here are therefore in significant part ones constructed by the articulate combatants in educational debates at the schools, especially Hamilton.

The majority of Canton's teachers espoused one of two positions, which I shall call incorporative and developmental. These positions, which provided the context for most common thought and debate at Chauncey and Hamilton, are treated at length in the first part of the chapter. The remaining, more extremely "authoritarian" and "permissive," positions which may be more common in other systems than in Canton are treated in the last part of the chapter.

INCORPORATIVE AND DEVELOPMENTAL EDUCATION

Academic Goals

Teachers taking the two majority positions believed that students either do or can share in the educational goals of a school and a classroom. They thus saw teaching as based upon a genuine relationship of authority. But they differed sharply over the kinds of goals which teachers should try to pursue with the children. A teacher at Hamilton who had served on two committees trying to mediate the open dispute among the faculty at that school over this issue summarized the two opposed formulations of goals in the following way:

> The conservative traditional viewpoint . . . presupposes the fact that there is a body of knowledge and this body of knowledge must be funneled into a student in the course of a school year. And that the teacher has not been successful if this body of knowledge, part of this body of knowledge, has been left out. Because therefore of course he [the student] will not be able to succeed at the next grade level without this complete body of knowledge.
>
> There are others of us—and I include myself in the second category—who feel that this body of knowledge has no meaning if you don't reach the person that it's designed to enlighten. I have said

before, and I'll say again and I think I'll always say, that I teach children. I teach them many different things. I do not specifically teach them my subject matter, which is English. I do not feel that I have a body of knowledge to give anybody. Instead I would like to give to students a curiosity about life, a curiosity about people, an appreciation of different kinds of writing, and an appreciation of their own kinds of writing.

And I personally feel that if a class is upset about something, that it's almost impossible for me to have them swallow anything [else]. . . . So I have made the decision that if I see something that my students want to talk about, we will talk about it. I will leave them with the decision.

Many times I can suggest to them many titles of books that are pertinent to what they are talking about. In which case they would be a lot more interested in reading that maybe, or discussing that, and I can bring that in.

The reader familiar with the educational debates of the thirties will notice the contrast between "teaching subjects" and "teaching children" which is brought up here. The teacher in this quotation expresses some of the ideas behind those catch phrases. She describes one group as conceiving of the knowledge to be taught as having a definite existence of its own. It is a tangible "body" of knowledge which must be "funneled into" the students. Interaction of the knowledge and the student in this process is not mentioned; the student simply incorporates the well-defined entity just as one's library shelf might receive a new book which is then "part" of the library. So this knowledge is now assumed to be part of the child, and he is ready for the next connected bit of knowledge in the next grade. This approach will be referred to as "incorporative."

The teacher here contrasts this approach with one in which the children are active rather than essentially passive agents. They learn certain attitudes and highly generalized skills and the learning goes with the grain of their interests rather than ignores it. In this approach the aim is to develop the child as a whole, to change his attitudes, interests, and skills in a way considered maturing but which works always from his current attitudes, interests, and skills as a point of departure. This approach will be referred to as "developmental."

This definition of the two approaches is made in terms used by a teacher clearly favoring the developmental one. Teachers favoring the incorporative one saw their own approach as that of passing on "basic skills" and a heritage of culture, history, and useful information to a new generation. School children necessarily had to be taught not only skills and information but also the values and attitudes which support the significance of these items of learning. To these teachers the developmental approach was pandering to childish whims and watering down a curriculum for whose contents the students would later have serious need.

Because the incorporative teachers saw themselves as standing squarely in a time-honored tradition, they did not elaborate upon their position at great length. Since they would not grant the educational seriousness of the challenging developmental teachers—who seemed merely to represent the absence of their own standards and content—they did not analyze the opposing position at any length either. Consequently, most of the comparison of the two positions by teachers comes from the developmental teachers, who in situations of conflict tend to caricature their opponents. This difference makes it hard to write a description of the two positions which does justice to the value of each.

The developmental teachers are also at an advantage because they are concerned with working with what might be; they stress the better moments of the children and emphasize their potential as it is occasionally revealed in their best actions. They try as much as possible to soften the limits imposed by the physical and social structure of the traditional school and classroom, and they speak longingly of innovations in everything from scheduling to architecture which would facilitate their efforts. The incorporative teachers, on the other hand, usually take the present situation as given and for practical purposes immutable. They teach in the present system with the children as they presently act. Thus the developmental teachers express a note of imagination, exploration, and faith in human nature which is appealing.

The incorporative teachers display an attachment to routine, combined with anger, resignation, or despair toward some categories of the children, which spreads a negative tone over their ideas. Because the changes and student potentialities of which the developmental teachers speak are relatively untested, they have an undue advantage in discussing their beliefs.

But there is one way in which the developmental teachers can be called the realists and the incorporative ones the idealists. The developmental teachers sometimes point out that the aims of the incorporative teachers are valid in themselves (if not bought at too high a cost) but that because of the total orientation of which they are a part, incorporative teachers do not in fact succeed in accomplishing their aims. In Canton the developmental teachers cited as evidence for the failure of the incorporative approach in practice the poor academic performance of a large proportion of the black students who had been exposed to it throughout elementary school. They also cited the frequent non-cooperation of some of the ablest white children also exposed to this approach throughout previous grades. The developmental approach allows the teacher to experiment until the child actually begins to learn and then to build more ambitious goals from there.

The developmental teachers think the incorporative ones unrealistic to keep on with the same goals and the same methods while the children fail to respond. The incorporative teachers think the developmental teachers unrealistic to expect children who do not learn well with incorporative aims and methods to learn any better with any other aims and methods—even though they might enjoy something else more.

Given the difficulty of measuring learning, especially in any but an incorporative mode, it is hard to settle this debate with empirical evidence. It is not the task of this work to judge the relative merits of the two approaches in the absence of such evidence. The reader is warned that his reading of the following descriptions will be colored by whichever set of assumptions about the way children learn best he happens to share.

It is undoubtedly the case that the learning which results from the developmental approach is considerably less systematic than that resulting from the incorporative approach. The content of what is finally learned will also differ. A social studies teacher who had come to the developmental approach through a gradual pragmatic process describes how she differs from the teachers in her department who take an incorporative approach:

> One of the things I see us as differing on is that . . . I hope they learn subject matter—but I put the child before the subject matter. He is more important than the subject I'm teaching him.
>
> And it's a very valid thing to have a discussion in class about Huey Newton or Black Panthers. Or civil rights. Or something that came in the paper. It's valid, if for no other reason than that this is a social science class. And these are things that are concerned with social sciences. One of the objectives to me in teaching social science is that the kid learns about his society, and he learns about himself. . . .
>
> On the other hand, I think many of the other teachers would put more emphasis on subject matter. We *must* cover the book. We *must* be on a certain chapter at a certain time, a certain page. The kids must have mastered so much factual data. Which to me is not very important. That is minute factual data, like a President has to be thirty-five years old. I don't think that's too important at all.

Nonetheless, the developmental teachers were as a group intensely interested in the students' academic progress. Some of them came to the developmental position precisely because they despaired of academic progress, especially at the lower academic levels, with any other approach. Further, despite the importance of students' interests to the developmental teachers, it was still the teacher who had the primary part in structuring each month's and each day's learning. Part of their plans included the use of class time to stimulate the students' interest in the curricular material.

According to the developmental approach, if students are not interested in material they will not learn it in any sense worthy of the name, though they might memorize some of it. Therefore, if one wants the students to learn one must either: (1) follow their interests and try to extend them toward what the teacher knows and the children do not yet, (2) use existing interests to excite curiosity about something else, or (3) create interest in something new or not previously valued even though it does not intersect with students' prior concerns.

The developmental teachers already quoted describe the first method. A teacher who had done considerable substituting at Hamilton before being given a class of his own for the remainder of the year describes the second method:

> In my experience the new [i.e., developmental] teachers are stricter with the kids and push harder for concrete knowledge. But they do it differently; they do it through the kids. You know the standard division, what's more important the kid or the material; they would tend to focus on the kid.
>
> Emma Yoland, when she started to get the kids to read *Don Quixote,* instead of passing the books out, will play a recording of *Man of La Mancha* that the kids like, follow this up with a brief introduction to the play *Man of La Mancha,* and then give them *Don Quixote,* which they will all then read. I think she's pushing academic subjects and academic excellence much harder than a person who would pass the book out and say, "Now do a book report."

The same teacher uses the third method in teaching his own classes in mathematics, since the majority of students enter with little pre-existent interest that is relevant. He was asked how he started the year:

> I set up an axiom system which makes *no* sense and ask them to work with it. And I do this over and over again. And they really, in a short period of time, are able to think about things without relying on their past experience. They answer a question to answer a question.
>
> One day in one of the classes I started by saying, okay, take a red ball and a yellow ball and you put them together and you get nothing at all. And whatever this means—it doesn't have any meaning—but we have to use it. And now what happens when you do?
>
> One of the things you do is ask questions that they cannot answer and that you won't answer. And you continuously ask questions and you build up a tremendous tension in the class; everyone's really high. And you help them to find the answer. When the answer comes from them, it's such a relief that they've really got it. Everyone was really listening.

Behavioral Goals

If academic learning is to occur, students must either already have or else be taught a minimal attachment to acceptable social behavior. They must learn to be reasonably still and quiet, to wait their turn, to be at least somewhat polite to one another and the teacher, and so on. If the children do not learn these basic elements of courtesy and social responsibility, the result will be disorder in the classroom sufficient seriously to interfere with academic education. But these behaviors can also be considered important learning in themselves under the rubric of character education, which is then seen as a complement to academic education.

Character education and the maintenance of order are easily confounded. Many of the same rules and procedures, and many of the same admonitions and discussions, can be seen as leading to either goal. It is always difficult, therefore, to tell how much a teacher is interested in character education for the sake of the students' development and how much simply in maintaining order. The rhetoric of the first seems often to be used in the service of the second.

The differences between incorporative and developmental teachers in the matter of character education were similar to those in academic education, but rather clearer and sharper. While both groups agreed on the necessity of decorum and consideration for others, there was wider variation in what was to be learned than in the academic context. The incorporative teachers generally argued that school and classroom rules are educationally valuable because they inculcate specific items of proper behavior to which the children should become accustomed. Thus one teacher explained her belief that schoolwide rules were important as an educational device in the following way:

> Well, I think children do have to learn to follow rules and regula-
> tions because when they get out in the world and hold a job they'll
> have certain rules and procedures. Like most jobs you have to be on
> time; you have to be at a certain place at a certain time. You can't be
> cutting or loafing. You certainly have to know the procedures for

handling your absences, who do you call, what do you do, and so forth.

Knowing how to behave, certainly, in the halls is necessary if they're going to be involved in other institutions, the theaters, various other places out in the community. And I think that knowing proper behavior is important, and I'm not too sure they always learn it at home. I think this is part of their education.

The developmental teachers stress that children must learn to behave responsibly, whatever that may mean in a given situation. Specific rules are less important than understanding the requirements of the situation and exhibiting sensitivity to the feelings and practical needs of others within it. One teacher, asked if she tended more to general guidelines for classroom behavior which were open to interpretation or to definite rules which were consistently enforced, replied:

No, I don't set up definite rules. Generally I'd tell them, "I expect you to act with common sense and in good taste." And I leave the interpretation of that up to them. And they know, in no uncertain terms, when they've overstepped the bounds as far as I'm concerned. Because it's usually not only as far as I'm concerned, but also as far as the rest of the class is concerned. And I usually find that if I can hold my tongue long enough, the students in the class will say to the offender what I was going to say. And I find that it's a much more effective thing when they kind of discipline themselves than when it comes from me.

So I tend not to be specific. This is getting back to my philosophy of having them be responsible for their own actions. This is the way I would like to see society in general. I do not like to see a lot of rules. I like to see people grow up by not having to obey certain things [so much] as to do them because they feel it's the best thing to do. They're considerate of other human beings so they'll act in this way rather than this way.

The contrast can perhaps be seen more concretely by comparing discussions by two math teachers of the way they establish rules. First, an incorporative one:

I: How do you start off the year with a class to kind of set the tone and get them going?

R: [She sets out the academic requirements and] . . . Then I lay down certain rules like you have to be in your seat when the bell rings. You can't be standing up, you can't be out in the hall, you can't be running for your seat as the bell rings. You have to be *in* your seat when the bell rings. And if not, you're going to be marked tardy, and you'll come to me for detention. And if you don't show up for my detention, you'll be referred to the dean, and you'll stay forty minutes for the dean rather than just a couple of minutes for me. And I will say that the kids do a pretty good job on getting in their seats right away. . . .

I: With discipline or classroom behavior, do you lean more toward setting up general guidelines for behavior and then interpreting them according to the individual and the situation or do you lean more toward setting up definite rules for behavior and then trying to enforce them consistently?

R: Ah, there are a set of definite rules like tardy rules. And when they're taking a test they can't talk. They know that they have to have their homework with them in class, that late homework is not acceptable. They know that tests must be made up or it goes down as F. Oh yes, with homework, if they don't do their homework it goes down as a zero; they know that I forgive three zeroes a marking period. On the fourth zero, I'll knock down their report card grade. And they know that their report card grade is based on test grades with some consideration for homework, just a little consideration for homework. Those things are just strict and definite.

Then I would say everything else is sort of guidelines which I will interpret. Whether an offense is serious enough to go to the dean. I do allow a certain amount of freedom. They know they can't—well they can't swear, and they can't call me names (laughs) or they can't—you know—I mean way out things are going to get them to the dean. Or they can't make it so impossible that I can't teach the class. Once it reaches a level where I *really* feel that child is hindering the class, then he goes to the dean. He knows that. But exactly where that point is, that's left to my discretion. And they sort of understand that. They just understand that when I no longer can teach the class because of an individual, I'm going to remove that individual.

Or if a child disobeys me. If I ask him to do something and he flatly refuses. I had one girl who had a note passed to her, and I said put it on the desk. Which all is standard procedure; if I catch them passing notes they put it on the desk, they lose the note. Well, she refused to put the note on the desk. Well, a *refusal* like that goes to the dean. I suspended her from my class for one week. And everything went down as F's which couldn't be made up. And that kind of thing is a definite rule.

Her statement stands in striking contrast to the following lengthy discussion of rules by the developmentally oriented math teacher quoted earlier.

I: Well then, with discipline or classroom behavior do you lean more toward setting up general guidelines for behavior and then interpreting them according to the individual and the situation or do you lean more toward setting up definite rules for behavior and then trying to enforce them consistently?

R: What I try to do is work out with the kids something that they can do which will enable them to learn. Then we work it out and sometimes we write it down on a piece of paper and we mail it home. And it is well understood that this is what is going to happen. It is also well understood that that can change. But no one person is going to change it because he feels like sharpening his pencil during a discussion.

We also decide what you do when someone doesn't cooperate and then simply follow it through somewhat automatically. If a kid runs up against a real problem, I never solve it in class; class is a group kind of thing, not really an individual thing.

I: When you talk about deciding on the rules, do you do that then as a group?

R: Yes.

I: You discuss it with the group and—

R: Yes. Right.

I: —does the group vote or something to make the final—

R: There's usually not a problem of voting. You hit upon something that works and everyone just sort of goes "yeah." It takes awhile. I mean you don't solidify it for a week or so. You try it out and people say things that can't be done. And rather than say, "Oh, no, we can't do that because you'll always get up and pull the shades down when it gets too hot," no matter what's going on you just try it out. You refine it. It usually takes a couple of weeks. You refine this to the point where it looks like its going to work and then we really solidify it.

In answer to some further questions, he explained his system in more depth. He said the students at first saw his methods as "outrageous."

R: They just have to somehow or other believe that you mean it and I'm not willing to be punitive about it. You know, bring your pencil or this is the punishment that's attached to it. I don't want to do that. And so sometimes kids don't bring their pencils for a long time and don't do the work. . . .

If there were a fight in class, I always let the fight go on, if it were between two people who were equally matched and if the class would leave them alone. And I almost never had a fight. Because most fights, fights in classes, are safe because you can't fight [laughs]. Kids really—for years, and years, and years, "If you hit him, you go to the dean," and suddenly, "If you want to fight, go ahead and fight." They really saw this as very outrageous.

I: You talked about not being punitive with the example of not bringing your pencil, but a little earlier you were talking about how the honors kids would come for detention if they've broken a rule . . . What's the distinction?

R: Oh. Rules don't include things like you have to bring books and you have to bring pencils and you have to bring papers and you have to sharpen your pencil between 8:00 and 8:05. They weren't ever set up like that. They were much more general. It was assumed that you knew to bring paper and books, and if you couldn't, you left your book in the room and you could leave your pencil in the room with your name on it.

The punishment would come in if someone else had your pencil. And a rule, for instance, would say that people may do things, legitimate things, which involve noise that will not disrupt the class. And we would talk about what would be the interpretation of this. We would set up the interpretations; first [what if] there's a discussion going on, and that sort of thing. But they wouldn't be very, very specific because too many people would get hurt all the time with that.

I: Also it sounds like it's a matter of whether you're interfering with someone else.

R: Yes. Right. Oh yes, I have never asked—I have *never* asked—a kid to work because he wasn't working. I've only asked a kid to work because he was talking. I mean I just thought it was better to say, "Do your math," rather than, "Be quiet."

Both the incorporative and developmental approaches to rules then provide for the orderly conduct of the class hour and in some measure for the learning of responsibility. But both the substance of the rules and the methods for forming and enforcing them differ.

In the context of character education, as in academic education, the developmental teachers retain their right to final definition of appropriate activity. The teacher quoted who has the children write the rules in such an elaborate way is more pronounced in his developmental orientation than most. The following English teacher takes a very firm and in some ways traditional stand in defining and enforcing rules whose content—on more subtle matters than those previously discussed—is of a developmental style:

And I kind of lay down the law at the beginning. And the law has gotten much less lawful each year that I teach. I was quite authoritarian when I first started to teach and was not sure of myself at all and relied upon rules and regulations a great deal. The more I teach, however, the more I feel that I can bend and I think this is a good thing, that there need not be as many specific rules, just common sense ones. You know, we're here to learn and be able to show courtesy and respect to each other. And you will know the consequences of your actions and then you'll have the choice to take whatever road you want to take. And I spell out very clearly what I intend to do if there is any misbehavior in the class. And I, in no uncertain terms, tell them that there are things I will not put up with. There are a few things I will not put up with. There are a lot of things I will.

I: What are some of the things you won't?

R: I will not put up with anyone infringing on anyone else's rights to express himself even if that expression is contrary to what everybody in the class believes. Everyone has the right to say what he wants to as long as the point is to express his opinion or to give his own interpretation of something. And no one will be discourteous to anyone else, at least within my hearing. For example, we do not use the word "stupid" in my class or "shut up." And if they do, then they have either sentences to write or detention after school because to me these are marks of impoliteness to each other and I try to get them to treat each other like human beings, which they don't always do when I get them. I don't know if they do that after they leave me, but in my classes that's how they must operate. And I spell out what I will do and then when an opportunity presents itself where someone has taken a choice, then I just do what I said I was going to do. And it soon gets around that I do it.

The Child's Role as Subordinate

Since the classroom goals discussed so far involve educating children, that is changing them in some fashion, they necessarily involve implicit definitions of the nature of the material which is being changed. The previous discussion of the goals of the incorporative and developmental approaches suggests the outlines of the Canton teachers' understandings of the nature of children and of their appropriate role in the school.

The teachers with incorporative goals generally see the child as an empty vessel, a small pitcher which must be filled with knowledge poured from the large pitcher of the adult. The child is more or less passive in this transaction, or more accurately, his actions and thoughts are of a standardized pattern activated by the directions of the teacher.

The teachers with developmental goals generally consider the child to be inherently active and inherently curious about his environment. The task of the teacher then is not so much to fill the void of his ignorance as to channel his spontaneous curious activity in directions which will yield the most useful harvest of facts, principles, and skills.

Ideas about the inherent nature of the children were rarely articulated explicitly by the teachers, and ideas about the students' appropriate role only slightly more often. This was especially the case with the incorporative teachers who focused on the material to be learned and the rules to be followed and took the children's part in the process more or less for granted. Further with both groups, their implicit assumptions about the nature of children were in general more extreme than either group might admit in an explicit statement. The average child in the classroom is not as able or willing docilely to incorporate a logically ordered curriculum as the incorporative teacher implicitly claims, but he is also not as spontaneously and actively desirous of learning about the world around him as the developmental teacher implicitly claims. Both kinds of teachers adapt to this reality in daily practice, at least if they are competent and serious about teaching, but nonetheless the differences in their points of view do make a difference.

The best expressions of the two points of view emerged in debates between persons with opposing philosophies, but these rarely occurred in direct face to face conversation. The following instructive exchange took place at Hamilton between a developmentally oriented volunteer, not yet aware that these matters were not openly discussed, and an incorporatively oriented teacher. The account is quoted from field notes made afterwards. The volunteer began by observing that:

> "Many of the children in lower academic tracks are having trouble because they are so bored with the petty trivia that a lot of teachers give them to work on." She said this in a tone which implied that she assumed everyone present [a group of "older" and therefore incorporative teachers] would find this obvious. I braced myself for a strong reaction; you just don't *say* that in this part of the lounge.
> Mrs. Immer asked what she meant. "Well, at Canton High, at least, I know there is one counselor who, when a child is bored and not doing well, will move him down!" answered the volunteer.
> "But if he won't work, what are you to do with him?" asked Mrs. Immer.
> The volunteer persisted. Much of the work they are given is terribly boring for them, and they don't have the kind of self-control that is necessary to do what they don't want to do. The exercises they are given [evidently to teach basic reading, grammar,

writing, spelling, etc.] are inane to the student; they have no relation to their values.

Mrs. Immer, who had colored slightly and seemed to be speaking with well-controlled anger, replied, "If they still need to do that work, then they can't judge the material."

"But," insisted the volunteer, "the teachers don't make any effort to give them material that will stir their interest, material that will be interesting to them."

"What about learning their basic skills?" asked Mrs. Immer. They pursued this for a few exchanges, each restating her case. Then the girl said, "They need material which will suit their tastes, which will be of the kind they are naturally interested in, because they don't have the self-discipline—that, granted, they *should* have—which would enable them to work at what they don't like."

That did it for Mrs. Immer. Her strained politeness broke and she scoffed openly, looking around at the rest for agreement as she spoke, (and this quotation is exact): "Tastes! It's not a matter of their tastes! We can't suit their tastes; we're here to teach them the tastes to have suited!"

The volunteer maintains here primarily that students are active human beings who will learn if they are interested in something. She also maintains that children in junior high have distinctive values and interests of their own which guide their action and which must be reckoned with, and even cooperated with, whether one approves of them or not. If students will learn eagerly when they are interested, they also will refuse to learn when they are not. No amount of insistence by adults can substitute for the desire to learn in the child.

Mrs. Immer expresses some of the assumptions of the incorporative position. If the students come to school with values other than those of the school, these should be studiously ignored and the school should insist that the students accept for themselves the values of the school in their place. Part of the school's goals is to teach its own values, used to justify its other teaching, to children who do not come sharing them already. Until the children learn officially approved values and interests they are to be formally regarded either as without any interests or values at all, or as already sharing those of the school which they *ought* to share in any case. In a similar way Mrs. Immer holds that the way to get students to learn their "basic skills" (the three R's) is to concentrate directly upon them and nothing else until they are learned.

A less explicit contrast of points of view about the child's role is evident in a comparison of the way two English teachers replied to a question about what they do "the first day or the first week to get things started and set the tone." The first teacher explains:

> I don't think there is any one particular thing I do. It depends on what's available at the moment. Generally speaking, I think, most teachers try to establish the firm but friendly businesslike approach. . . . I just start off business as usual in my groups. We just start off on whatever it is we're going to do, whether it's a book or a paper or what.

The second teacher takes a different approach:

> Well, I try to find out who they are and I have them write some kind of personal autobiography or some kind of thing, to find out what their abilities are and who they are and how they feel and how they think. And I give kind of an overview of what we will cover and how we will cover it. And I like to sound out their feelings on what I have in mind and to see if they have any suggestions as to how these things might be done or if they have any additions or changes that they would like to make. And I kind of set up the requirements, which tend to be a little bit more rigid at the beginning and then as they get to know me and as I get to know them and they see what they like to do and what they don't and what's effective and what isn't, then I may change these in the course of the year.

The first teacher assumes that groups of a given level are all the same and simply starts giving the children what he planned with no attempt to learn their particular characteristics, let alone what their own interests or desires might be. The second teacher adjusts to each group of children and gives them some voice in what is done.

The incorporative teachers must justify their dismissal of the values and claims of those students who are in disagreement with their own. They do this on the grounds of age. For these teachers students in junior high school are, as one of the more vehement

ninth grade teachers said, "barely out of diapers." Like babies in
the culture generally, they are not-yet-persons. Their interests
and values can therefore be dismissed without serious treatment.

An implicit theory of child development is involved here on
the part of the incorporatively inclined teachers. They believe that
if children will for an extended period absorb and accept the
values, knowledge, and rules for behavior given them by adults,
they will finally have a basis on which to act and make decisions
as adults themselves. Before they have absorbed these things,
they are "mere" children and not competent to judge what is and
is not important, moral, or even relevant to themselves.

A developmentally inclined teacher makes explicit a constrast-
ing theory of child development. She believes that the capacity
for self-directed activity grows gradually from practicing with
what capacity a child has in a situation in which responsibility is
still shared with an adult:

> And I think teachers have to be able to . . . have students kind of
> involved in the decision-making processes about how they want to go
> about things. And [have them] practice making decisions, because
> this is what they're going to be doing in their lives. And I don't
> think that responsibility and decision-making suddenly comes upon
> someone because they turn the age of eighteen or they enter college
> or they become the age of twenty-one. That it's a learning process.
> And if students or young people are continually told what to do or
> guided by someone who has the word, whatever the word happens
> to be, kids are not going to have to figure things out for them-
> selves. And I think doing this is important.

In a situation where students accepted the school as a
representative of knowledge and the society they were growing
into and where they trusted the teachers to teach them appropriately, these differences among the teachers would not make a
great deal of difference to the life of the school. But in Canton,
significant numbers of children challenged the schools' goals and
the teachers' styles or alternatively simply refused to cooperate or
to learn. Teachers turned to their theories of child nature to ex-

plain the failure of their teaching efforts. The consequence was an exaggeration and polarization of the teachers' beliefs.

The Teacher's Role as Superordinate

The character of educational goals and the appropriate role for students which a teacher espouses determine much about the kind of role he or she will expect to play. It is quite possible that psychologically the teacher's role is the point of departure in shaping pragmatic pedagogical philosophy, but logically it comes last in a description.

In broad terms, teachers who take an incorporative approach expect to have an essentially exclusive prerogative to articulate the values and goals of education and to determine the particular activities which will serve them. They reply to requests for the justification of a given command with reference to their superordinate status as teachers. A child's challenge of a command will rarely lead to any change except in the case of a technical error. Teachers who take a developmental approach are more likely to let the students make suggestions or choose between alternative ways of translating educational goals into action. They reply to requests for justification with explanations or demonstrations of the ways in which particular commands are related to educational goals. A child's challenge to a command on the grounds that it does not serve those goals may lead to a change in the command if the reasoning is cogent, but the teacher retains the right to make the final decision.

Within these outlines, there were some variations in the roles which teachers took. Because the teacher's role is rather vaguely defined, it was common to model it upon other roles. Some incorporative teachers saw themselves as the equivalent of *parents*. They claimed personal discretion within the bounds of custom. In response to challenges from students, they would justify a command with reference to their personal wisdom validated by their teaching status. The answer would take some form like "Do it because I am your teacher and I know what is best," or even, "Do it because I say so."

The teachers' interview included a series of stories of classroom incidents ending with a question about what this teacher would do next. One about a challenge to a teacher's command drew replies which provided good indicators of teachers' conceptions of their own roles. The story ran:

> When you collect the homework during class one day a girl says she hasn't done it. You tell her she will have to do it, but she retorts angrily that it was a stupid assignment and she isn't going to do it.

The teachers whose general approach to their role was on a parental model were the only ones of the incorporative or developmental group to become highly concerned about the simple fact of a challenge and to feel that it must be suppressed as subversive of the very relationship. One replied in a typical fashion:

> I would be inclined to follow through and see to it that she did do it. Whether she thought it was stupid or not. Because I feel that a student should—then it becomes a matter of just absolute dis-obedience, and not—I would insist that she do it. Or have her stay after school and do it. She would have to do it.

In discussing the next story about a boy who mimics the teacher's voice this teacher pursues the answer to the story about the girl:

> I would reprimand him, because there again he's showing *disrespect for authority, for the teacher.* . . . If he persisted in doing it . . . I would give him a dean's detention. [Emphasis mine]

These teachers with their view of their role as rooted in broad tradition perceive it as having a very wide scope. They feel free, as *in loco parentis,* to give the children directions in spheres which do not have an obvious bearing on academic activity. Dress is the area most often in contention in such relationships. But in the complex world of the classroom many fleeting issues arise where these teachers may take a stand on the basis of their parental role that exceeds a teacher's prerogatives as students or teachers with other models understand them.

Other incorporative teachers envision their role as similar to that of a *bureaucrat*. They are unlikely to use that word but speak rather of the children's need to learn to obey teachers as they will need to obey a supervisor or superior or boss when they get a job. These teachers tend to pay special attention to the structuring devices which spell out the school's goals and procedures in tangible terms. They place great weight on curriculum guides, textbooks, and school rules. They perceive themselves as impersonal conduits for the generalized curriculum and rules of the school. In the fluid classroom setting such teachers must and do make many personal interpretations, but they make them appear as impersonal as possible by anchoring them to rules or curricular documents. Their typical response to a student's challenge is "Do it because the rule (or textbook) says you must." One of these teachers met the fictional girl's accusation that the assignment was stupid with a reply which was almost a parody of bureaucratic reference of a challenge to an unavailable superior:

> I'd say in this case, if she'd like to write to the author of the book and get a reply, I'd be very happy to give her credit for that assignment. That I didn't think it was very stupid, that the rest of the class turned it in. But, that I didn't write the book and maybe she'd get an interesting reply from the author, because there are lots of things that I don't agree with in these textbooks myself. I think in the case of this girl, she's just trying to get into an argument. And I don't argue with students.

A more common bureaucratic response came from the teacher quoted earlier who makes it a rule that children may skip the homework and be "forgiven" three zeroes a marking period. She never thinks of questioning the validity of the assignment but simply reasserts her prerogative to give assignments and the students' duty to do them:

> I'd tell her that was her choice, to take the zero then. And I don't get worried about it. I just don't make an issue of it. I say, "OK, you think it's stupid, all right. It was assigned; it's your job to do it. This will be one of your zeroes. I hope you don't find any more than two

more stupid assignments this marking period. Because then it's going to start hurting your grade." And I just don't make a fuss over it.

These teachers limit the scope of their directions to students to matters which are clearly related to academic performance or are covered by school rules. But they often have strong feelings about non-academic matters and will exert pressure for the establishment or retention of school rules covering them.

Both incorporative and developmental teachers sometimes took a role which can best be described as that of *expert professional*. Rather than relying upon their office as justification for their commands, they relied upon their academic expertise. The typical response to a student's challenge was "Do it because it will help you [or others] to learn." Developmental teachers were likely to add "for these reasons. . . ." The following exchange from field notes on a Track One class taught by a teacher with a generally incorporative philosophy but flexible practice who took such a role illustrates its style:

> She read off the answers to the homework. This class had lots of questions, and they went through several problems together. They were working with equations which required that they subtract a term from both sides in order to be able to find the solution. Mrs. Theobold included a step in which she changed all the subtraction signs to ones indicating adding the additive inverse, and then proceeded from there. Several students objected that it would be easier to do the process more directly. Mrs. Theobold replied that they should do it the way the book says to, (i.e., as she had done it also) for if they don't do it that way they will find that they get confused when they get to more complex problems next year. But several of them persisted that their way was more straightforward and hence better. She said, finally, that she had learned it the way they wanted to do it, but had learned this method later. And she found that this method really did eliminate more mistakes. So, she added, if you have learned it another way elsewhere, and some of you may have, try to forget that and do it this way. Whether convinced or not, the students stopped arguing at this point.

Because this role relies on academic expertise, its scope is very narrow. It applies only to academic matters or those, such as obvious disruption of a discussion, which bear directly upon academic matters. Most teachers supplemented it with another role in dealing with matters of courtesy, safety, or routine procedure.

There are few models outside the school for the role the developmentally oriented teachers most often claimed. The name *facilitating leader* is vague itself but perhaps best describes their activities. Many combined this role with that of expert professional.

These teachers justify their right to give commands on the grounds that they have a better understanding of academic and social goals and greater skill in translating them into practice than the students do. But they do not claim that they have exclusive superiority in these matters. They will grant that students may see equally good alternative routes to the same end. And they will also grant that educational ends are open to interpretation in which the students may share. It is significant that these teachers are generally in the fields of English, social studies, and arts or crafts. In these subjects educational ends are vaguer and there is a greater variety of routes to one skill than in fields like mathematics or elementary foreign language.

These teachers therefore take challenges to their directions which are seriously given as occasions for reconsideration as well as explanation of the reasons for their plans. A social studies teacher responds in this way to the story about the girl who found the assignment "stupid":

> I'd ask her why it was stupid. Right then I would have a discussion with her about whether it was or not. She might be right. This is one thing that I'm very concerned about, is that homework not be busy work. And I think many, many times that it is. And I try not to do that. But I have a very strong conscience about that. And if she thinks it might be so, it might be so. So I would just talk with her about it. But I wouldn't categorically force her to do it at all. She might be right.

It is important that this teacher does not accept the student's objection automatically, but questions her further, requiring that she make a reasoned case for her claim. Thus that she "might be right" also implies that she might be wrong.

These teachers modify their approaches for principled challenges where possible, but many, probably the majority, of challenges are not principled. Another developmental teacher in replying to the same story considers this probability first. But if she is convinced of the student's seriousness, then she is willing to modify the assignment even though she does not agree with the student's reasoning. However, it is important that this modification occur in private over the matter of a student's written work. A teacher cannot be as responsive to individual needs in dealing with a whole class. This English teacher describes her probable response:

> If she retorted it was a stupid assignment and she didn't want to do it, I would say, "Well that's your privilege to feel that way. However, I think that perhaps the time to have mentioned this was when the assignment was made, not when the assignment is due. And I would have encouraged you to come and speak to me if you didn't understand the assignment or if you didn't agree with it. And perhaps I could have changed it in some way to suit you. Like can you be specific and say"—This I think I would say in private. I would say, "I would like to talk to you about this. Please see me after class."
>
> And then I would say, "Well, what specifically upset you about the assignment? What didn't you like?" And I would listen. And if I thought that she had some validity then I would see if I could modify it for her, so that she would want to do it or feel that she could do it. *As long as she wasn't trying to pull something over on me,* if she really does feel that it was a stupid assignment and she didn't see any need to do it, then as far as she's concerned that's the way it is. No matter whether I think it's a worthwhile assignment or not, that's how she feels. You see. And so I have to act upon the way things are for her, not the way I think they should be for her. So I would talk to her and I wouldn't take it personally or feel affronted or anything by it. [Emphasis mine]

Teachers who take this role try to focus activities closely around academic goals and to keep their non-academic directives to basic questions of courtesy and protection of classmates' pride, property, and person. Their typical justifications in persevering with challenged directives are "Do this because it will help you [or the class] to learn," and "Do this so you won't hurt someone else." To both of these they generally add "because . . ." and an explanation of the consequences of the requested or forbidden act. It is important, however, that these explanations of commands come in response to challenges. They are not routinely offered. Their use in response to questions was a demonstration of the teacher's competence and good faith as an agent of shared school goals. If the demonstration is successful the students will trust the teacher to give appropriate commands most of the time, so that he need not routinely give explanations for his directions.

PROTO-AUTHORITY AND NON-DIRECTIVE GUIDANCE

The majority of teachers I observed even briefly in the Canton schools espoused some version of incorporative or developmental education. They had in common a belief that the students either shared or could be persuaded to share a common set of educational values and goals. They also regarded academic education as their primary task. But there were a few teachers who did not believe the children shared educational goals with the adults. In the light of that fact these teachers stressed the development of students' character above their academic development. These teachers were of two quite different kinds.

The first group started from a philosophy of human nature which pictured children as resisting any activity which requires effort. And they believed effort to be the source of virtue and the hard road the only profitable one. The teacher's most important job therefore was to be a taskmaster requiring his unwilling charges to put forth effort. A teacher at Darwin expressed this philosophy forcefully:

> I think that overbending in a child-centered situation can become very exaggerated and more damaging than when a youngster knows what he has to do, what is required of him, and to see that he *does* it. And this is, perhaps, an old-fashioned philosophy, but it's the one

I hold. I don't think that a youngster, regardless of what track or what level of intelligence, will do anything unless it's required of him and unless he sees that he *has* to do it, that there is no other door, that the line of least resistance is to do it and to be successful at it. I carry this throughout; perhaps it's a little militaristic in terms of philosophy, but it's one I find gets results. [Emphasis the speaker's]

These teachers often had missionary zeal in propounding their point of view. The following more detailed statement comes from field notes on a conversation with a teacher at Darwin who was not in my sample to interview, but who hailed me on the street and delivered his views for an hour.

He said that he teaches mathematics; that he does not preach communism like some of these teachers. He does not believe in coddling the students. They get brought along with everybody feeling sorry for them, "You poor thing, you're from a culturally disadvantaged background." (He says all this with dripping sarcasm.) He believes this is mistreating them, because all of a sudden they will have to get a job and they won't be able to read, do arithmetic, or write their name. He allowed here that he was taking the most extreme case.

But he believes you should make them work and if they don't want to do it, then he says suspend them. Make them stay away from school for a while and make their parents bring them back. And then maybe their parents will do something about it. But people say, no, that's putting them out of the school and you want them in.

He kept coming back over and over to the theme that the kids don't want to work and that they must simply have it demanded of them. They have been coddled all their lives and nothing demanded of them. If they have been able to get through the easy way nine out of ten times, they figure it's only common sense to keep on doing it the easy way and take the odds! Who wouldn't?

He fears things are going to get worse in this school because of what he hears is happening in the elementary schools. They are getting a lot worse. I asked what was happening. They are filling them with all these *aides* (the word was said distastefully) and really spoiling the kids. I asked if perhaps the kids might end up learning more so they wouldn't come to ninth grade with fourth to sixth grade skills (as he says they do). Perhaps, he said, we'll have to wait five or six years and see. But he was obviously skeptical.

It seems fairly clear that this man's concern is not primarily with the students' academic progress but with their willingness to accede to demands for hard work and literal obedience to adults' commands. He believes unremitting effort and reliable obedience to be not only the sole path to learning, but the sole means to getting along in the adult world at all.

It is important that teachers who take this extreme position show little engagement with their academic subjects even when teaching capable, interested students. They also often speak with obvious enjoyment of their forceful exercise of power over the students. They publicly relish the chorus of impotent protestations of injustice with which students frequently respond. These were the teachers most likely to use questionably legitimate forms of coercion such as public insult or physical force upon their students. Still, despite the part their lack of intellectual zeal and their enjoyment of untrammeled power must have played in their choice of a definition of the situation, there was often a very genuine moral element in their actions. The teacher just quoted at length clearly believed that the school was in his words "letting the kids down" by not treating them as he would. He had a genuine moral passion for the good of the children as he understood it.

The relationship these teachers envision with their students is not one of authority. It resembles authority in the existence of a moral order which justifies the relationship, in the super-ordinate's right to give commands in the service of that moral order and in the subordinate's duty to obey them voluntarily. But it lacks a direct tie between the subordinates and the moral order. Subordinates may acknowledge that educational goals exist and legitimate the activities of superordinates, but they do not embrace them as their own. These teachers did not expect the children ever to share educational values. They hoped only to teach them that industriousness and obedience are a line of least resistance. I will refer to this pattern as *proto-authority*, because of its resemblance to, yet difference from, authority.

In such a context the teacher's role stands squarely between the students and the justifying basis of the teacher-student relationship. The student knows the nature of educational goals only through the teacher's directives. The teacher therefore need accept no challenge to his decision whether the student claims an appeal to educational goals or not. The typical reply to a student's challenge is "Do it because I say so." The teacher's role can perhaps best be compared to that of a *sergeant,* though these teachers were more likely to refer to that of parent. Significantly, many of the teachers taking this role were retired military men. Women rarely followed this pattern in its pure form but leaned toward an incorporative model with a parental role.

The other group of teachers who did not believe that students and teachers share common goals, held that they should not. They believed students should in large part define their own educational goals. They saw such goals as primarily ones of personal development, which differ for each child. They did have certain broad values which they believed should be a framework for personal development, but the details were variable. The role they took can be compared to that of a *therapist* who attempts to shape the interaction—and the patient—in the broad directions he considers to represent "growth" but does not command in the sense of an ordinary superordinate in a relationship of authority. Their directing of the children consisted mainly in providing them with opportunities for experiences and then using comments and suggestions, but not commands, to help the students build upon those experiences. I will call this pattern of teaching *non-directive guidance.*

There were so few of these teachers in Canton that none fell into the samples I observed even briefly. Those I believe to have had this pattern I knew only from reputation and conversation. There were three teachers among those I observed all day who attempted this pattern but did not have the skill to sustain it. They either practiced a developmental pattern which gave them more structural supports, or slipped over into abdication from teaching, discussed below. Teaching of this kind is a model much discussed in educational writing. But it is a style which is not well suited to a large public school or to the secondary level, for reasons I will discuss at the end of the chapter.

ABDICATION FROM TEACHING

All the types of teachers discussed so far are seriously interested in teaching the children something, though they differ in their priorities. Some teachers abdicate their responsibilities. Whether through inability or disinclination, they make no serious effort to teach the children anything. Some such teachers in Canton used the rhetoric of a developmental or non-directive approach while others used that of an incorporative approach.

The first group granted the students freedom more out of desperation than conviction, or else they were so lacking in skill and insight that their attempts to use a developmental or non-directive pattern amounted in practice to letting the children simply do as they pleased.

One such teacher ran a tightly structured class with those groups which would tolerate it, even though his subject was family living, usually treated in an at least partially open-ended way. But with groups that resisted structure, he went to the opposite extreme. With children who will accept structure, it requires the least effort, with children who will not, a laissez faire approach is easier. This teacher expressed his inconsistent philosophy in his interview. He listed discipline among his most important goals in teaching, but when asked whether he leaned more toward general guidelines or definite rules in his classes he replied:

> Well, first of all, I try to set up definite rules. But then again [if] there's too many disruptive kids, like in second period, you can't stay rigidly to your rules. If the kids want to get up and look out the window, you almost have to let them do it. In a class like my second period you can't expect some of those kids to sit for 40 minutes in one place. Now I thought we had a good session yesterday. They all wanted to talk. The subject wasn't really important to me. The main thing is they wanted to express themselves. I think this is good therapy. Anything. Something they want to express to an adult. So I'm very flexible with my second period. But the rest—[I'm not].

In answer to another question about handling of students determined not to cooperate, he elaborated on the same theme referring to his experience as an elementary school teacher:

> You could be much more flexible because you have a self-contained classroom. And a kid like Ronald [who bid for attention repeatedly in the second period class observed the previous day], you find something of interest for him. If he wanted to do it the whole day, it didn't bother me a bit, because he was busy engaged in something that was of his interest. It was sort of an interest-centered curriculum I used to run. . . . [Here he does that only with the second period class.] I didn't care if the kid didn't have math the whole year, because that same kid had so much problem that he was lucky to get to school in the first place.

Phrases such as "good therapy" and "interest-centered curriculum" are here thin garments trying to clothe the naked reality of abdication of responsibility in exchange for relative peace in the classroom. Their use in this context serves as a reminder that teachers can spin rhetoric, either incorporative or developmental, to cover practices which any serious teacher, of whatever persuasion, would reject.

Other teachers who were also unable or unwilling actually to teach or even to control the children used incorporative rhetoric. Some of these went further than the teacher just described. They were obviously and frankly timeservers in the classroom. With the most difficult classes they often simply withdrew behind their desks leaving the children to create a ceaseless din during the period, or even to wander in and out of the classroom at will. These teachers made occasional strict disciplinary sallies into the class, but because the activity, the time, and the student all seemed to be randomly chosen, these had next to no lasting effect. Yet these teachers generally spoke as though they were pursuing incorporative goals. Sometimes there was no relationship at all between their practice and their description of their goals and activity. Even after I had observed one teacher of this kind for a whole day, in her interview she spoke repeatedly in earnest

tones of her deep desire to push the children so they would learn.[1]
If the noise level is not high in these classrooms, other teachers
may accept such teachers' claims.

A TYPOLOGY OF TEACHING PHILOSOPHIES

If we hold abdication from teaching aside as a practical adjustment, the philosophies of teaching described here are separated along two dimensions. They are divided according to
whether or not teachers and students share educational goals. And
they are divided according to whether or not it is appropriate for
students to participate in defining classroom goals and specifying
classroom activities. These dimensions are presented in Figure
Two.

FIGURE 2

Dimensions Underlying Teaching Philosophies

	Goals Not Shared	*Goals Shared*
Teacher (Superordinate) Alone Directs Action	Proto-Authority 1	Incorporative 2 Approach
Student (Subordinate) Participates in Direct- ing Action	Non-Directive 4 Guidance	Developmental 3 Approach

The incorporative and developmental approaches are similar in
assuming that the children do share or can come to share educational goals which the school is seeking. It is possible to elicit
cooperation and effort by calling on the importance of these, and
possible for the teacher to expect obedience as their faithful agent.
Proto-authority and non-directive guidance are similar in claiming that educational goals are not shared.

1. This incident underlines the importance of combining observation with
interviewing of teachers. For teachers who lack this one's striking capacities for
departure from reality, observing not only provides a check on the veracity of
general statements but actually constrains the speaker to separate practice from
ideals.

Proto-authority and an incorporative approach have strong similarities in their emphasis upon the teacher as the sole definer of the situation within the classroom. Non-directive guidance and the developmental approach share a belief in students' capacity to participate in defining the situation.

Following the numbers on the boxes in Figure Two, one could picture these approaches as a progression or continuum. Teachers may take a position anywhere along a line stretching from proto-authority to non-directive guidance. This image allows for the many teachers who hold elements of two positions.

It is important to remember that these different goals and different teacher-student relationships are part of mental models of the appropriate character of a school which may be brought by members of a single staff into the operation of a single school. The possibilities for conflict or chaos in such a situation are legion.

THE LIMITS OF VARIETY IN CANTON'S TEACHING PHILOSOPHIES

These four approaches to teaching do not exhaust the possibilities. At either end of the continuum there exist more extreme positions. Teachers may see themselves with almost a duty to punish children for values that deviate from their own. They may be determined not only to make them work but to make them suffer. Descriptions of the desperate polarization in large city ghettos suggest that teachers sometimes take such an attitude. At the other end of the continuum, teachers may on principle refuse to guide students in any way, holding that their natural wisdom should be left to unfold without hindrance.

However, in Canton neither of these extreme positions was really represented. Teachers far less punitive than the first group were under heavy pressure to resign. One was dismissed despite tenure after repeated use of physical constraint, ending with an incident in which he grabbed a student by the collar and shoved him by the seat of the pants in view of other teachers and students in the corridor. Teachers of the second group would also come into irremediable conflict with the Canton schools.

These schools were not a congenial environment even for teachers who chose proto-authority and non-directive guidance. Those who chose proto-authority felt undercut because the district tolerated a good deal of noisy and expressive behavior from students and favored persuasion over coercion. Those who chose non-directive guidance had more subtle problems. Their approach requires building a generalized curiosity and initiative in a child. This is difficult to do when his other teachers insist upon his following a carefully structured pattern.[2] Similarly the rules and patterns of routine and supervision set up to keep physical order in a large school—which are discussed in Chapter Seven—create an atmosphere which is inconsistent with the one needed for this approach. Even within a single classroom, the patterns of control used to prevent children from interfering with one another which are consistent with this approach do not work well with a large and socially heterogeneous group. It is not an accident that most of the examples of non-directive guidance in the literature are located in small, socially homogeneous schools.[3]

There are further problems for non-directive guidance in the curriculum of the secondary school. Unlike the elementary school where children can learn basic skills through any substance, the secondary school seeks to give its students at least a basic acquaintance with specific facts and skills which will not be spontaneously absorbing to all of them.[4] In Canton, the teachers

2. In a study of third and fourth graders, Bossert found that the behavior of children, including peer relationships, varied significantly with the structure imposed by teachers in self-contained classrooms. When classes were reconstituted in the next grade, within a few weeks students assigned to contrasting teachers changed their behavior to accord with the new structure in which they participated. Steven Bossert, "Tasks and Social Relationships in Classrooms."

3. See for example all of the following well-known accounts: A. S. Neill, *Summerhill*; Sylvia Ashton-Warner, *Teacher*; George Dennison, *The Lives of Children*; and Lawrence Cremin, *The Transformation of the School*, passim.

4. Even at the elementary level, such patterns face organizational difficulties. Gracey describes in vivid detail the problems faced by the principal and a few teachers in a suburban elementary school as they attempted to introduce individualized, interest-centered instruction into a generally traditional community and school. (See Harry L. Gracey, *Curriculum or Craftsmanship*.)

who even attempted this pattern without exception taught subjects with fluid curricular aims such as art, music, and family
living.

The typical teachers of Canton were thus incorporative or
developmental in their teaching philosophy. They were also
reasonably competent and dedicated.

While the pedagogical philosophies of teachers make a difference in the way they approach their teaching and define their
classroom experiences, the characteristics and activities of their
students are at least as important in determining what they
actually do every day. Let us now turn to the students' ideals for
the school.

CHAPTER 4

Students' Definitions of Classroom Relationships

JUNIOR HIGH SCHOOL students are experiencing puberty. The eighth grade is the year of the greatest transition and the greatest variety amongst individuals. This study focused upon eighth grade students because their moral understanding, like their bodies, seemed to be in the process of transformation. Eighth grade classrooms are the scene of unusually high amounts of moral conflict and debate.

Eighth graders, especially the more articulate, displayed remarkable moral insight and moral passion. They would take stands and refuse to yield a point even at some cost to themselves. But half an hour later the same children might engage in a childish prank without thought to its consequences. Further, they were naive and thoughtless about practical matters. They often did not think that the consequences of an act which would be harmless if done by one person would be seriously disruptive if done by thirty-five. They did not in general look at the classroom as a system where all activities and persons are interdependent or imagine themselves into the teacher's responsible role.

They raised moral issues with purity and energy, but they lacked the sense for logistical necessity and for the social implications of individual action which must shape a teacher's specific decisions about classroom activities. Eighth grade classes are thus difficult places in which to practice authority but excellent places to see issues of authority made explicit. Seventh graders retained more of childhood's trust and raised fewer moral arguments, while ninth graders had slightly more appreciation of practical complexities and adults' dilemmas in administering them.

Though the teachers were aware of the special characteristics of eighth grade children and sometimes discussed them as a major factor in their choice of teaching strategy, other variety among the children in each school attracted much more of their conscious energy and comment than did the effects of age. Teachers often catalogued this variety in terms of the tracking system. The children were sorted into five tracks—though special Honors sections were not officially called a separate track—in the academic subjects of English, math, and social studies. In foreign language they were separated into two tracks, and in other subjects grouped heterogeneously.

CHARACTERISTICS OF THE TRACKS

Classes of various tracks took on a special character because they were sorted to rough homogeneity not only in academic performance but in social compliance, race and social class. Officially, a child's academic achievement in the classroom was the only criterion for his track placement.[1] But since teachers were given wide discretion in judging whether a child's achievement warranted a change in track, some rid themselves of disruptive children by moving them down a track. The lower tracks therefore consisted of a mixture of children who were actually slow to learn, children who were capable but did not try, and

1. Scores on aptitude tests were claimed to have an effect only when a child seemed to be performing well below his capacity and a teacher judged that more challenge would help.

children who were able but also rebellious, disruptive, and spotty in their academic effort.[2]

The tracks differed visibly in race. The school population was 32 per cent black, but there were only two black children in eighth grade Honors classes at the two schools together, during the year of the study. Track One was overwhelmingly white with a sprinkling of black children. Track Two was about evenly divided between white and black children. The majority of Oriental children were in this track, though a few appeared in other, especially higher, tracks. Track Three was black, with a sprinkling of whites, never more than one fifth of the group. Track Four was essentially all black with an occasional lone white or Oriental child.

The racial composition of the tracks was bound up with the effect of social class[3] and elementary school origin upon academic performance. Canton's neighborhoods were homogeneous in

2. Leacock found among elementary school children in a middle income school that teachers and children both liked those children best who had high IQ and high reading scores. But in a low income black school, the teachers were most *negative* toward the children with the highest IQ scores. IQ was not correlated to reading test results in this context. In contrast to the teachers, the children preferred poorer readers with high IQs to better readers with average IQs. (See Eleanor Burke Leacock, *Teaching and Learning in City Schools*, pp. 136−37.) These poor readers with high IQs are the kind of students who were leaders in challenging teachers in Canton's lower track classes. Leacock suggests teachers' dislike may play a part in creating their poor skills (ibid., pp. 195−97).

3. The schools did not compile data on the characteristics of students in each track, so that there were no convenient summaries of their racial composition or range of IQ scores. Since children were tracked independently in each subject and movement up or down during the course of the year was common, such information would have been difficult to compile—even if it had not been so sensitive.

From observation I could get fairly systematic data on race, but not, of course, on IQ or, very reliably, on social class. Three kinds of indicators form the basis of my judgments about class: first, cues picked up in observing, such as the dress and speech patterns of children combined with their comments about their own and their parents' outside activities; second, the occupations of parents listed on the registration cards of children considered for interviewing; third, statements of teachers and counselors about the distribution of the usual indices of social class in the various tracks.

social class and in race—though not absolutely segregated. The
elementary schools reflected neighborhood patterns and reinforced the advantages and disadvantages of the children attending them. The tracks in junior high school, chosen on an academic basis, then reflected social class patterns.[4] Black children
from the better neighborhoods and elementary schools gained
access to higher tracks.[5]

Differences in the tracks were sharpened by the lack of a large
middle status group in Canton. The school population was
bimodal in both social class and IQ. (In each of the junior highs
graphs of IQ scores showed a mode just below 100 and another
significantly above.) Consequently, though the social and racial
groups overlapped in the middle track, classes in the high and
low tracks were relatively homogeneous. The analysis here will
concentrate upon the high and low tracks with their distinctive
social, racial, and academic style.

Even these classes behaved somewhat differently according to
the particular assemblage of individuals each group contained,
but there were still definite common elements among them. The
socially diverse composition of Track Two classes made the
behavior of individual groups far more variable, depending upon
the weight of the social mix in any particular group.

For all the classes, a few vocal and active individuals are by far
the most important in affecting the relationship of authority

4. It would be extremely instructive to be able to look at the effects of
academic capacity and academic performance, classroom compliance, race and
social class separately. But it is also useful to study the effects of the constellation, since in most schools geographic boundaries or academic tracking create
groups which are homogeneous in just such constellations of characteristics.

5. The original track placement was done by sixth grade teachers, and then
readjusted by seventh grade teachers in the early weeks. Children were also
moved relatively easily in mid-career. There were instances of blatant racial
favoritism and racial prejudice at work in this process from time to time, and
the subtle prejudice which results from the meeting of cultures was more
pervasively active. But in general the pattern seemed to reflect the association of
social class background and social class segregation in the elementary schools
with conventional academic accomplishment. For a discussion of the factors
affecting counselors' placement of entering ninth graders in college and non-
college curricula in a suburban setting see Aaron Cicourel and John I. Kitsuse,
The Educational Decision-Makers.

between the teacher and the class. The assertive students who give the most pungent responses—whether positive or negative—set the mood for all. Unless their definition of the situation clearly clashes with that of the majority, they will both express and shape the attitudes of their peers. The numerical majority in almost any class are more accepting, more quiet, and more passive than the leaders. They rarely expressed their point of view directly in class, though some of them were able to articulate their position in the research interview.

The discussion of students' definition of the situation which follows will therefore deal primarily with the vocal and expressive students who determine the tone of the class. The quiet followers will be discussed separately at the end of the chapter.

HIGH TRACK STUDENTS' DEFINITIONS OF CLASSROOM RELATIONSHIPS

The children of white professionals who dominated both Honors and Track One were quite articulate about the goals of education they considered appropriate and also about the proper roles of teachers and students. They were not reticent about expressing these ideas either in class or in an interview.[6]

Values and Goals

The vocal students in the top tracks had lost faith in the validity of tradition and the wisdom which has guided the older generation. They felt that the world they were growing up into has changed and that they themselves were different from children their age who were in school twenty years earlier.

They saw education not as the passing on to them of the knowledge accepted as important by adults but as the answering of their questions about the world and themselves. For this reason

6. The children at Hamilton were more thorough and expressive in holding the positions described here than were those at Chauncey. Greater numbers of them also held to this philosophy. Chauncey children took a position between this one and that of the quiet children described at the end of this chapter. See Chapter Ten for a thorough discussion of these differences.

a criterion of learning was that it involve them in an active rather than a passive way and often that it be in some way enjoyable.

One student stressed the students' distrust and even rejection of a traditional curriculum. She had just described the teacher she liked least as "conservative all over":

> I: Well, can you describe a little bit what's the difference between a conservative teacher and a nonconservative teacher in the way they run a class?
>
> R: If a teacher can bend to the ideas and the change [in] the ideas of the students and how they would like to run the class and how they would like to learn, I feel this is more what a liberal [teacher does] . . . There are some teachers who have exactly the same notes; and they're teaching the class exactly the same way that they taught them twenty years ago when they were at this school and it hasn't changed. And so the kids then took it—I mean, that was what it was then. But I'm sure the teachers have felt "Well, the kids are getting worse and worse these days and I don't know what the world's coming to." It's because they haven't changed their way of teaching to the changing of the students and their ideas. Because I feel that students are becoming more aware of what is going on, and the teachers need to change to them.

A boy described the teacher he liked least, his social studies teacher, with the following comments:

> R: I dislike her because she doesn't know how to teach. . . . She's teaching in a very old-fashioned way. . . .
>
> I: And what is it she does that's old-fashioned?
>
> R: Mainly I dislike her because there's no time for discussion or anything like that. She just works straight from the book and all this. And when she has discussions they're very highly organized, and so nobody can really express himself the way they want. And the only way people do is by just yelling out and no order.

He continued:

> And one thing I don't like about a lot of the teachers is that a lot of them are just teaching and they're not really helping people learn and it just doesn't—people aren't interested in that.
>
> I: And what's the difference? That is, what's it like to help—

R: Well, teaching is—well, they tell you this, here's what you have to learn; now go do this and that. But when I say learning, is that they give you things that you can learn that are interesting. And if you have questions about it, you ask them rather than them all of a sudden giving you all this stuff which is unnecessary.

When a teacher simply expected the students to incorporate the contents of a textbook, to "memorize" as some of them complained, these students could become angry and withdrawn. Repeatedly they characterized those teachers they liked least and learned least from as those who taught "straight from the book," who would not allow students to ask questions on related topics not included in the lesson, and who would not allow them to discuss their own understandings of the matter. One social studies teacher was chosen as the least-liked teacher by every higher track interviewee who was in a class of hers. They described her as both knowledgeable and capable in presenting material. They disliked her for insisting on her own structure in each lesson. For example, she would summarize statements by students, changing their meaning (at least as the student saw it) to support a point she wanted to make, and then refuse to let the student speak again.

Many students in top tracks would simply stop working, at least temporarily, in courses they found distasteful. Their record cards revealed a pattern of wildly erratic grades.[7] These students also cut class with a frequency on which both they and their teachers remarked. Both groups also agreed that it was the most verbal and capable students who most frequently cut. These were

7. It is important that students who took this point of view and who would stop working in some courses did not seem at all concerned about their grade or college entrance. They mentioned their grades in interviews only if they had slipped to D or F. Because the state university was both academically and socially acceptable to elites, the students were not under competitive pressure for grades, especially as early as junior high school. This is a relative statement, however, comparing Canton to contexts where the Ivy League is the goal. There were individual parents who put pressure on their children to maintain good grades, and at Chauncey there was more underscoring of good grades and, according to some students, more pressure to work for high grades, than at Hamilton.

also the ones who took this educational position in its most developed form.

However, these students applied the position thoroughly only to subjects such as English and social studies, which have a content that is vague, subject to change, and of personal relevance. They reluctantly admitted that there were certain skills and information to be acquired in school which, though unexciting, would be useful and even necessary for them later. In the interview with the boy quoted above who found his social studies teacher old-fashioned, the interviewer asked about learning a subject like math. He replied:

> Well, the way I feel about math is there are certain subjects that can be lenient and some that can't; and math has to be taught straight because you have to learn math. There's no other way. And I don't really enjoy it, but I learn it. You have to learn it to get through. I just don't think there's any way of changing math.

Class observation also indicated that top level students were less persistent in challenging math teachers than others.

The Teacher's Role

Students in the top levels were quite capable of carrying on debates with teachers who disagreed with them about educational goals. Since they saw the validity of a teacher's superordinate status as based upon his competence and good faith in bringing about those goals, they might challenge his specific commands on the grounds that they did not serve education as the student understood it. These were not challenges to the teacher's right to be a superordinate, but to the validity of a given command.

Consistent with their belief that they should share educational goals and have a part in defining them, these students expected their teachers to take a role such as expert professional or facilitating leader. They required a teacher to justify a challenged command with at least a generalized explanation of the way it served education. They rebelled when a teacher taking a parental or a bureaucratic stance refused to give such a justification but replied in effect "Do it because I'm your teacher and I say so," or "Obey the rule and don't ask why."

Encounters between the most convinced students and teachers supporting these different roles quickly became vicious circles. The teacher read the student's request for explanation as a denial of the legitimacy of his superordinate status. He accordingly treated it as misbehavior or rebellion. The student was angered when his principled request for justification was treated as illegitimate. The teacher was likely to construe the student's anger as disrespect or defiance and to impose coercive sanctions. The student interpreted the punishment as a sign of the teacher's inability or unwillingness to control the class through what he understood as legitimate authority.

A boy at Hamilton expresses much of the students' perception of this conflict in answer to a question about the correspondence or independence of fairness and strictness:

> Last year I had Mrs. Cosgrove. She didn't have to be strict because we respected her. And that's what I don't dig about the dean and stuff like that. That they [the teachers] have this as a tool, and if they can't get the kids to have respect for them, they send them to the dean and the kid gets detention, when it's their fault because they can't earn respect. They demand respect and there's a lot of teachers I just don't respect. And their thing is you have to respect a teacher, and I don't believe that. I believe if somebody wants respect, they have to earn it. And those teachers demand respect right away. . . .
>
> If you're strict, the kids will do it [disobey or challenge] anyway. You'll send them to the dean but they'll do it anyway even though they'll have detention or something. And it's just no answer. . . . Whenever there's really respect for a teacher, then you learn.

This is not to say that these students required every teacher to justify every command. Once a teacher established a reputation for giving commands that were based upon sound reasons related to learning, the students would trust him to continue giving commands of this legitimate kind. Further, the students also allowed the teachers a certain amount of freedom to have idiosyncratic preferences, so long as they were frank about the nature of these and did not make them into moral laws.

The Students' Role

These leading students were emphatic in their belief that as students, or as eighth graders, they were not *qualitatively* different from teachers. This belief came out most clearly in several accounts by children at Hamilton of conflicts with teachers. The teacher would reprimand the child for interrupting or for rudeness. In telling the story the student would often admit that the charge was true and that he had therefore done wrong. But he was still indignant because the teacher had interrupted him or been rude to him and had done it first. That also was wrong in the child's eyes.[8]

These students believed themselves capable of grasping at least the outline of the justification for curricular choice, and they thought they should be given the voice of junior partner in making some decisions about what particular materials to study and what particular procedures to follow.[9] However, they were desirous of a fair hearing and an explanation for the acceptance or rejection of their ideas rather than of having the final say. They praised teachers who "respected" students, which seemed to mean those who listened to what they had to say and took it seriously, whether or not they always agreed with it.

In matters of classroom decorum, they were willing to admit that they and others occasionally engaged in activities which were lazy, inconsiderate, foolish, or malicious, and they considered it appropriate for the teacher to prevent them from con-

---

8. Some teachers occasionally told of similar incidents and I witnessed some (though more often in lower tracks). The teachers were often astonished and puzzled by the responses of children to remarks or actions of theirs which they would clearly have considered outrageously rude if directed *toward* them by a child, but which seemed perfectly routine when directed *by* them toward a child.

9. This belief again varied according to the subject. Students expected much less voice and choice in the study of mathematics or elementary language than in English, history, or family living.

tinuing with such behavior.[10] However, they also believed that
there might be either a rational reason or an emotional difficulty
behind any act seemingly calling for discipline. They believed
that the teacher should try whenever possible to find out the
reason for a student's misbehavior and to respond to the cause
rather than simply to the behavior. In response to the five
incomplete stories of classroom incidents presented to both
teachers and students in interviews, vocal students from these
tracks recommended with monotonous regularity that the teacher
find out the reason the student had acted as he did before taking
other action. Sometimes they spelled out the logical implication
of this position that a teacher should not see a class as a group of
similar students, but rather as an aggregate of unique individuals.

While it is difficult to identify the sources of these children's
stance on these issues, clearly both the events of the times and the
status and practices of their parents played a part.[11] The children
watched television news and often read mass media magazines
such as *Newsweek*. They were intensely aware of adults' conflicts
over the Vietnamese War and of President Johnson's "credibility
gap." Not only the mass media, but the diversity of their own

10. There was one student interviewed who did seem to reject virtually all
controls. But he also rejected the legitimacy of the school, claiming that the
teachers "don't know one single thing" and that he learned nothing in school
(although his grades for the last two marking periods were all A or B.) But
rather than actually rejecting adult guidance, he seemed to me to be radically
testing it. He did this even in the interview, playing games with the questions
and turning them around on the interviewer. Observations indicated there were
a handful of students like him who, at least explicitly, granted the teachers
scarcely any claim to legitimate control. They seemed to take delight in presenting the teachers who would accept no challenge as legitimately principled
with a stream of challenges, sometimes puerile and sometimes jesuitical.

11. Since Coleman's classic study of the effect of peer group values on
students' valuing of academic pursuits and on their actual achievement (James
Coleman, *The Adolescent Society*) there has been considerable controversy about
the relative salience for these outcomes of parental values and class background
versus "adolescent culture," immediate peer pressure and the "climate" of
schools. Much of this literature has been based on survey data measuring school
climate by comparing aggregated questionnaire responses of students. The controversy and the literature are reviewed in Edward L. McDill and Leo C.
Rigsby, *Structure and Process in Secondary Schools*, pp. 1–22.

school taught them something of the social and cultural realities of a stratified and racially separated society. Protests and programs at the University underscored all these issues.

In such a context, they did not see the school and the teachers as representatives of a unified adult society into which they needed initiation. Rather the ends of their education and for that matter the character of adult society were matters for debate. Similarly, they did not believe that a teacher could claim status as a moral mentor or even as someone who would tell the truth and act in good faith simply because he was an adult. After all, the President was politely but generally being called a liar. And large numbers of other adults seemed to be acting immorally as well.

The parents of these students contributed to their attitudes in a number of ways. Many opposed the Vietnamese War and questioned the principles and good faith of powerful figures and institutions in both government and the private sector. They established and reinforced their children's reluctance to accept adult society or adults on faith.

Furthermore, these children's parents were for the most part of higher status than the teachers. At the least they were not awed by teachers, and they communicated their feelings to their children. At the most, they questioned the teachers' capacities and judgment and did not hesitate to believe that their child might be right and a teacher wrong.[12]

This study provided only scanty evidence on family interaction, but what there was suggested that these parents had accustomed their children to asking for explanation and justification when an adult asked them to do something they did not want to do. One may speculate that these families have sufficient material affluence and few enough children so that they can lead each child to expect that his unique needs and wants will be

12. The most rebellious high track student interviewed asserted that his teachers knew little and were not bright, but that his counselor was "intelligent." Asked how he could tell the difference, he retreated, saying he supposed the counselor wasn't intelligent really or he wouldn't be a counselor in a school but would be working at the university or in some similar job. According to school records, the boy's father was an architect and his mother a teacher.

accommodated in family activity. The children carried this expectation with them to the classroom.

In contrast to the high track students, those in low tracks did not have a developed normative definition of the way schools should be run. Rather, they took the school as they found it and did not question the administrators' and teachers' right to define what they should learn, how they should learn it, or how they should behave. However, though they accepted these definitions as inevitable, they did not embrace them. And they frequently failed or refused to cooperate in the activities the definitions implied. They did not question the school's proper character, but they held themselves apart from it. They remained alien and separate within it.[13]

When asked in their interviews which teachers they liked best or least, these students preferred teachers who were not "mean" or "always hollering" at you, who treated everyone alike (did not play favorites), who made accusations of misdeeds only when justified, and who explained the material so the student could understand it. Many of the same criteria were adduced in explaining why the student learned most from one teacher or least from another. To these were added that the teacher should give neither too much, nor too little, work.

The requirement that a teacher who was to be liked must make a genuine and coherent effort to teach indicates students' insistence that a teacher's power over the student be justified by *some* educational goals. But these students did not specify the kind of educational goal or the kind of role a teacher should take. They were concerned primarily with the human decency and sense of fairness with which he treated them.

In reply to the question giving them unchecked power to

13. The pattern described here was more pronounced at Chauncey. See Chapter Ten.

change the school, those who did not reject it completely improved the plant to make it pleasanter or more "modern" or changed the deans, counselors, or teachers to make them "better," "nicer" or not so "mean."[14] The most salient characteristics of the school were not its official educative purposes and works, but the degree to which life within it was endurable.

Unlike the students in the top tracks, these students considered adults to be people really very different from themselves. This belief appears in their interpretation of confrontations over conformity. The students, at least the enterprising vocal ones, as a matter of course denied anything they were accused of unless they were caught red-handed. Even then they might try to talk their way out of the situation. This was all part of a legitimate game of wits. But nothing would make them more indignant than to be punished for something they had not done despite their protestations of innocence. Though their aim in the first instance was to fool the teacher, it did not occur to them that they were asking him to be omniscient in the second.[15]

Despite their behavior, the children in the lower level classes accepted a normative requirement for unquestioning obedience from all students. In their interviews, as they responded to the five stories of student non-conformity in the classroom, these students were the fastest to recommend that the teacher turn to punishment and they gave the most severe punishments. They almost never had the teacher inquire into the student's reason for his action, as the top level students regularly did.

In these answers they may have been speaking of what teachers actually *did*, rather than of what they thought they *should* do.

14. A significant proportion of the students with no disciplinary referrals during the year mentioned that they would also stop the students from so much hostility or troublemaking. One girl at Chauncey barely breathed that she would stop all the "hate." On further questioning she seemed to be referring to both students and teachers.

15. There may also be a cultural misunderstanding at issue here. Black students may use a different tone when protesting innocence as part of the game of wits and when protesting it in all seriousness. White teachers, not trained in the game, may miss this difference in inflection. Compare the misunderstandings discussed in Herbert Foster's *Ribbin', Jivin', and Playin' the Dozens.*

Teachers were most peremptory in lower level classes. But even so, these students' acceptance of teachers' actions reflects their attitude that it is the teacher's prerogative to do all the defining, deciding, and initiating in the situation, while the student merely responds.

The children in the top level were far more critical of the school in a direct way. They felt that the school belonged to them, that it was there to serve their needs. While they were willing to grant its staff some right to tell them what those needs were, as well as how to meet them, they expected and demanded a part in shaping the school's endeavors.

The children in the bottom tracks seemed rarely to think of the school as a place which they could affect in any way, and certainly not as one which they could shape as an instrument to meet their own experienced needs. It was rather a given, unalterable phenomenon which must be endured. Generally it was unpleasant and often unfair. Teachers could make it tolerable if they were fair and nice, but the most one could hope for was an absence of active pain.[16]

It is important that while this passive and alienated attitude was clearly linked with the racial and socioeconomic backgrounds of these students, in ways to be discussed below, it was not shared by all children from these backgrounds. Some black children were in upper track classes. Many of these, especially at Hamilton, were articulate in complaining to teachers that the curriculum was geared to a white and European context which left out the current culture and experience of blacks and their nonwestern heritage. They made pungent protests, but they recognized the usefulness to themselves of success on the school's terms and generally kept up their grades.

Other less sophisticated black children, many from the poorer parts of the city, also believed in the potential usefulness of the school's curriculum to their own ends. Whatever their feelings about it, they did their academic work well enough to qualify for

16. Remember that the school modified these attitudes. The children in high tracks at Chauncey were less independent and the children in low tracks at Hamilton more hopeful.

Track Two, some moving out of lower tracks as they caught on to required skills and behavior. And they were sufficiently diligent and cooperative to remain in Track Two or to move up.

But for those who remained in the lower tracks, not only the content of the curriculum in fields like English, social studies, and the arts, but also the full range of skills to be learned seemed alien and of little use. They could not see the world of their elders, let alone their own current concerns, reflected in what the school was telling them they needed to become adult.

A black English teacher describes their puzzlement over the usefulness of the curriculum:

> I can't think of anything more deadly to them [Threes and Fours] than we just sit down and worry about a verb. Because they can't see any *need* of it. To tell them that they cannot perform or get a job if they don't know how to use verbs is absurd to them because, "My God, I'm sitting here talking and I'm being heard and people understand me." They are capable of communicating. "So what's all this verb and grammatical bit?" So you have to kind of sneak it in or make a game out of it. Then they like it because if they can do it they know their grade will go up, but as far as going out and applying it, they won't for quite some time. Some of them never will.

These students were not well aware of the skills that they would need for even modest occupational success. They knew little of the adult world's requirements and judged relevance by their immediate needs.[17] But they were also expressing a feeling that their kind of people are shut out from any but the most menial of work since they have failed already by ascription. There

17. Werthman found in an intensive study of fifty-six members of black and white gangs that they did not work in junior high school because they saw no rewards from doing so. When they realized in high school that graduation was not automatic and that it would be useful to them for tangible economic rewards, those not already in hopeless academic trouble began to work. (See Carl Werthman, "Delinquents in Schools." Schrag in a study of lower and upper middle class students, and Rhea, in a study of upper middle class ones, found that students were willing to be both diligent and unquestioning even though they found their studies uninteresting and of no direct use. They conformed in order to get good grades, which they thought would be of use to them later. (See Peter Schrag, *Village School Downtown,* and Buford Rhea, "Institutional Paternalism in High School.")

is no point in doing school work as a means to occupational success. Such an attitude is self-reinforcing, for it creates failure in school.[18] The children were all aware of their track level and would sometimes refer to it in addressing teachers. In classes I observed, lower track students occasionally told teachers they were only Track Fours or Threes and so the teacher should not expect so much of them.

An English teacher describes this attitude:

I: Well then, I was going to ask about what you see are the main differences among the levels . . . in the way the class hour proceeds. The things that they do that you have to adjust to?

R: Well, I use the term faster learners and slower learners because this is the way I see them. It seems to me that the faster learners come into the room more with an attitude of "Well, let's see what we have today." You know, "I may not like it but maybe I'll put up with it, and if it's interesting, I'll even like it. Because I can do it. I can usually do the work and I might even enjoy it."

I think the faster learners have a medium or high degree of self-esteem or a personal confidence. The two low ability classes that I teach made up of slower learners, come into the room with an attitude of "Good grief, not another time here. I wonder what it's going to be today. I won't like it anyway—I don't even wonder what it's going to be, I'd rather be out playing baseball. I can't do it anyway. Whatever it is, I can't do it and if I can do it, I'll be shocked and if I do like it, I'll be shocked also."

Some of these children had genuine difficulty in handling the work expected of them. Others in the lower tracks demonstrated that they were perfectly capable of doing work at a higher level, but rebelled at the requirement to do it. These children had more spare time in class, more agile imaginations, and more motivation for creating distractions and entering into conflicts with the

18. John Ogbu documents this pattern of self-fulfilling prophecy at length among children from a poor black and Mexican-American section of Stockton, California. He explains the students' attitudes and behavior in the context of the conscious ambition and experienced frustration of their parents and the stereotyped negative images which many of the school staff maintained even though dealing with a variety of students and parents. (See John Ogbu, *The Next Generation*, pp. 97–100, 133–69.)

teacher. They were thus the visible students and the leaders in the lower track classes. A conscientious math teacher, disturbed by the unwillingness of his lower track classes to work faithfully, gave the following account of these students' behavior:

> If a kid really is bothering me and he's just talking and he won't pay attention and he's just cutting up, I say "O.K., you don't want to learn now, so I'll send you down to the dean's office. It won't go on your record, you can come after school." And I can just mention this and the class quiets down, . . . they don't want to come after school. And it's amazing, the times that I have done this. The first kid that talks I just send him out; it seems like I have to make an example of some kid. And then once I make the example, everybody quiets down. And they work the rest of the period.
>
> And when this kid comes after school—most of the kids—they sit down and *they do the work that would take a period, forty minutes, they do the work usually in ten or fifteen minutes. And it's correct and it's done well.* And this is the sad thing that if you can get the right pressure on them they'll do the work and they can do it very well. But they don't want to work in class. This is probably the best tool I've got. But it's hard on me because I teach another class with them. [Emphasis mine]

For all of these children not working, not trying, provided protection from experiencing genuine failure. But for those who really could do the work without difficulty, a more important motivation was their response to the alien character of the school and its curriculum and its apparent uselessness for people who are black and poor. Some may have gained a kind of superiority and expressive control by their refusal to work.[19] The young math

19. Stinchcombe found a similar pattern in a white small town high school in the west. Students who faced unsuccessful later careers were more likely than others to rebel in school. Both those who were capable but socially disadvantaged and those who lacked individual capacity followed this pattern. (See Arthur Stinchcombe, *Rebellion in a High School.*) Hargreaves's study of the effects of tracking in an English secondary modern school confirms Stinchcombe's findings. Though the students were socially homogeneous white working class boys, the tracking system led to opposed subcultures. The higher track boys identified with the school's values and looked forward to relative success within the working class context. They were diligent and cooperative. The lower track boys looked forward to occupational failure. High status in the

teacher just quoted was concerned about a student who was one of the better known "discipline problems" at Chauncey. He was easily capable of doing work beyond the Track Three math class in which he was placed. The following excerpt from field notes records this teacher's observations about him as we talked after a day's observation.

> Percy, the boy with the process, is also very bright. But usually he just won't work. He'll work literally one day in two weeks perhaps. Mr. Evans said he talked to him for all of ninth period one day. Percy said that he doesn't need to know math to make money. He's making it now without math, so why should he learn math? Mr. Evans argued that to get any kind of a job he'll need it. Percy was un- impressed. If he needs it, he'll learn it then, he said. Mr. Evans tried to persuade him it would not be possible to do that. (Possibly if Percy has been in classes below his ability, it is his experience that he can catch up on two weeks work in one day, more or less at least. So his experience suggests that if he needs to learn anything, he can pick it up as he needs it.)
>
> I said I would think Percy would get bored. Mr. Evans said he had asked him if he didn't get bored sitting in class. Percy said yes, he did. Mr. Evans then suggested that if the class was boring he'd better take note that he was heading for a life of sitting in rooms just as boring, at home out of work or in a jail cell. Percy was still unimpressed.

At the same time that the black children in the lower tracks might find the school's curriculum both irrelevant and useless to them, they recognized perfectly clearly that the school is the agent of the larger society and must represent its values. If what the school teaches is irrelevant to their lives, then their lives are irrelevant to the larger society. It is therefore usual for such children not simply to reject the curriculum but to have a highly ambivalent attitude toward it. It is in this context that one can understand the importance in these students' eyes of a teacher's genuine efforts to teach. Teachers who do not continue to try

---

lower track peer group was inversely related to academic effort and classroom cooperation. (See David H. Hargreaves, *Social Relations in a Secondary School,* especially pp. 159–81.)

despite the students' resistance are telling them they cannot learn what the society calls important. They are offering an insult.[20] One teacher who consistently yelled at children and occasionally hit at them was universally chosen by her students as their least-liked teacher. But the reason given was less often her angry attacks than her disinclination to explain the work or to help children who were having difficulty with it.

In sum, then, the students who set the tone for the lower tracks had opposing normative and practical responses to class-room relationships. At an abstract normative level they accepted unquestioningly the school's legitimate societal mandate to pursue any of its traditional goals, the teacher's right to play any customary superordinate role, and their own duty to be obedient and diligent students. They did not have any moral quarrel with the imposition of punishment for their non-cooperation as long as the punishment was consistently and evenhandedly meted out.

But in practice they rejected the school's goals as useless for them though they took their own need to reject them as a negative judgment on their social worth. While they granted that teachers were only "doing their job" they would still almost universally fail to cooperate with them and tease them on a daily basis—though with varying degrees of good humor. While their model role for a student was a cooperative and diligent one, they practiced and admired boisterous play and little work.

20. Werthman reports with his delinquent gang boys, that it was very important to them that the teacher actually attempt to teach them, take an interest in whatever attempts they made to learn, and grade them on the basis of actual performance. This was a condition of their cooperativeness with the teacher, even though they might in fact still not make the effort to learn. (See Werthman, "Delinquents in Schools," p. 60.)

Herndon found similarly that it was very important to his lower track classes in a virtually all black junior high school that they be doing "real" schoolwork. They wanted to have the books for their own grade and they wanted a teacher who would assign them the usual kind of work. They were delighted with a substitute who did this while Herndon was gone for a month. But he discovered that despite their pleasure in her assignments, they did them incorrectly, carelessly, and most often not at all. (See James Herndon, *The Way It Spozed to Be*, pp. 101–04.) Lower track children in Canton also sometimes objected to "baby books" intended for their academic level and were pleased with ones that looked advanced. But they did not necessarily work in them.

QUIET STUDENTS' DEFINITIONS OF THE
CLASSROOM SITUATION

Vocal students who dominate classroom interaction have been the focus of attention of this chapter. However, at all track levels, especially those in the middle, there are students who generally conform to teachers' directions, are easily corrected when they do not, and rarely offer challenges to the teacher.

In general they seem to have a definition of the classroom situation very like that of the incorporative teachers. They believe that there is a body of knowledge and of proper decorum which they should learn in school and they expect teachers to teach it to them in good faith.

These children need not be prigs; some are even mild discipline problems. But their misbehavior is that of excess energy, high spirits, thoughtlessness, or an occasional urge to tease the adult. Teachers are more likely to speak of those who do create classroom problems affectionately as "rascals" than angrily as "discipline problems." Though these students do not always obey, they do not question the legitimacy of the teacher's claim to authority, nor do they purposefully set out to make his life difficult.

Interviews with these children were usually rather brief, for they had little to say about the school. They accepted the curriculum and did not comment on it. They accepted the teacher's right to give them commands by virtue of simply being a teacher, and they accepted their own duty to be obedient and diligent. (Some, especially in the lower tracks, might not be diligent, but they considered that to be a matter of their own dereliction.)

When asked at the end of the interview what they would change in the school if they had the power of a dictator or wizard, they sometimes changed nothing at all saying they liked the school (and so had not thought about how it might be different), or they changed some detail, making the food better or the architecture more modern.

Despite their generally incorporative approach, these children often named developmental teachers as those they liked best or learned most from. But, unlike the philosophical leaders of the upper tracks, they did not analyze these teachers' style or difference from other teachers, but simply said they chose them because they were "nice" or they "make it interesting." They usually chose the teachers they liked least or learned least from not on the basis of a general approach to teaching but because the teachers reacted with disproportionate anger to small misdeeds, punished students for acts they had not committed, or were so disorganized that they communicated little of the subject matter.

When these students were presented in the interview with the standard set of five imaginary disciplinary situations, and asked what they would do as teacher, they neither administered strong punishment like the typical low track students nor attempted to question and reason with the student like the high track ones. Instead they usually gave a mild punishment. If a student persistently talked, they would move his seat, rather than either sending him out of the room or talking with him to find out why. If a girl refused to do an assignment she found "stupid," they simply gave her an F without asking her why, but without other punishment. Their responses to these situations were very like the typical responses of incorporative teachers to the same imaginary situations.

It is very difficult to say what proportion of the students followed this pattern. It is all the more difficult because students, like teachers, do not fall neatly into distinct types but hold positions in combinations or gradations. And children who would themselves never challenge a teacher to give a reason for a command may share the anger and withdrawal of a challenger when the teacher refuses to give such a reason.

Each school in Canton contained within its solid walls and standard routine a rich variety of understandings of its goals and of the relationships of the persons pursuing them. Teachers differed with one another; students differed with one another. And the two groups differed as they faced one another in the classroom. Let us look now at what happened as persons with such different understandings of their common activity interacted day by day and week by week in the confines of a full classroom.

CHAPTER 5

Classroom Interaction: The Teachers Adjust to the Students

TEACHERS ARE RESPONSIBLE for creating a change in students, for transforming them as raw material. While the analogy should not be pushed too far, it is relevant that the good craftsman whenever possible works with the inherent qualities of his material and not against them. In the schools of Canton, teachers, vastly outnumbered by their students and trying to transform them in educative ways, went further in adjusting to the students than the students did in adjusting to them.

They did not always experience their adjustments as such, and they certainly did not always make them explicit. But observation made it clear that almost all the teachers altered their teaching in the same general ways to meet the needs and demands of classes at the various track levels. Adjustment to track differences included adjustment to different academic competence, different models of authority, and different ethnic and social class styles. This chapter deals with similarities among teachers as they responded to differences among the classes. The next chapter discusses variations among teachers as they interacted with similar classes.

STUDENTS' CHALLENGES

Before describing teachers' adjustments to the students, it is important to say something more of the distinctive characteristics of students' actual behavior in the various tracks. For teachers one of the most important aspects of students' behavior is the challenges which all classes make as they try to get to know a teacher and try to get their own way in areas of disagreement. Teachers were all asked about these challenges in their interviews and all agreed that they are a fundamental fact of classroom interaction. Most agreed that students in Tracks Three and Four posed theirs primarily through overt physical or verbal disorder, while those in Track One and Honors classes most often test the teacher's mastery of the subject and related intellectual matters.

A teacher who had considerable experience as a substitute and so had seen and dealt with a larger number of classes of each track than most teachers, gave the following interpretation:

I: Well then, what about the challenges that children will give to test you out? Are there differences among different groups of children and what they'll do that way?

R: Well, I mean, maybe I'm oversimplifying, but I think people challenge teachers in an area in which the child is good. If it's a slow class they will challenge him physically or verbally, and if it's a bright class they will challenge him intellectually.

It's a very rough assignment to take an Honors class as a substitute teacher because you're faced with thirty-five wise guys. And it's a rough assignment to take a Third Track because everyone suddenly becomes more destructive, walks around more, throws balls. I think they just present you with what they're good at.

I: And then with the Honors kids, they won't do any of the spitball business?

R: Oh no. No. They'll let you get started and they'll correct every word that you pronounce poorly and they'll—if there're two ways to say something and you say it one way, they will *really* fight for it being done the other way.

The teacher has illustrated the style in which top level children give their challenges. The following excerpt from observations illustrates a case in which a boy in a Track Four class completely disrupted a relatively orderly math class with clever use of physical action about which the teacher could do little.

> Most of the students were paying attention to what Mrs. Theobold was doing on the board, and the room was pretty much quiet except for her talking and their replies. There was a bit of desultory whispering and some shuffling and movement. . . .
>
> But while they were still working on the board there was a commotion around Charles, who said he couldn't get his foot unstuck from the chair in front of him. A couple of boys gave some advice. Then a girl said, "Silly, just turn your foot sideways." But that didn't work. She went over to him to offer serious help, and the class started to gather around.
>
> Mrs. Theobold did not try to get their attention back but watched as the foot was struggled with. Charles seemed to be playing a skillful game. He gave signals that he was genuinely stuck, genuinely in difficulty. But when someone would make a suggestion or actually move the foot, he would cooperate with an expression which indicated pleasure with all the attention, yet was not an obvious grin of delight. Then he would yelp in pain, with comic effect, and yet not so loudly or dramatically that the teacher could accuse him of pretense. He made the situation dramatic and funny and became the center of class attention, yet he underplayed his role enough so that it stayed within the bounds of legitimacy despite his comic actions.
>
> The whole class got to grinning, even the initially scornful girl. [Eventually the foot was free, but the class remained talkative and inattentive to the teacher.]

Even when the children in the top and the bottom tracks engaged in explicitly disallowed behavior in class, there was a difference in the kind of misbehavior they chose. A teacher at Chauncey pointed out the boisterous, expressive, and public character of the disallowed behavior in the lower tracks, in contrast to the more private and quieter play of children in top tracks who don't pay attention:

> I: And I wondered about the kinds of challenges that they give you. What sort of things do they do to challenge you, and is it different among the different classes?
>
> R: Yeah. Usually the Level Fours are just generally disruptive.

They're boisterous or they're out of their desks or they're very active in some very overt way: they'll yell across the room or they'll bang on the desk, drum on the desk, this kind of thing.

Whereas the Level Ones will do sneaky things more. They might shoot rubber bands, they'll go through a period of this, or throw paper wads, or they might be playing games with each other. This kind of thing. It's usually quietly distractive. Primarily the problem is that they're not paying attention and the people that they're doing it with aren't. It's not disruptive to the whole class, usually.

Reference to the "sneaky" quality of the high track white children's misbehavior was common. They would break rules because there was something else they wanted to do, or to "get away with something," not to tease the teacher openly or to challenge the rule in itself. The black children in the lower tracks seemed more often to break rules openly and partly for the fun of flouting a rule or the teacher.[1] This difference seemed to be associated with race as well as with track level. It was nicely illustrated in one incident in which two boys in Track Two were asked by a teacher to come after school because they had left class a minute early at the "warning bell" which preceded the end of each class at Chauncey. The following account and analysis are from field notes:

> The two boys whom Miss Liu had told to come back for detention came hurrying in very shortly after the end of ninth period, which ends at 3:15. One, Dan, was a tall, dark, good-looking black boy. The other, John, was a short white boy.
>
> Dan came in now, talking the minute he entered the door. How long did they have to stay, he asked. "I just *have* to be home by 3:30." His parents were counting on it, he said. Miss L. said, "Then you can tell your parents why you are late." She said they would have to stay until 3:20. (The idea was to make up the time they were shaving off class.)
>
> But Dan was not to be stopped. He went on, saying, "You never

---

1. Systematic observations on this point were not made, but it seemed that the lower track classes were no more likely to become boisterous if the teacher were called from the room briefly than were high track classes. In fact if they had been previously boisterous, the level might even subside slightly.

told us we couldn't leave at the first bell. We've been doing it all along and you never said anything."

Miss L. replied that Dan knew very well he was not supposed to leave at the first bell.

"But we've done it anyway, and you never said anything before," he persisted.

"Well . . ." she said, hesitating.

Dan decided to press this home. "Most of us leave then," he added.

Miss L. smiled at this. It was plainly not true; she evidently thought it possible that some had been getting out, but this was clearly an excuse. "No," she said.

So Dan tried again. His parents would be terribly angry, he said. He just *had* to get home. And besides it's not fair keeping us here for something we didn't even do!

"Now wait," said Miss Liu. "You just said you do it every day!"

Dan smiled at being fairly caught in this inconsistency, but drew breath for another try.

John intervened, "Be quiet! Or we'll never get out of here!" (Not exact quote, but the idea is.)

But Dan was not to be quelled. "I've got a paper route and I've got to get started on it."

John cut in, "That doesn't start until four!"

"But I have to get started or I won't get through on time!" countered Dan.

"You have until five, and you know it!" replied John with some heat. He seemed surprised, amused, but somewhat outraged too at Dan's cheerful fibbing.

Dan was silent just a moment with his confederate now also on the attack. John put in, "Since I've been good can I go?"

Miss Liu replied, "When are you going to leave tomorrow?"

"After the second bell," said John.

Dan mumbled another reply which I couldn't hear, something like, "When I want to."

"All right, you can go," Miss Liu told John. She asked Dan again, "When are you going to leave tomorrow?"

"After the second bell," replied Dan meekly.

"All right." Miss Liu nodded. Both boys left. It was 3:19.

This whole exchange occurred with good humor on all sides. Dan affected a voice of desperation, but there was always a light touch implied in his tone. . . . He may indeed have lightened his sentence by being so good-humored in his pretended distraction. Since Miss Liu had some sense of humor and of proportion, Dan made it hard for her to take her administration of punishment much more seriously than she could take his protestations.

This anecdote is a lovely illustration of the different styles of the black and white children. . . . Dan does not take either his crime or his punishment too seriously, but he is willing to use any handy device to get out of the punishment if possible. He enjoys playing on the teacher's character; her insecurity about possible oversights, her sense of fairness, her sympathy, her sense of humor. The white boy, on the other hand, feels it dangerous to be anything but outwardly penitent and ready for reform. Whether he actually is any more penitent than Dan is quite another question.

Dan makes the crime and punishment the occasion for a friendly contest, risking in the game the possibility of receiving a heavier punishment. John is intent upon his separate purposes and soberly seeks the most efficient means of evading the teacher.

In the daily rhythm of classes, the lower track groups were far more restless and subject to collective activity distracting from the lesson at hand than the top track ones were. It was harder for the teacher simply to get their attention. All tracks (and meetings of teachers for that matter) would break out into conversation if there were periods when nothing was happening, for instance if they had to wait while the teacher performed some mechanical chore. But in top track classes, it was often possible for the teacher to start or resume the class by simply starting to speak about the material; silence would fall on its own. In lower track classes it was necessary to call for attention and even then it was harder to get.

Further, top track students responded more quickly to simple reprimands for inappropriate activity, and, if the teacher was firm, were less likely to start again as soon as the teacher's attention was elsewhere. In a lower track class one or more children might engage intermittently in disallowed behavior throughout the whole period. Keeping the level of distracting activity at a low level, without trying to eliminate it, could require a good deal of a teacher's energy in such a class.

However, cooperation even in the top tracks was not automatic. But it could be established for the week, the month, or the year with only brief efforts necessary to strengthen it, while in lower track classes it frequently had to be negotiated daily if not even several times daily.

A generally incorporatively oriented black teacher, sympathetic to the lower track children, described the tracks on this matter:

> But, of course, you have to get down with the Three Level[2] as far as discipline is concerned. You have to yell and scream and hit them over the head and then kiss them. This is about the only way to handle the situation. They cannot conform to someone who insists upon their sitting in their seats and staying there and having their paper and having their pencil and no humor; they have to have humor. They have to be able to laugh at me; I have to be able to laugh at them. And, you have to kind of play it by ear. A One group, you don't have to worry about this too much because all you have to do is raise your voice and say, "Sit down" and they do it. But if you don't, they will make sixth period [her most difficult group of Threes] look like a dream in comparison.
>
> I: If you don't do what?
>
> R: If you don't control them they will. If you sit back and let them go, a One group will chase you right out of the room. And they're capable of doing it.

TEACHERS' RESOURCES FOR CONTROL

As the teachers faced the children's challenges on a daily basis, an acceptable relationship of authority was a necessary, but not a sufficient, basis for maintaining control, for ensuring both order and constructive activity. Teachers mustered other forms of control on a regular basis, and there were clear patterns in the kinds of control used in various situations. Let us consider for a moment the forms of control available.

2. Tracks had been officially renamed "ability groups" in the year of the study. And they were often referred to—as here—as Levels.

One of the most important might be called *arrangement of the situation.* Teachers in Canton were left free within broad limits to determine the physical, social, intellectual, and temporal structure of their classes. They arranged the objects in the room (and rearranged them for different classes), set up rules within the school code, and determined the activities for every class hour. The teachers thus could define the class hour as a context for performing structured exercises or as one for free ranging group discussion. They could establish it as a place to sit still and face front or as one for moving about the room or school consulting books, experiments, or persons. This power to define the situation is important. Routines confidently established take on an air of inevitability. Students come to see them as an inherent part of school, of math classes, or at least of classes with Miss Smith.

Teachers arranged the routines of the class hour differently for different track levels as a means for controlling the different kinds of students. In establishing different routines for the sake of control, they shaped the children's activities without personal direction, without the use of command or request.

Another very important resource for control is the use of *exchange.* When employees are paid there is an exchange of money for dutiful service which becomes a strong incentive for conformity. Students are not offered this incentive. Grades, the most obvious parallel, are an important source of exchange, but their salience varies. For junior high school students they are less important than for high school students who are closer to using them as references. For students who perform poorly they have little value as an incentive. At Chauncey and Hamilton even the children in the top tracks—or many of them—were little concerned with grades because of both their age and their belief in their capacity to make the B average required for entrance to the state university despite an erratic pattern of grades.[3]

3. Seeley, Sim, and Loosley describe the tensions which arise when a school system which decides to stress the idiosyncratic development of the whole child exists in a context where students will ultimately be competing for limited access to universities and high status careers. (See John R. Seeley, R. Alexander Sim, and E. W. Loosley, *Crestwood Heights,* Chapter 8.)

Aside from grades a teacher has few resources for direct exchange with his students. Eighth graders are growing too sophisticated for gold stars. Favors such as field trips do not work with individual students, (except as something to take away) and the enjoyment of learning can not be doled out in reward for conformity.

However, exchange need not be a direct barter of compliance for specific rewards. A superordinate may build up obligations of exchange through many kinds of indirect, even half-unconscious interchange. He may be helpful beyond the call of duty, or informally suspend formal rules, thus building up gratitude and obligation in his subordinates. Such obligations may even be enforced by members of the subordinate group who are aware of, or share in, favors done.[4]

Persons desiring to exercise control of others in any situation may resort to personal *influence.* However, this form of control does not carry the weight of obligation and it depends heavily upon personal resources, which individual teachers possess in varied degrees. Those who had these resources used them. Others made do without this form of control. At the extremes of warmth and hostility, a teacher's personal attitude toward students made a great deal of difference. But these marked feelings of warmth and hostility tended to be associated with a teacher's educational philosophy, and so will be discussed in the next chapter with the effects of variation among teachers.

Analysts of schools sometimes speak of *manipulation* as a significant source of control. It is not really an analytically distinct form of power, but rather is the deceitful use of influence and sometimes is supported by arrangement of the situation and exchange. It is distinguished by the fact that the person using it conceals his true reasons for suggesting a given activity to someone else. It obtains voluntary cooperation which might be withheld were the initiator's actual purposes known. It is the stereotyped method of control of the vulgarized "progressive"

4. This process as a source of informal control has been analyzed at length in an industrial setting and in a government agency. (See Alvin Gouldner, *Patterns of Industrial Bureaucracy,* pp. 172–74, and Peter Blau, *The Dynamics of Bureaucracy,* pp. 215–217.)

teacher who abjures control on the surface but in practice keeps the reins in his or her own hands. It probably is heavily used in some contexts, especially with younger children.[5] It was used from time to time by Canton junior high school teachers, but usually not to accomplish purposes the children resisted but only ones to which they were indifferent. Children of junior high school age are likely to see through the deceit involved in any but this marginal kind of manipulation. Their trust in the adult, needed for the exercise of authority, will then be seriously undermined.

When outsiders think of school "discipline" in a common sense way, normally all these forms of power recede before an image of *coercion*. But in fact the teacher's coercive resources are sharply limited. This is especially the case with classes which engage in punishable activities most often, so that the children develop a familiarity with, and an immunity to, the teacher's arsenal.

Although there are quite a variety of coercive measures available to a teacher, most are relatively mild. Thus teachers in Canton might firmly reprimand a child, make him or her move to another seat, assign him extra academic work, make him come after school for detention, or send him out of the class to the dean, a special officer concerned primarily with discipline.[6] If a child is chewing gum he can be made to come forward and spit it out in front of the class; if he is playing with a toy it can be confiscated.

There are somewhat stronger sanctions which some teachers use but which others consider illegitimate. Thus teachers can engage in brutal insults or in biting sarcasm. They can make the child a butt of humor for the rest of the class. They can hurt him physically. But most teachers in Canton, though not all, abjured

5. Some of the literature advising teachers on discipline suggests manipulation as a major tactic without calling it by that name. An example dealing with the elementary school is Katherine LaMancusa, *We Do Not Throw Rocks at the Teacher!*

6. Elizabeth Eddy catalogues punishments used by teachers in the "slum schools" of a "large Northern City" with a list essentially similar to that used here. (See Elizabeth Eddy, *Walk the White Line*, pp. 149–53.)

these methods as inappropriate. Some, such as physical punishment, were against district policy, and teachers were warned by
principals that they would not be supported in front of parents in
such actions.

In Canton sending a child to the dean is seen by those teachers
who abjure sarcasm, shaming, and physical pain as the single
really forceful coercive weapon available. There was a good deal
of anger in all three schools at the deans, especially deans of boys,
for not using strong enough coercive measures once students
arrived in their offices. But the dean, like the teacher, has a
limited arsenal—and especially so in Canton. His strongest
weapon is expulsion from the school altogether and the next
strongest, temporary suspension. But these were used extremely
sparingly in Canton. Short of these punishments, a dean could
reprimand a student, keep him after school, make him run laps,
have him write essays on appropriate topics, or assign him to
assist the janitors. At most he could call the student's parents and
sternly inform them of the misbehavior, perhaps while the child
sat in the office and listened. For some of the children some of
these punishments had real coercive bite. For the generally well-
behaved, merely being sent to the dean's office was a strong coercive sanction. But with those children most frequently prone to
cause disorder, who were the source of the majority of the teacher's serious problems, the punishments available to the dean soon
became familiar and thereby lost much of their force.

THE EFFECT OF TRACK LEVEL
ON TEACHERS' ACTIVITIES

The Teachers' Arrangement of Classroom Routines

There were striking similarities in the response of teachers of
virtually every philosophical persuasion to the differences in the
behavior and attitudes of the different tracks. They all responded
with patterns of arrangement of the situation adjusted to the
characteristics of each track.

The following two descriptions of a teacher's adaptation to the
characteristics of the students come from a developmental social

studies teacher and an incorporative English teacher, yet they are strikingly similar. The social studies teacher put it this way:

> I think that maybe the clue would be in the way I conduct a class. Groups One and Two . . . I try to conduct as oral discussions, interaction with students, you know, "express your own idea." And everybody, I hope, if they want to, has a chance to talk. Because they seem to be able to handle it without getting too far out of line. I think that's really important in social sciences that people be able to talk and discuss things. But in Threes and Fours I find it very difficult to do it that way. I use a worksheet and work around this, and this keeps the kids more in control. I don't use the discussion method a lot because it seems to really get out of hand then. A little bit at a time I do, and then I'll cut it off and we'll do the worksheet.

The incorporative English teacher expressed her experience and strategy thus:

> I have found, of course, that dictionary work with Threes, particularly, has been successful. They love it. They like to be busy. Isn't that strange? They like to be able to sit down, open a book, and work on something . . .
>
> Discussion—they haven't been able to handle too well. (Hesitation) Because it's still, "Let's outshout one another." I tried discussions with them and found them unsuccessful. I keep trying a little of it but cutting it down, making it pretty short to get kids to express their ideas. But never anything more than five minutes because they go *completely* up and they won't relate to the subject material at all. They will relate particularly on a personal basis. And of course this is part of the difficulty anyway. What *I* did in connection with such and such a thing, or what my mother did, or my girl friend or boy friend, or something of this nature. They cannot state a situation where they are not directly involved.

The use of much written and individual work in lower level classes was partly a technological response to the constant threat or presence of distracting activity. One child making editorial comments or even just talking to his neighbor can effectively destroy a lecture or discussion for everyone. But if students are working individually it is possible for those so inclined to progress with their work despite the colorful or noisy activities of one or more others. The use of written work and its constant presence during discussions was a means of allowing some students to learn while others played. It also provided a way to focus yet divide the class's attention, thus decreasing the likelihood of collective play or teasing arising out of a group interaction. Teachers usually kept their plans flexible in lower level classes, and if the tempo of irrelevant activity started rising so high that the whole class was likely to become involved, they would often cut short collective activity and assign individual written work. In the class cited above where the boy artfully involved the whole class in the drama of his foot and the chair, the teacher brought her lecture to an earlier close and gave more time for the class to work examples than in another class at the same level on the same day where such a collective distraction did not arise.

Still, teachers used structured written work as a device to quiet a class or to keep it calm, partly because most students in Tracks Three and Four actively preferred this kind of work. Several teachers mentioned that other teachers—never themselves—kept orderly classrooms in lower level classes by giving the students well-structured assignments, sometimes even on material already thoroughly covered, which did not challenge or teach them but at which they were happy to work quietly.[7]

Most teachers took both this preference for written work and the boisterousness of the lower level students at face value. But it is important to consider how these pieces of behavior relate to the students' definition of the school and their relationship with it.

Structured written assignments are less mentally taxing than more open-ended tasks; they are more manageable for children who lack the ability or inclination to take on more challenge. But more important they are private activities; a student's mistakes are not publicly visible as they are in oral recitation.

Such tasks also involve less of the student's whole person than

7. Herbert Kohl found that his Harlem sixth graders liked to use a social studies book with structured written exercises even though they would not learn the material it presented which described an American life quite alien to their experience. (See Herbert Kohl, *Thirty-Six Children*, pp. 28–30.)

do either unstructured or oral tasks. He need involve less of his mind to find a right answer to a specific question than to respond imaginatively to a broad one. And he exposes far less of himself to social scrutiny in writing down a short answer than in responding orally to a teacher, a situation where the tone of certainty or uncertainty, meekness or defiance with which his answer is delivered will be visible to both the teacher and his peers. Exchange and discussion with classmates which includes opinion and debate exposes even more of a student's person to public view. For students who lack academic confidence, it is much safer to confine academic activities to the narrowest, most private space available.

These students seemed to prefer a fixed daily and weekly routine. They would ask explicitly for clarification of the routine and for confirmation that it was being followed. And they would object to doing a given kind of task at other than the appointed part of the hour or week. According to teachers they would also become much more active, talkative, and disorderly whenever some unexpected event created a departure from usual procedure. In a situation where they feel unsure of themselves, the presence of routine protects them from unexpected situations with which they fear they may not be able to cope effectively. Further, since the school is experienced by most of these students as part of a racially and socially alien world, as well as one which demands skills they lack, both routine activities and a routine schedule have the advantage of minimizing the thought, effort, and personal commitment which they must invest in a threatening context.

The generally alien character of the mainstream society is often embodied for the student in the person of the teachers. Teachers are usually members of the middle class by either birth or mobility and share middle class expectations for classroom behavior. Many are baffled or angered by lower class students' boisterous ways. Perhaps more important their own self-esteem as teachers is threatened if their students fail to make significant academic progress. They may escape negative reflection upon themselves through vehement blame of the children or radical downward adjustment of expectations mixed with an attitude of condescension. Either attitude will be painful for students. They can protect themselves a little from the teacher and his image of them by engaging only in highly structured routine academic activity in which they neither invest nor expose themselves.[8]

These students' boisterous tone and frequent clowning in class likewise protect them from a negative image. If a student jokes and clowns in class, he defines both the situation and his own performance in it as matters to be taken lightly, as not appropriate for taking the measure of his serious worth or capabilities.[9]

The Teachers' Response to Distractions

Not only did teachers make similar alterations in the kind of activity classes engaged in according to academic track, they also made similar alterations in the way that they treated officially inappropriate activity. The atmosphere of the class hour and the relationship of teacher and students was quite different in the top and the bottom level classes.

With all teachers there was a certain air of intensity in the top level classes. The children were expected to pay close attention at all times except during administrative lulls such as the passing

8. Wax and his colleagues document this pattern of response with unusual clarity in their study of American Indian children. They were able to observe the same children in the Indian village, in the classroom, and in the physically and socially intermediate setting of their own office. They saw that what the teachers took for shyness and academic inability among the students was often simply withdrawal from the uncomfortable school situation with its negative reflection upon them. The children would stumble in school over recitations they had given perfectly the night before at home. They seemed incapable of initiative or of organizing themselves at school in matters which they handled very capably in other settings. The teachers saw them only at school. Their withdrawal and seeming lack of academic and social abilities in that setting increased the teachers' negative stereotypes and their belief that the children could not learn. A vicious circle therefore grew up. (See Murray L. Wax, Rosalie H. Wax, and Robert V. Dumont, Jr., "Formal Education in an American Indian Community.")

9. Herndon gives a dramatic example of this use of clowning, as he describes the behavior of four students in his seventh grade class who could not even read their names. Each refused to admit that he could not read and each was adroit at creating humorous diversion when called upon to read in class. However, one learned to read during the course of the year and then poured forth his former painful feelings to the class, according to Herndon, like a reformed sinner or alcoholic. (See James Herndon, *The Way It Spozed to Be*, pp. 91–93, 186–87.)

back of papers. The pace of activity was brisk; teachers would discourage any quiet whispering or even silent inattention as soon as they noticed it. In general the students did in fact pay good attention and engage in little non-academic byplay.

In the lower level classes the atmosphere was in one sense more relaxed. The pace of activity was slower and there was considerably more inattention, conversation, and often even movement about the room. The teachers would reprimand the perpetrators of these activities if they were prolonged or especially disruptive, but they did not attempt to eliminate them altogether as they did in the top level classes.[10]

However, in another sense the top level classes were the more relaxed. A child who engaged in some physical activity such as throwing spitballs would be mildly told to stop; one who made an angry outburst or mocking comment at the teacher might be only coldly ignored. But in the bottom level classes overt teasing of others or disrespectful comments toward the teacher were treated far more peremptorily and severely. Teachers were often articulate about these differences in their treatment of different groups. For example, one observed:

> R: Of course sometimes you will allow in a Group Three something you wouldn't allow with an Honors student. And conversely, sometimes you allow an Honors student to do something that you couldn't condone in a Track Two because of the tone of the class and so on. For instance, an Honors student might do something which if done in a Track Two class would really upset the whole group.
>
> I: What would be an example of something like that?
>
> R: Oh, jumping up and taking somebody else's book. You know, some sort of overt act. Or even saying something to the teacher in a tone of voice which in a lower track would be regarded by the other kids as a victory over the teacher. In an Honors group it might be

10. Leacock describes similar differences in comparing fifth grade classes in middle income and low income schools. She attributes the difference to teachers' different expectations for appropriate adult behavior in the graduates of the different schools. (See Eleanor Burke Leacock, *Teaching and Learning in City Schools*, pp. 116–35, 151–70.)

regarded simply as bad manners on the part of the student and so would need to be dealt with differently.

It seemed that with the top children the main focus for disciplinary sanctions was attention to academic work, while with the children in the bottom tracks the main focus for disciplinary acts was displays of anger or attempts to rile either other students or the teacher. Consequently, it was with the very children who were most reluctant to engage in academic work that the teachers exerted least disciplinary pressure in that direction.

There seem to have been two general reasons for this difference in the teachers' focus with each track. First, with the top tracks the ground of battle, even when students were truly furious with a teacher, was likely to be academic work. The students in the lower level classes lacked the skill and confidence for such attacks and so always expressed their anger in non-academic challenges. In the top tracks a teacher could therefore keep his focus in the academic realm even when he was in serious conflict with a student. The conflicts were not consequently easy to handle. On the contrary, the students often chose academic ground for their battles because it was very difficult for a teacher to pin down punishable actions. The students would spend considerable energy plotting strategy and weaving traps into which an unwary teacher could easily fall.

The following example is typical. This student who was in Honors groups at Chauncey had come in conflict with her Spanish teacher after the teacher had encouraged her to write a play in Spanish for presentation in class, but had changed her mind after it was written and not allowed the student to present it. The student, Eleanor Starling, speaks:

> I just couldn't stand her and she couldn't stand me. And I'd do anything I could to make her mad. And so I'd put my head down on my desk and I'd pretend I was asleep, but I'd be ready at all times.
>
> Like we were supposed to study these four paragraphs about Mexico City. So I was sitting there [with my head down] and so she pulls my name out of the deck of cards and says, "Eleanor Starling, describe as much as you can about Mexico City." So I just recited off four

paragraphs [laughs] with the book closed. She was kind of floored. It was really a sense of satisfaction.

And I got a very high grade on that. I think I got the only A in the two eighth grade classes on this one test. So she's just lost all hope of outdoing me.

A student in a lower track class finding himself or herself equally furious at a teacher would be much more likely to express it with loud angry protests on the spot than to plan a drawn-out but quiet vendetta. Lesser anger would be likely to be expressed with noisy talk or play or sullen non-cooperation. These styles of response were far more likely to induce classmates to join in the conflict than were the conflicts in the top tracks, which might not even be clearly interpretable to classmates.

The second reason for the difference in teachers' use of restraining sanctions with the different levels was the much greater volatility of the lower tracks. Since the children in the top tracks generally embraced the academic goals of the school and expected most teachers to represent them in good faith, conflicts in most classes were individual matters. But in the bottom tracks where most of the children felt divorced from the school's values and accustomed to conflict with the teachers who represented them, a conflict between one student and the teacher was much more likely to ignite the whole group into rebellion. Those few teachers who seriously violated upper track students' expectations of the teachers' role had to deal also with general volatility in response to single conflicts. I will say more of this in the next chapter, but here the exception helps to make the general point.

In responding to outbursts of anger or really noisy diversion in the lower track classes the teachers used stronger disciplinary measures than they usually used at all in higher track classes. A census of all referrals to the dean (sending a child out of class to the disciplinary officer) from September to January reflected this pattern. The vast majority were for children in Tracks Three and Four. In seeking interviewees from these tracks who had no such referrals, I found there were very few indeed. Most of the rest of the referrals were for black students in Track Two, many of whom share the social characteristics of those in the lower tracks.[11]

Because there was so much distracting activity in lower track classes, the teachers had to employ restraining comments and devices fairly frequently simply to prevent uproar. These actions used up their resources for control, which were especially slim in these classes because of the students' lack of spontaneous attachment to the academic enterprise. Consequently, they did not have capital left to push children to academic effort. At best they established enough quiet so that those who wanted to work could do so.

But the teachers never talked in terms of the allocation of limited resources for control. They simply observed that the students in the lower track classes would not stand for too much pressure to get them to do their work. Academic pressure, they said, had to be applied gently, indirectly, intermittently. But their statements carry the unspoken implication that too much direct pressure will so raise the level of noisy distraction that it will defeat its very purpose.

In practice, if not in intent, the teachers engage in exchange with the lower level classes. The teacher permits inattention to the academic task and minor breaches of classroom etiquette in exchange for the students' willingness to refrain from really disruptive noisy activity or overt angry attack upon the teacher.

Such an exchange may allow every one to get through the hour without unduly intruding upon one another. But it does not result in the most academic progress for the majority of students. Some teachers tried to alter the pattern, either through better sources of coercive control or, more frequently, through increasing students' intrinsic interest in the academic task. But most found it very difficult to change the pattern significantly. And in fact there was

11. Race was a very important factor here. Some teachers associated black children with classroom disruption. They sent from the room children who had no conflict at all with other teachers. On the other side, some black children were particularly sensitive to slights because of their experience of being criticized for their race. They might take offense at a teacher's action and enter into conflict with him when otherwise similar white children would not have.

evidence that over a long time teachers gradually come to adopt an
educational philosophy which justifies the strategies that yield the
minimum of conflict with the students of the schools they find
themselves in.

THE MATCHING OF TEACHERS' STYLES WITH
DISTINCTIVE STUDENT BODIES

The pedagogical philosophies of teachers identified in Chapter
Four were not distributed randomly in each of Canton's schools,
but rather were found in clusters where they matched the characteristics of the student body—or former student body. The sampling method of this study did not allow for a direct count of the
incidence of each philosophy in each school, but each school had a
recognizable faculty culture which reflected different emphases.
Positions were raised publicly at one school, but never given voice
at another. Positions were argued boldly at one school, defensively
at another. Each school had informal leaders among the faculty
who were particularly articulate in arguing the dominant position
or positions for that school.

Proto-authority and the Incorporative Approach

Teachers who had taught at Darwin when it was still called
Lincoln had served exclusively the predominantly black and
working or lower class clientele which later filled the ranks of
Tracks Three and Four and some of Track Two at all the schools.
Among these teachers proto-authority was far more common than
in any other group of teachers. (It was not universal, however.)
It was only at Darwin, where there was still a large cadre of these
teachers from the old Lincoln, that this position was clearly and
openly supported in teachers' formal and informal discussions. If
one ignores the assumptions about child nature included in proto-
authority, it provides the closest match to the behavior of the children Lincoln was working with. They do fail to share academic
values and consequently the patterns they evoke from most
teachers resemble those of proto-authority in their preoccupations

with order and behavioral conformity and their lack of emphasis on academic learning.[12]

There was nearly unanimous attachment to an incorporative approach among the teachers who remained at Hamilton from its earlier days as a school for white middle class children of a more trusting time. The majority of these students probably resembled the quiet students of the late sixties; certainly that was these teachers' memory of them. There was again a match between the student body and the faculty.

It is not clear how much this "fit" of the characteristics of the students and faculty at a school is the result of socialization of the teacher while on the job, and how much is the result of migration of teachers with preexisting attitudes to schools with appropriate children. Administrators and teachers at the various schools confirmed that teachers who had difficulty with children not of the white middle class (children who would not fit the assumptions of the incorporative approach) had often transferred to Hamilton while its population was still nearly homogeneous. Nothing was said of a migration of teachers to Lincoln, although there had been complaints from the community that the teachers sent there were

12.   It is important to remember that the process is always a circular one. Hargreaves's intensive study of an English secondary modern school, educating working class boys who had failed the examination for the selective "grammar school," is instructive here. Hargreaves describes classroom interaction in which the teachers played a part in creating the kind of resistance to learning in lower track boys which then pushed the teachers into patterns resembling proto-authority (or in some cases laissez faire abdication). With high track boys from the same neighborhoods and social status who had also failed once in not gaining admittance to grammar school and had only modest occupational prospects, teachers' relatively high expectations and favorable treatment helped to create patterns of dedication to learning. (See David H. Hargreaves, *Social Relations in a Secondary School,* Chapter 5.)

Rist describes the effects of kindergarten teachers' stereotypes of students based on parental occupation and readiness tests. Not only teacher—student interchanges but students' participation in the class and its subgroups and their academic performance were affected. These effects followed the students as Rist observed them through the second grade. (See Ray Rist, "Student Social Class and Teacher Expectations.") Ogbu indicates class and racial stereotypes can lead parents as well as students to change their behavior to fit teachers' expectations. (See John Ogbu, *The Next Generation,* pp. 133–40.)

the least competent academically, a trait which is conducive to proto-authority. Becker's study of Chicago public school teachers suggests that migration is more important, but that some teachers when forced to remain in an originally uncongenial setting adjust to it and gradually become reluctant to move to another kind of setting matched with their initial style.[13]

In any case, it seems that, given a stable situation in the school, there will come to be a complementarity in the definition of the situation of the majority of the students and the majority of the teachers. The wide variety of students in each Canton school at the time of the study precluded such an adjustment, or rather made it more difficult. The closest approximation of it was at Chauncey, the school with the longest history of such diversity and with the least turnover of students and faculty during the reorganization of the schools. The adjustment of Chauncey's teachers will be discussed later in treating the question of the mutual accommodation of students, faculty, and administration in the schools taken as a unit.

The Developmental Approach

Most developmental teachers had been in Canton less than five years. They arrived in number only after the schools were desegregated. With the exception of a few strong teachers of long service, the members of this group were in their first ten years of teaching, often their first five. Some were young, in their twenties and early thirties, while others were middle-aged mothers starting or renewing a career.

One reason for the scarcity of such teachers among the experienced ones in Canton was the preferences of the man who was chiefly responsible for hiring for a very long period ending in 1963, just when developmental teachers started to be hired in number. Still, the developmental style of teaching is probably the most taxing, and one can legitimately ask whether some teachers tire with the years and fall into easier modes of teaching or into other kinds of work.

13.   Howard Becker, "The Career of the Chicago Public School Teacher."

One must also ask whether people entering teaching are newly likely to have a developmental orientation as they respond to changes in the times and in the students.[14] It was only in the sixties that the idea became widespread that lower class and especially black children who resist the traditional school style might, if approached in the right fashion, be both capable and willing to learn very ably. And it was only in the late sixties that really large numbers of upper middle class children as young as junior high school began seriously questioning traditional school patterns out of principled argument.

The developmental teachers then can be seen as responding to new groups of children, in one case new only in the definition of the adults who deal with them, in the other case actually different from their older brothers and sisters. Whatever the case may be nationally, it was clear that the developmental teachers in Canton shaped their teaching in response to these two groups of students.

Between these teachers and the leaders of the classes at the top track levels there was a ready matching of ideas about the proper character of classroom relationships. There was also a visible sympathy and ease in their interactions. But many of these teachers had entered teaching or at least decided to work in Canton because they were interested in teaching the kind of children found in the lower tracks. In all their conversations they talked primarily about their work with these children. Yet despite their interest in the children, they could not establish the kind of mutually satisfactory relationship that came rather easily for them with the upper tracks. Their goal was to make academic progress with these classes. To do that they had to change both the children's feelings about the school and the patterns of interaction described in the last section. This was no easy task.

14. On the basis of a study of the teacher corps, and a comparison of its interns with other graduate students in education, Corwin argues that such a change is taking place. He attributes part of the difference to increased recruitment of teachers from the upper middle class. In Canton, wives of graduate students and of middle aged professionals constituted a special pool for recruitment of such teachers. (See Ronald G. Corwin, *Reform and Organizational Survival*, pp. 114–16.)

The strategy had two major thrusts. First these teachers tried to increase the students' personal commitment to learning academic material and their trust in the teacher's acting as a good faith agent of the learning process, thus increasing their attachment to classroom authority. They hunted for materials the students would find inherently interesting, and they experimented with methods that might add to the appeal of more traditional material. They were scrupulous in their efforts to make it clear that the basis of their directions for classroom activity lay in the requirements of the learning process. They tried to avoid giving commands which did not visibly bear upon either learning or elementary courtesy. When they made rules or comments designed to limit distracting activity they pointed out their connection with the learning process.

Second, and probably more important, they tried to break up the pattern described in the last section in which teachers concentrated their resources for control upon order, reserving little capital with which to induce efforts for learning. To this end, they generated as much personal good will, which could be used for personal influence, as possible. And they built up resources for exchange with a number of improvisations.

To generate good will they tried to keep their personal relations with the children as pleasant as possible. They made efforts to maintain a quiet tone of suggestion or request even when they felt considerable frustration, and they allowed the students to let off steam from some of their frustrations even on occasion directly at the teacher.[15]

To create resources for exchange they ignored minor school rules and relaxed demands for traditional school demeanor. For example they allowed students to chew gum or to comb their hair in class. They allowed as much nonacademic activity which did not distract others as they could, permitting each child to set some of his own

15. Many incorporatively oriented teachers also used a few of these methods in an attempt to strengthen their hand in exchange with the students. But they were less thorough and planful in so doing, and they used much of the capital they gained for preventing serious disruption rather than for pushing academic effort.

pace of work and to spend some time in other activities which made him feel at home. They interfered as little as possible with emotional expressions.

Some of the developmental teachers even settled on a strategy of more or less explicit bargaining with students in which they allowed activities not officially acceptable as part of a class hour some of the time in exchange for reasonably concentraed effort at another time. Thus one teacher frequently told her Track Three and Four classes that she had work for them planned so that, if they worked conscientiously, it could be completed in thirty of the forty minutes. If they finished they could have the last ten minutes of the period to themselves as a reward. On the day she was observed, the students completed the work in approximaely this time, and the teacher then withdrew to work at her desk leaving them to talk among themselves. In both classes they did so in a quiet and amiable way.

One teacher would occasionally promise a class that if they continued their conscientious work to the end of the week, they could choose the activity for Friday's class. Another more spontaneously allowed the students to play on occasional days when it was clear that no one was willing to work anyway, thus building up general good will which paid off in concentrated work on other days. On the day of observation one of the bottom level classes worked as a group with good attention throughout the period, while members of another resisted gentle but firm urgings until the teacher suggested they work individually, thus allowing those so disposed to work and those undisposed to do as they pleased so long as it was done quietly at their desks.

It is difficult to measure in any very exact way the amount of serious work done either by a class as a whole or by individuals. But the visible signs of concentration in classes where the teacher used either direct or indirect bargaining techniques were above average for those academic levels. The differences were modest, not miraculous. Still, by allowing some forbidden activities in class in return for concentration, the developmental teachers got their students to work seriously for a larger proportion of their time in class than did teachers who officially required them to work all the time but were pushed by constant disruptions into using up their resources for control on matters other than directly academic effort.

It is even more difficult to know whether developmental teachers' attempts to stretch the curriculum to meet children's interests and to incite interests to meet the curriculum bore much fruit. The same slightly higher levels of attention to academic activities in these classes might or might not reflect such a difference. The problem is compounded by Canton's policy of moving children who excel in low tracks into the next higher track at the end of six-week marking periods. A few teachers spoke of their ambivalent feelings upon promoting a child who had caught fire with interest and successful effort and had become a leader and exemplar for the rest of the class. His move up to a more challenging class left a gap sorely felt in his old one. Thus observation of classes does not give data on teachers' relative success in inducing individuals to become attached to the school's curricular aims because the successes are drawn upward and out leaving the bottom tracks always populated with the slow or unwilling.

The Importance of Competence

It is important in understanding the interaction of the developmental teachers with the children of both the top and bottom tracks to note that these teachers shared some crucial personal characteristics. The developmental approach if it is to be successfully practiced demands these characteristics. This approach requires greater academic competence than do others. It opens up a much wider field of legitimate questions from students, and allows a broader spectrum of perspectives from which questions may come. A teacher must have a wide and thorough grasp of his field in order to be able to respond to such questions at all, and doubly so if he is to respond in a way which moves the whole class to a better general understanding of the field. With such an approach no two offerings of the same course will be identical; so the teacher must be sufficiently knowledgeable and intellectually active to be able to cope with a new structure and new material in every course every year. Such teaching may be challenging and stimulating, but it also requires a great deal of mental and emotional energy.

The developmental teachers in Canton in fact gave the impression, essentially without exception, of being especially academically competent and confident in their subjects. They made fewer mistakes than most teachers, both as detected by their students and by another adult. They were willing to admit freely that they did not know the answer to a student's question. They gave an air of enjoying the study of the material at hand and pointed out sidelights and subtleties which other teachers omitted.

In addition to these intellectual qualities, Canton's developmental teachers seemed to have more personal and social energy than most teachers. Their classroom personalities were vivid and assertive. They also had a gift for understanding and organizing both individual and group activity. The invention of structure to fit the needs of the student and the class demands that the teacher be able to respond quickly, imaginatively, and yet firmly to changing situations. Canton's developmental teachers seemed to have this gift and the stamina to keep using it five classes a day five days a week, though many confessed that it strained their resources to do so.

The importance of these personal characteristics to the developmental approach was underlined in Canton by the different personal characteristics of other teachers who used a developmental rhetoric, but did not in fact practice such an approach. Some of these teachers had a good sense of their own strengths and weaknesses and worked out combination approaches which gave them the support of routine structure where they needed it and allowed them to work developmentally where they were able.[16] Others talked like the developmental teachers, but in various ways failed to follow through in their behavior, most often lapsing into a laissez faire pattern where they let the children do much as they pleased. Such a pattern requires less competence, energy, or social responsiveness.

16. Teachers who taught two different subjects were sometimes explicit in interviews about having to use a more structured incorporative approach in their weaker area. Those less skilled in social interaction imposed more detailed rules for classroom behavior than did purely developmental teachers, in order to cut down on demands for individual decisions in this area.

Thus it seems that the developmental approach to the student – teacher relationship is special in that it *cannot* be practiced by any but a highly competent and dedicated teacher.[17]

However, if all the developmental teachers were highly competent, not all the highly competent teachers were developmental. There were some very capable, dedicated and lively incorporative teachers in Canton. However, although their philosophy, especially concerning goals, was of the classic incorporative kind, these teachers tended to take the role of "expert professional" in academic matters. In other words, these most intellectually competent incorporative teachers moved in the direction of a developmental approach in the manner in which they presented academic material. They justified their academic, if not always their disciplinary, commands with reference to academic goals, and they usually gave a schematic explanation of the connection between the required action and the goal if it were at all possible. While competent incorporative teachers almost all moved toward this more developmental style of presentation, teachers who seemed to be less competent gravitated toward the roles of bureaucrat or parent.[18]

Thus, while there are significant differences among competent teachers, they occupy a relatively small sector of the possible range of variation in teaching styles discussed in Chapter Four. This attraction of competent teachers to roughly similar styles suggests

17. The same analysis applies to non-directive guidance if it is to be educationally productive and not to slip over into laissez faire abdication of responsibility.

18. Signs taken to indicate incompetence were obvious mistakes, especially when not admitted in the face of students' objections, defensiveness in response to straightforward academic questions, attempts to evade, change, or cut off student requests for information or clarification, etc. There is some problem with these indicators of incompetence for such refusals could be—and indeed often are claimed to be—signs of a thoroughgoing belief in an incorporative approach where it is the student's obligation only to listen and absorb, not to question. It is the contrast with competent incorporative teachers, often also firm believers in conventional and docile student demeanor, which makes this behavior in the academic context look like a protective device to cover incompetence. Incompetence as used here may be a matter of capability, of academic preparation, or of unwillingness to take the effort to explore new facts or perspectives.

that competent teaching may require an assumption that teacher and student share goals—or perhaps better it may require the creation of such sharing in actuality. It may also require that a middle ground be struck between total dominance of the teacher and predominance of the student.[19]

When students come to school already believing that they share the general goals of the school and that their teachers are especially qualified to spell out specific appropriate behavior for them, an incorporative approach with any of its usual teacher roles fits these requirements. But the more skeptical a state of mind the children arrive with, the more a developmental approach is required to get their trust and cooperation.[20]

It may also be that for an academically incompetent teacher to be able to avoid rebellion he must move toward the outer ends of the continuum of approaches, either demanding that students do precisely as he says with little opportunity to question or participate in the situation on their own terms, or else, at the other extreme, allowing the students to do much as they please.[21]

19. Lewin and his colleagues came to a similar conclusion on the basis of their classic experiments with leadership styles in play groups of boys slightly younger than junior high school age. They found the groups most cooperative and free from conflict and most capable of taking initiative and carrying through a project when they were under a pattern of leadership in which they were given some say but not left entirely on their own. It is perhaps significant that the boys' productivity of finished projects was highest under the pattern of strict adult direction, but that they showed less interest and involvement in the projects, worked on them less when the leader left the room, and included fewer imaginative elements in them under this condition than under the middle one. In the context of a school, we are still left with the unanswered question of whether tangible productivity or independent involvement are more important to the learning process. The competent teachers in Canton, even the developmental ones, gave more direction than the optimal middle group in Lewin's experiments seem to have, but they were operating in the context of a classroom, not a play group. The most complete report on the experiments can be found in Ralph K. White and Ronald Lippitt, *Autocracy and Democracy.*

20. St. John's summary of a group of studies suggests that teachers play a crucial part in the academic and social progress of black children in desegregated schools. They have less impact on whites. (See Nancy St. John, "Thirty-Six Teachers.")

21. Hargreaves found that teachers who were weak both in academic background and in capacity to control students moved toward the extremes of

The fact that all teachers adjust as they move from classes of one track to another, and that they do so in roughly similar ways, indicates that the students have considerable power to define the classroom situation in practice if not in principle. Similarly, the development of faculties at Darwin and Hamilton the majority of whom initially or eventually shared the students' definition of school relationships suggests the students' power to change or drive out teachers who disagree with them. The developmental teachers—competent, energetic, enthusiastic, and determined to change the definition of the situation of lower track students—find their work slow going. In the process their approach, too, is strongly shaped by the expectations of the students, even though they resist changing their one central conviction that the students can and will learn if only they can be brought genuinely to want to.

Actual interaction wears down the sharp edges of the diversity of definitions of their common situation with which teacher and students enter a classroom.[22] Whether they admit it or not, each allows himself to be brought to act for substantial parts of their time together as if he believed in portions of the other's way of seeing the situation.

In this chapter I have stressed the accommodations which students collectively incite in their teachers. Despite these accommodations, there were notable differences in teachers' behavior in classes of all tracks. These differences were clearly related to the teachers' beliefs about the proper character of teaching. Given the differences between the beliefs of some teachers and some students on these issues, one would expect conflicts to arise. In the next chapter I will treat occasions of actual classroom conflict which seemed to stem from students' principled rejection of a teacher's definition of their relationship of authority.

---

control. Some imposed rigid quiet while others withdrew allowing the class to be disorderly. Both patterns tended to inhibit learning. (See Hargreaves, *Social Relations in a Secondary School*, pp. 103–04.)

22. In his early study of the school as a set of interdependent systems, Gordon found that a teacher's acquaintance with students in their extraschool and extracurricular activities also affected his classroom interaction with them. Students' classroom response to teachers' efforts was affected by their recognition or non-recognition of status in the peer hierarchy. (See C. Wayne Gordon, *The Social System of the High School*, pp. 43–48.)

CHAPTER 6

Classroom Interaction: Principled Conflict

CLASSROOM ORDER is fragile. One child intent upon his own purposes can easily destroy the concentration of thirty-six others. One might expect that classes would be in a constant turmoil as a result of someone's intervention. But in fact most classes in Canton were conducted with civility and some semblance of concentration. Upper track classes even proceeded with decorum.

This relative peace is created by the students as well as the teachers. Classrooms have the peculiar quality of being intimate yet compulsory settings. Everyone must exist and interact in physical and social proximity for forty minutes a day, five days a week, for a whole school year. Everyone is motivated to reach an acceptable modus vivendi. The accommodation of teachers to students described in the last chapter is part of this adjustment. But beyond this, both teacher and students have reason to keep their conflicts with one another within bounds which will be tolerable during their long mutual association.

Nonetheless, conflicts do occur and they are occasionally sharp and in some classes frequent. Some of these conflicts arise over students' inclinations to engage in various pleasant activities which distract themselves or others from their schoolwork. The teacher intervenes to restore concentration upon the task at hand. Other conflicts occur when the students are motivated to disregard or to resist the teacher over a matter of principled disagreement about the character of the activity or the relationship they are mutually involved in.

The first group of conflicts is by far the more common. Virtually every teacher in every class must cope with at least one incident such as students whispering with their neighbors, sailing paper airplanes, drumming rhythms on their desks, or reading a novel in math class. The students recognize freely that such activities are illegitimate and will not be angered when told to stop. The amount of such activity varies noticeably from day to day with a given teacher and class. According to teachers, it varies with factors such as the weather, the day of the week, and outside activities ranging from domestic quarrels in someone's home to lunchtime ball games.

A few of the teachers observed handled this kind of disallowed behavior in ways which brought to the fore principled disagreements with the students. But in general, though a teacher's success in keeping this kind of distraction to a minimum required that his style of authority be accepted, it depended more directly upon his skill in classroom management, arrangement of the situation. To avoid these problems, a teacher needed to be adept at such devices as creating smooth routines for classroom chores, having alternative calming activities ready for days when the students came in excited from some previous event, or planning activities which were more interesting for sleepy Monday mornings or less taxing for energetic Friday afternoons. He also needed adroit use of personal influence in handling the hyperactivity or dreamy-eyed distance of particular students who were reacting to something other than the central activity of the class.

In Canton these conflicts occupied a good deal of time in class and a good deal of a teacher's attention, especially so if he were inexperienced or lacking in skill. But little more will be said about them here. Distracting though they might be, they did not stem from the core of the teacher—student relationship.

The occasional conflicts which arose from students' refusal to accept a teacher's definition of their relationship were far more bitter and lasting than conflict over a simple matter of distracting activity. However, these conflicts were not a direct result of students and faculty entering the room with different conceptions of classroom authority. The accommodations described in the last chapter and a certain mutual tolerance and respect smoothed relationships when students perceived teachers to be making a consistent effort in good faith to engage in *some* normatively defined form of authority. The sharp conflicts arose when students perceived the teacher to be defaulting on his obligation to establish a relationship of *any* kind of authority.

Nonetheless, some combinations bred more of these perceptions than others. In general, the better matched the students and the faculty member, the less conflict they had. The smoothest relations of all were between incorporative teachers and those few classes with even the dominant students also inclined to an incorporative pattern. These classes sometimes ran their whole course without challenge or conflict. High level classes with developmentally inclined students and developmental teachers also often passed without serious conflict, but there was likely to be at least debate or exchange, if only of an appropriate and allowed kind, over some point in the material. The least smooth congruent pairing was that of teachers who took a position of proto-authority and low track children. These classes often also passed without direct challenge or conflict, though usually not without some negative sanctions or at least warnings from the teacher. But here there was always a feeling of an underlying restiveness and often pantomiming between students, muttered editorial comments, and the drumming of fingers to express it.

The lower level groups engaged in relatively more restlessness and conflict than the top ones for any given amount of agreement with the teacher; so it is not clear that the pattern of proto-authority was a poorer match with these students than were other adult patterns with their corresponding students. The expectations of the students may have been equally well matched, but their willingness to cooperate still considerably lower than that of other groups.

Since teachers favoring proto-authority were generally as much interested in obedience as in academic progress, it is also open to question how much academic material was learned in their classes, despite the relatively good order. One of the most striking examples of the orderly consequences of matching teacher's and students' expectations occurred in a Level Four class in which the teacher succeeded in keeping the class operating as a group listening to him talk for forty minutes while they remained almost completely quiet. It was a nearly unique occurrence in classes of this track. The exercise at hand was the reading of answers to math problems, their correction, and the answering of questions, but it was clear that at least half the class were not even looking at their papers after the first few minutes of the period. The teacher carried on as though they had been following, and the class did not interrupt him.[1]

The most harmonious combinations next to matched ones seemed to be ones of classes whose predominant approach was incorporative with either developmental teachers or ones using proto-authority. There was some restlessness in both cases. In the first, the students were partly testing limits and trying new patterns; in the second they were sometimes resentful in response to heavy-handed treatment of minor misdemeanors.

Classes combining lower level students and developmental teachers were, as pointed out in the last section, slightly more peaceful and more industrious than other lower level classes. They were more noisy and active than those with teachers using proto-authority and they included considerably more challenge to the

---

1. Under other circumstances, at least some did learn. One such teacher at Darwin asked for the Track Three classes where programmed self-instruction was being tried. This clear written task fit his teaching style, but also gave the students an opportunity to learn despite his shaky competence. A lively student in Track Three who was more intelligent than diligent named this teacher as the one he liked least, giving the laconic justification, "He a mean man." He also named him as the one from whom he learned *most,* giving the reason that there's nothing to do in that class but work!

teachers, but they also seemed to include more genuine attention to the academic task assigned.

The teachers whom students most vehemently opposed were *some* of the incorporative teachers with both top and bottom tracks and most of those devoted to proto-authority with the top tracks. However, these conflicts did not come simply from disagreement over the character of the relationship, but from other qualities which were correlated with the pedagogical positions of the teachers. The incorporative teachers who got into difficulties were ones who believed very strongly in the importance of teaching conventional behavior and academic content. They also believed strongly in their right to roles like that of parent or bureaucrat which should bring automatic deference and obedience. The resistance of children in the top and bottom tracks to both their teaching and their right to deferent treatment made them extremely angry and they responded with open hostility. Unlike the generalized disapproval of the proponents of proto-authority, this hostility was direct and personal in tone. The strong feelings behind the students' response grew out of their receiving that hostility.

Some of these teachers and many of those espousing proto-authority were shaky in their academic competence when facing the knowledge and the style of questioning of the top tracks. These students perceived this lack of competence as a lack of the quality on which a teacher's claim to authoritative status is based. They therefore were not ready to accept these teachers' orders without question. But the teachers exercising proto-authority considered unquestioning obedience a necessity. Conflict ensued.

When students were asked directly in interviews whom they liked most and least, their responses seemed to be based primarily on teachers' friendliness or hostility to students. There were a few teachers in each school who were outstanding either in their positive attitude to the children and faith in their capacity to learn or in their vehement hostility to any student who did not conform instantly to academic and behavioral expectations. These teachers were named as most or least liked, respectively, by nearly every child interviewed who had them in a class or even a study hall, and occasionally by students who encountered them only in extracurricular activities or the hall.

Often the same teachers were named also as those most and least learned from, but a surprising number of students even in low tracks made judgments about learning on the basis of some form of competence. Those in the low tracks would choose teachers who had ceased to try as those least learned from. Those in the top ones would name teachers who could not meet their academic challenges or those who refused to answer their questions or to let them speak in class.

Students systematically tested and assessed every element of the relationship of authority claimed by a teacher. They devised trials to find out if he could play the superordinate's role in a competent fashion. They discovered and assessed his conception of their own role. And they made judgments about whether his actions as a superordinate actually served to promote the educational goals which justified his claim on their obedience.

REJECTION OF THE TEACHER'S CAPACITY
TO PLAY THE SUPERORDINATE ROLE

All classes of children challenged teachers to find out if they were personally in control of the skills which qualified them to act as agents of the goals of the school. If they lacked the capacity genuinely to represent these goals, then they lost their claim to the right of command over students.

As indicated in the last chapter, children in the top tracks chose academic ground upon which to challenge the teachers. The teacher who made mistakes or displayed a lack of confidence in the face of such a challenge would, in these students' eyes, lose his claim to act as a legitimate agent of academic learning. He would be barraged with niggling questions and corrections as a demonstration of the students' lack of faith in his claim to authoritative status. However, if a teacher passed this test decisively he would be trusted to be capable of imparting knowledge and leading analysis, trusted to be a legitimate superordinate appropriately claiming authority.

One of the academically best prepared English teachers, who was teaching at Darwin, described this process. After some experience he had developed a quick recognition of such challenges and a strategy for unanswerably demonstrating his capacities.

> The Honors kids instinctively test each teacher they get to see whether or not they're smart enough to teach them. For instance Dick Stein. The first day in class we were talking about what literature was, what our purposes were to be, and he talked about *Tristram Shandy*. Well, so I just gave him some of his talk back again, exchanged some rapid conversation about how this book related to that, how this concept related to the other. And piled it up over his head and buried him in verbiage.
>
> That was the end of any problems with Dick. Dick and I get along beautifully. And he has a lot of troubles with his other teachers. Because he can put them down. He really knows a lot about some areas. But he's only fourteen years old.

Students in the lower levels had difficulty judging teachers' academic competence, unless they made blatant mistakes or failed to try to teach. These students did mention repeatedly in interviews that some teachers explained well or badly or were especially willing or unwilling to explain and to help a student if he were having difficulty. Faithful performance of academic duties and the capacity to meet the child's mode of comprehension was the test of competence here.

Lower level students made their most direct challenges of a teacher in matters of regulation of distracting physical activity. For these students part of the necessary qualification for occupation of legitmate superordinate status was the capacity to insist that students engage in official classroom activity. They would be boisterous, clearly watching a teacher to see if he could stop them, and they would make fantastic fibbing excuses like Dan's in the last chapter to see if the teacher were capable of directing their activity or could be fooled, distracted, or defeated by their energetic nonconformity. A teacher who could not successfully stop them was not considered competent to hold the office and would meet teasing and boisterous play all year.

Just as lower level students did some testing for academic competence, upper level students would also test to see if a teacher could keep them working, though much of the play they would try to get away with was verbal, including long digressions by the class as a whole from the subject officially at hand.

These tests of a teacher's competence to claim superordinate status were serious, and a teacher who failed them could have a great deal of difficulty in controlling a class. The students could often be cruel in their teasing and persistent misbehavior in such situations, but the cruelty was not purposeful, but a by-product of a childish joy in getting away with something. While such a teacher would not be respected and would be willfully disobeyed, he would not necessarily be resented or disliked. In fact students might even find him personally pleasant and congenial, especially if he lacked competence because he was an inexperienced teacher or was teaching outside his field of expertise.

I observed a clear demonstration of this attitude in following a first year teacher at Chauncey through her day. At the beginning of the year she did not know when and how to be firm. When she began belated and not very forceful attempts to take a stronger hand, her classes had long since learned to take advantage of their opportunity for recreation. However, she was a pleasant young woman with a sense of humor and clear good will toward the students. They took advantage of her but did not express any resentment toward her. Their actual good will became clear in a class during which the principal sat in to observe for the teacher's evaluation. During the period a window rattled loudly in the wind and a wall decoration fell from its place. The principal got up and fixed each, making clatters and bangs as he did so. This over, two workmen strolled in and spent most of the rest of the period hammering on some cabinets. Such noisy events would normally seize the attention and comment of much better controlled classes. But the children saw the principal and apparently understood his mission. Throughout the class they were deaf to the din, giving rapt attention and appropriate answers to the teacher. Though they would tease her for fun, they would help her when it counted.

However, though classes bore no enmity to teachers who lacked academic competence or the knack of controlling restless play, they quickly became bitter if the teacher attempted to compensate for his weakness as a superordinate in authority by controlling their actions through coercive methods. These teachers lost their right to control in not representing the values of the school. It is illegitimate for them to use coercive resources— which are granted as a supplement to authoritative control—as a substitute for effective moral claims.

An extended example will illustrate the difference in the students' response to simple incompetence and to incompetence controlling through coercion. The class was a Track One math class at Darwin taught by a teacher who provided one of the purest examples of proto-authority in the sample. The class was probably the single one most affected by my presence. My day's observation suggested to me that this teacher lacked academic competence, but when he mentioned before the last class of the day that it would be dealing with probability, I thoughtlessly made pleasant conversation by saying I knew a little about that. His response was suddenly defensive, and the events of the class suggest that he was afraid to display his grasp of the material before a knowledgeable visitor. The following is a briefer paraphrase of my field notes describing the class.

In the early part of the class the students pushed the teacher's statements when they had half a chance and haggled over small points where they could. But they did this in a good-humored, more or less jocular tone, and the teacher also responded with a jocular manner. For example this exchange:

Mr. Taylor asked a boy what the probability of the number on a die showing three is. The boy replied zero, because dice don't have numbers, they have dots. Mr. Taylor walked over to an alcove containing a window and looked out, hidden from the class. He turned around and said, "All right, shall we go on with the class?" The boy replied, "All right. It's 1:6 (the correct answer). The boy's tone was good-humored, and seemed to imply that his first reply had been a game which was now concluded. However, the teacher twice more made derisive references to the boy's comment.

The class grew gradually more talkative and more challenging. The teacher apparently let them go further than usual, for they started turning frequently to look at me and point me out to one another, something which occurred very rarely indeed during the study. He taught almost nothing during the period and even ended the lesson early, reminding the class of the homework assignment and retiring behind his desk. But when the class started to get out of their seats and mill about near the door waiting for the bell, he grew suddenly stern and angry. He warned them he would give them a very difficult test the next week. The students were sitting at various angles in their desks and looked unimpressed. He started adding to the punishment. One of the boys in the back when directly addressed, replied "You've said that before." The teacher said yes, but this time he would do it. He kept adding to the punishment as they looked lethargically on, saying it would count equally with the mid-term, then adding that he would include earlier work. "That's cheating" replied someone. The class gradually began to grow more serious, to sit facing him, and to take on a sullenly resentful tone.

Two girls made protests appealing to the principle that the punishment did not fit the crime, but the teacher was unmoved. He replied with accusations which were exaggerations at best, most of which he left half-finished. He kept the class three or four minutes after the bell for the end of school, a fairly strong punishment in itself. Most of the class departed in haste when finally released, but the two girls stayed to protest more. One clearly was arguing that his punishment was for my benefit. Since I suspected they were right, at this point I thought it best to depart.

This class clearly had limited respect both for the teacher's academic abilities and his capacity to control them. But he and the students seemed to have reached a modus vivendi so that their usual relationship to him was one of gentle teasing. When he suddenly tried to assert his power over them by using the only real coercive weapon available, that of grades, they were at first unbelieving that he would seriously try to defeat them on their own intellectual ground, then bitterly resentful of his use of a coercive measure which went against clear customs about material appropriate for a test.

This teacher probably departed from his accommodation with this class because of my presence. His behavior with the class was very different from that with his lower level classes and must have violated his self-image. He attempted to reassert this image at the end of the period.

He was a retired sergeant in the armed forces with many years of teaching experience at Darwin. He was extremely proud of his capacity to control students in the lower track classes and spoke repeatedly and with pleasure of his power over them. And he did have such power. It was he who taught the only Track Four class I saw which consisted of the whole group facing front while the teacher talked for the whole period—the math class referred to early in this chapter. There he was able to keep restless movement and sound to a minimum with the use of a truly peremptory tone and harsh warnings hinting of physical coercion such as "I could shorten you up real quick," and "It would be very easy to put a straight jacket on this class." Vague as these warnings were, they clearly carried some force with students of a group who were not easily daunted.[2] His normally jocular manner with the upper track class, which must have been a psychologically difficult adjustment, underscores the social necessity of teachers' changing their styles to fit their students.

REJECTION OF THE TEACHER'S
DEFINITION OF THE STUDENT ROLE

The students would engage in conflict with teachers who seemed to picture their own character or their school role in a way they found insulting. The lower track students' vehement rejection of teachers who made no serious effort to teach is an example

2. Despite this iron control lower track students did not name this teacher as among the least liked or learned from. Counselors said that he was generally accepted by lower track students. When asked why, the counselors explained that this acceptance was based on the fact that he was predictable, consistent, and impersonal in his treatment of students. So long as they obeyed his rules, they got along with him.

of this attitude. The students took the teacher's reluctance as a sign of his belief that they were incapable of learning and responded with hurt and hostility to such teachers. Because these students liked and were accustomed to structured written lessons, even some of the teachers who attempted nondirective guidance in good faith seemed to these students not to take them seriously. They responded with anger. A student in Track Four at Chauncey describes the teaching of a man who attempted this pattern with only modest skill in a class in family living. Since he was not attempting to teach as she understood it, she held that he had no right to interfere with the students' activities in class.

I: Which of your teachers do you think you like the least?

R: Mr. Mundt.

I: And what's he like?

R: He don't never do nothing in his class but talk and pick at people and things like that.

I: Umhum. Well, when he picks at people, do you mean he tries to get them to talk or he picks on—

R: He bothers them. Like if you were minding your own business— See he don't never do anything in there, but he talks and he never give any written assignments or anything. And once in a while he'll show a movie. And if he's not talking, nobody's talking, and then if you turn and ask somebody something, he gets mad and tell you to be quiet.

The students in the top tracks were most likely to reject teachers for their picture of the student role when they treated students as consistently frivolous or as younger than they were. They wanted, like the lower level students, to be taken seriously, and their demands were higher. An example of a teacher rejected on these grounds was Miss Bock, who had taught in the primary grades for most of her career and maintained much of the style and even the language which she used in that context. She was disliked by students at all track levels. An upper track student describes her classroom manner:

She treats the kids like kindergarteners. And when she's angry, it's just like the old schoolhouse. See she goes (he claps his hands),

"Let's come to order now." . . . She addresses the class as "children" all the time and these are kids that are thirteen and fourteen years old and it sort of bothers them to be, you know—I mean they won't say this is why I don't like it, but it's just the atmosphere of the classroom. And I don't know. I think she'd probably be a good elementary school teacher.

This teacher was the only one in the study to speak of problems of classroom disorder as "naughtiness."

REJECTION OF A TEACHER'S CLAIM TO SERVE HIS PROCLAIMED EDUCATIONAL GOALS

The strongest classroom conflicts occurred when the students perceived the teachers to be claiming the right to demand obedience while they clearly failed to serve educational goals. An incompetent teacher was *unable* to serve them, and so less strongly condemned than a teacher who willfully betrayed or neglected them. Such teachers seemed to be asking students to be personally subordinate to them, to obey their whims rather than the needs of the educational process. When students of any level perceived a teacher to be making such a claim, they rose in angry rebellion.[3] Students judged a teacher's good faith in serving educational goals according to their own definition of those goals. Thus disagreement over educational goals could appear to the students as the teacher's bad faith in their service. Similarly, in cases of disagreement over the relationship of the superordinate's role to the justifying goals, students often perceived teachers to be acting arbitrarily when the teachers perceived themselves to be defending their status as agents of the school's educational mission.

This kind of conflict often arose between high track classes and teachers who took an incorporative stance and a parental role, especially when they were teaching in the poorly defined subjects of English and social studies. (Similar teachers who took a bureaucratic role, followed proto-authority, or taught in more structured subjects such as mathematics, stayed close to texts

3. Their perceptions need not be correct from an observer's point of view, and they certainly were not right from most of the teachers' point of view.

which provided justification for most of their directions.) But these teachers lacked a clear textual referent and when asked by the students to justify a command referred to the teacher's right to personal discretion. In the students' definition of the relationship, the teacher's right to command rested upon demonstrating that his directions served educational goals. His status was questionable if he could not make such a demonstration.

Consequently confrontations occurred in which students said, "Why should we do it?" and the teacher in essence replied, "Because I say so!" To the student this reply looked like an attempt to impose simple personal subordination in the name of authority and he would grow angrier. "What does it have to do with what we're supposed to be learning?" he would ask, in effect. And the teacher would reply, in effect, "If your teacher says it has something to do with learning that is all you need to know. Now stop this impudent questioning." For the teacher, to give an explanation would be to weaken his claim to complex personal wisdom as the basis of his superordinate status. For the student, *not* to give an explanation was to undermine almost completely the teacher's claim to be an interpreter of educational goals as the basis of his superordinate status. But because their definitions of the elements of authority were different the insistence of each upon his own definition destroyed his standing in the other's eyes as a person responsibly participating in a relationship of authority.[4]

An example of this kind of conflict arose in an English class at the Track One level taught by the teacher described as treating children like kindergarteners. The discussion concerned Faulkner's short story, "A Rose for Emily," which the class had read in preparation for the hour.

> Max kept calling out answers. Sometimes he would raise his hand and Miss Bock would recognize him. Sometimes he would get to make his point even though he called out because Miss B. did not cut him off before most of it was out. On one of these occasions when he

4. It is informative to compare the issues which arise in such clashes over authority to those in the moral dilemmas Kohlberg uses to delineate stages of moral reasoning. (See, for example, Kohlberg and Turiel, "Moral Development and Moral Education.")

did get to make the point, but Miss B. then cut him off, Dick spoke up saying, "He's right though." Miss Bock cut off Dick too, saying, "Don't call out."

Max had raised his hand by now and a girl named Sally with shoulder length straight blond hair had hers up. Miss Bock said she was going to ask Sally what she thought. Dick protested, but Miss Bock replied, "You didn't have your hand up; you have to wait your turn. Sally had her hand up first, Max is second, and you are third. Sally?"

Both Dick and Sally were saying "But . . . but . . ." during this reply. Sally responded to being called on by saying that Dick was first. Miss Bock said "All right then," and listened to Dick. The class was making restless movements.

Dick argued that Max had a good point because the theme of the story is—but Miss Bock cut him off, saying, "Don't tell me what the theme of the story is, that's not an answer to my question. That's the problem with a lot of you on your tests. You talk about something that's only tangentially related to the question."

Dick was sputtering "but," but Miss Bock put up her hand, and wouldn't let him get it out. She said, "Wait. I want an answer to my question. I'm not saying what you're saying isn't true or valid, or that it isn't important, but it's not an answer to my question. I asked about the meaning of that one sentence."

The class as a group was plainly restless and seemed annoyed at her handling of the situation. Dick seemed to be trying to say that to understand the sentence you had to understand the meaning of the story as a whole, but Miss Bock was trying to do little more than unscramble a Faulknerian sentence and see in a simple sense why the various parts were there. It took some time for her to be able to get the discussion going again at all, but she did get some answers out of some of the girls, two or three.

Miss Bock does not explain why she wants only the answer to her questions. Her refusal to let someone say how the theme of the story affects the sentence uses up a good deal of time and good will from the class. But it seems to be important to her that she establish her right to get the kind of answer she wants, simply because she is the teacher and that is the way she wants things done. Max, the instigator of the incident, was one of the most persistently rebellious of all the high track students in the school.

But Dick was far more conforming and in an interview spoke critically of Max's general behavior. Sally was a quiet student in the rest of the hour and in other classes. They insist on pursuing the point of the sentence and the story together because it seems to make sense. If the teacher refuses, she should explain why it does not make sense.

In lower track classes students most often perceived a teacher to be failing to act in the service of educational goals either when he clearly did not make any effort to teach or when he gave a child a punishment but refused to name the crime or refused to believe the student's protestations of innocence.

A classic case is the following incident observed early in the study at Darwin. The boy in question was later interviewed and turned out to be a quiet and wary boy recently come from the South. Though the incident was never mentioned, the boy spoke angrily in general of teachers who punish you but won't tell you what you did.

[The students were working at their desks.] Miss Brown looked up and said to Stillman, "All right, go in the back corner without your books." There had only been a very quiet murmur in the room. I don't know whether Stillman was the source of it or not.

Stillman asked very quietly, almost in a mumble, what he had done. Miss Brown simply told him to go on, without his books. Stillman asked, this time clearly audibly, what he had done. Miss Brown said, "Don't talk back, Stillman. Go on back in the corner." Stillman said he was not talking back, he was simply asking what he had done. Why should he have to go back there?

Miss Brown said, "Because I'm telling you to." She looked down to her work again. Stillman just sat there. She looked up again and he mumbled that he wanted to know what he had done. Miss Brown said, "We'll discuss it later." Stillman still insisted that he must know what he did. Miss Brown picked up the pad of referral notices and told him warningly to go on back. He kept his ground silently and she said, "All right," and put down the pad. She told him to go out in the hall without his books and wait until she brought him the referral notice. "Go on, hurry up." Slowly and reluctantly but without pausing, he went.

In a quiet way Stillman was offering Miss Brown ferocious resistance. He stoically accepts a much larger punishment than his original one rather than yield to her in this matter of principle. It is not clear whether or not he was guilty of making the noise that caused her to look up, but the issue quickly became one of his right to have a justification for punishment versus her right to unquestioning obedience.

In the intimacy of the classroom, even the tone of voice in which a teacher gives a reprimand or punishment is important in a student's acceptance of its legitimacy. If the teacher's tone implies personal dislike or an attempt to humiliate, his action will be taken as a personal attack rather than an action in the service of legitimate classroom order and education. The students in the lower tracks have a finely tuned sensitivity in these matters.

This process can be illustrated with an example of a set of encounters in which the teacher very carefully kept her sanctioning of a boy who was testing her rather severely at an impersonal level. A long account from field notes of the interaction of the two through a whole period will give the reader some sense of the delicate intricacy and the fantastic speed of crucial interactions in the classroom. The account is from the same Track Four math class reported in the last chapter in which a boy got his foot caught in the chair ahead of him and became the center of attention for the whole class. (Italicized sections are reflections made as I was writing out the events at length the following evening. They are set off from actual observations which are not italicized.)

Earlier Guy, a very big black boy seated in the back, was out of his seat. Mrs. Theobold told him to sit back down and asked rhetorically, "Do you wonder where your points go?"[5] He replied, with only the slightest edge of irony in his tone, "Yeah, where?" Mrs. Theobold didn't understand, asking him to repeat. He did. *I think she just gave a straightforward answer.*

5. This teacher kept a chart of points for good and bad behavior in her Track Four classes.

Guy thus came to the near edge of mocking her, but by using a rather
factual tone, stayed clear of it. She kept control by treating the question
as serious and passing over it quickly. Thus there was a kind of stand off,
with each keeping face. Guy questioned her definition of the situation
publicly, but didn't push it; she refused to understand his questioning of it,
and he allowed her to misunderstand him. . . .

Incidents like this are often so minor that I don't notice their significance,
or not totally, at the time. It is only in looking back that I see how im-
portant they are. These duels of definition or for status occur in a matter
of one or two seconds and scarcely ripple the surface of the main inter-
action and yet they are very significant.

Note that Mrs. Theobold gave Guy fairly stern treatment the rest of the
period. It may be her attitude was a response to the questioning of her defini-
tion which she publicly did not even understand.

Thus Guy tried two or three times to get out of his seat during
the course of the period. Each time Mrs. Theobold would speak to
him before he had gone more than a few steps, telling him to return.
Usually this was simply a peremptory, "Guy, you have no reason to
be out of your seat!" Or "Guy, sit down please!" Sometimes it was
just "Guy!" and gesture of direction back toward the seat. This
was all said in a very firm tone, but not an angry, hostile, or be-
leaguered one. Once Guy replied that he had to get some paper—
this was just before they started to work on their own. Mrs.
Theobold replied, "It will be handed out later and you know it,"
with some slight annoyance.

After the incident with Charles's foot, Guy started demanding
attention frequently, by getting out of his seat, making comments,
etc. The comments were pretty neutral, impersonal, that is they
were comments on the students' interaction with each other, not
comments directed toward the teacher. At one of the first of these,
while Mrs. Theobold was talking, she stopped and looked at him
sternly with arched eyebrow. "O.K., Teacher, I'll be quiet" said
Guy. At least one other time the same silent stern look got the same
response out of Guy. He addressed Mrs. T. often by name, as it
were, but always as "Teacher." She accepted this without comment.

But like much of his other behavior the name is a way of putting dis-
tance between himself and her definition of the situation. He refuses to
accept her as an individual, but only as "Teacher" and repeatedly insists
on this definition. But he says Teacher, not Teach; he doesn't mock or flaunt,
just firmly states his perspective.

Just before the foot incident, Mrs. Theobold was going through the problems as they should do them on the board. She looked up toward Guy and said "Guy do you understand?" Guy replied, "No, I can't do it." Mrs. Theobold started to back up and explain it to him, but someone else did something that distracted her. After that was settled she went back to the main explanation, then said they were to work some problems. She turned to Guy who was being rather noisy as the whole class started restlessly moving and said she would come and work with him as soon as the class got started. She did this, and was with him quite awhile. Then when she left he was soon staring into space. She went back, asking him what he had done. She worked with him awhile more. Then she left again to help others and he started calling out to her to help him. He said he was stuck.

It seemed that he wanted attention more than that he was having real difficulty. In calling for this help he also publicly pointed to his difficulties, in a kind of acceptance—and possibly simultaneous rejection—of the values of the classroom. Very good symbol of the black children's frequent ambivalent response. He simultaneously (1) annoys Mrs. T. by calling for her to spend all her time with him, disrupting her work with the others, (2) points out to the class that he can't do this stuff, this isn't his important work in life, (3) admits failure in the task set, (4) accepts the teacher's importance and her definition in asking for both her presence and her help with the work.

There was one more incident with Guy. Right after Charles and the foot the class was restless and noisy. Mrs. Theobold said, "Charles I don't know what's the matter with you today, this isn't normal for you." Guy started to make a comment, and Mrs. Theobold said "You are acting normal for you. Now try to be unnormal and do some work." Guy said something like "You want me to be unnormal?" in a tone as though asking for clarification, but it was a bit defensive too. Mrs. Theobold said "Unnoisy. I want you not to be noisy and to do some work."

The first comment to Guy had been the bitterest of any she had made or was to make all day. It had a definite impact on the room. (Just how I know this is hard to say. I could feel it go right down my spine and the class gave some kind of response, a little laugh or a little silence.)

Again, Guy's response was subtle. It carried two messages. At the first level it was a naive request for clarification but also challenged Mrs. Theobold to "say that again slowly." At another level he was saying,

"You want me to act unnormal, lady, I can. Is that what you want?"
The second meaning was more subterranean, and Mrs. Theobold backed off
from even the more surface challenge. She changed the word "normal" to
"noisy" thus making the accusation much more trivial. She essentially
backed off from the personal level of attack on character to the impersonal
one of appropriate classroom behavior. Thus Guy once more held Mrs. Theo-
bold at a distance, actually got her to retreat, without an open challenge,
using a simple informational tone of voice. And Mrs. Theobold was able to
save face by insisting on the relevant but less hurtful definition of appropriate
classroom behavior.

Guy and Mrs. Theobold play this game rather adeptly, each keeping
his piece of territory with sparring in short but loaded exchanges where each
has a finely tuned sense of how far to push. Mrs. Theobold remarked to me
that by this time in the year {spring} you have gotten to know the children
and have worked out a modus vivendi with them. I doubt this one is con-
scious, but it is clearly present.

Note that Mrs. Theobold is restrained in these exchanges. She was over-
wrought over the reaction to Charles's foot when she made the "normal"
accusation, yet she backed off where I have seen teachers sail into a student
with a personal attack in similar situations. So she has a sense for leaving
the students room to express their feelings while she concentrates on reasonable
order and reasonable work.

Finally, the black children in all tracks check very carefully to
see if their teachers seem to treat all students alike. This is
particularly the case when the class is racially integrated. It is far
more important to a teacher's claim to be acting in authority
rather than out of a desire to be personally superordinate that he
treat everyone similarly than that he be either lenient or kindly.
One boy explained this in an interview. He was very angry at his
French teacher who treated different people committing the same
offense in very different ways. Asked what the relationship
between strictness and fairness is, he explained it this way:

> Like my French teacher . . . she gives me a bad time *and* she's
> unfair, you know. But other teachers they give everybody a bad time,
> you know, then that's fair. Like they give white, colored, Chinese,
> everybody gets a bad time, just mean teachers.

CONCLUSION

The chapters of this part have documented the diversity of ideas and practices which both teachers and students in a single school bring into its classrooms. Not only the teachers but the students consider the classroom and the student—teacher relationship to be governed by norms growing out of the educational process and out of general principles of fairness and respect. The most fundamental of these have to do with the goals, roles, and relationships which constitute authority. Definitions of these norms use similar broad language to cover quite different specific ideas. Unless both parties are sensitive to these differences conflict can result.

In the long run the teachers adjust to the students as a body as much as the students adjust to them. Adjustments in the activity and style of interaction which take up the class hour are the most striking. Some teachers make these adjustments out of conscious analysis of the students and their needs and behavior. Others make them more gradually as they are pushed by events.

It is especially notable that in the lower two tracks essentially all teachers emphasized written work individually performed, and all used much of their resources for control more to keep noise levels down and tempers calm than to press for academic accomplishment. While there were still significant differences among the teachers as they dealt with a single track, the differences in a single teacher's behavior with different tracks were at least as important. One sees here the necessity of order as a precondition to learning in a school setting, and the relationship of students' willingness to embrace learning as a goal or moral order which supports authority to their willingness to be voluntarily orderly.

Where there was disagreement over the definition of authority, over the character of roles, relationships, or the moral order of school learning, some teachers adjusted to the students' definitions out of an analysis of their claims and arguments, while others did so out of an unarticulated sensitivity. Others never realized that students might have a serious normative model of authority different from their own and found themselves in chronic conflict with their students without ever comprehending its source.

The variety of students in each of Canton's schools and their challenging character made it difficult for teachers to develop smooth adjustments to them. The students were difficult to teach and they were difficult in varied ways. Perhaps the only classes which did not present a "problem" of some kind were top track classes with developmental teachers and those with only what I have called quiet students with incorporative (or developmental) teachers. The other matched pair, low track classes with teachers endorsing proto-authority, may have followed an uneventful course satisfactory to the participants, but it was one in which both concentrated on order and ignored learning.

Where students and teachers were not matched, one or both had to adapt or put up with persistent conflict. The top tracks could make life very hard for a teacher, and they might feel themselves put upon and fail to learn as much as they were able to. But it was the bottom track classes which presented the most serious problems for both teachers and students.

In these classes the pressures on teachers to stress order alone, or nearly so, were very strong. Even the developmental teachers who were energetically dedicated to inducing these students to learn were less than spectacularly successful in their efforts. Their attempts to lure the students to their own pattern of authority by finding substance which would catch their intrinsic interest were helpful but by no means sufficient. More striking were their efforts to gather other sources for control by using personal influence and by generating obligations for exchange through ignoring minor school rules and changing the classroom routine. All of these efforts helped, but they did not transform the classes into anything like a resemblance to upper track classes. Further, these practices complicated the maintenance of order in the school at large, as later chapters will indicate.

The pressure on teachers to adjust to their students is important not just in the understanding of the character of a school but also in understanding teaching and teachers themselves. As teachers adjust to the particular students they encounter, they will develop distinctive outlooks which make them importantly different from teachers from different contexts who may use the same rhetoric.

My characterization of teachers in Chapter Three is thus colored by the nature of Canton's students, because these teachers' beliefs and activities were colored by them.

For the incorporatively inclined teachers the resistance not only of the poorest but of the best students could not but be discouraging and disheartening. Many teachers responded with a rigidity in pronouncement and practice which they probably would not have displayed in a context where students were more amenable to their efforts. Further, some of the developmental teachers in Canton were persons who had started with an incorporative philosophy and had gradually changed to a developmental one as they experienced the difficulties of applying an incorporative approach to Canton's students. These teachers tended to be above average in intellect and energy, thus adding to the relative luster of the developmental group. But in a context where students accepted an incorporative approach these teachers would have been likely to continue in an incorporative style.

The district's support of the developmental teaching style— discussed at more length in the next chapter—was likely to have a similar effect, making some incorporative teachers defensive and moving others away from this style to a developmental one.

For teachers originally inclined to proto-authority, the effect of the district was probably even stronger. Its educational optimism and its support of developmental methods could be expected to make the true pessimists, convinced that obedience was all that could be taught to certain students, feel defensively entrenched in their positions, while other persons who might have taken a position of proto-authority in a school where it prevailed moved to a more hopeful incorporative approach.

The students and the district provided a context which encouraged developmental teachers to insist on a considerable degree of structure and traditional academic learning, despite their willingness to let students help define goals and instrumental activities. The public was unusually aware of the need for literacy and computational skills for success in the labor market at this time and the lower track students clearly lacked and needed these skills. The district's concern to help these students and to stimulate the students in the top tracks also supported these teachers' faith that such efforts could be made within a traditional school context.

These observations suggest that studies of the effectiveness of various teaching styles can only be meaningful when they specify in subtle detail the character of the children taught and the context of the school and school district. The age of the students should also make a difference. High track students' greater responsiveness to incorporative goals and methods in math classes and the limitation of teachers attempting nondirective guidance in Canton to a few subjects suggest that the character of the subject taught is important. But this study does not provide systematic data on these points.

It is time to look at the wider school beyond the single classroom. Students inhabit not just classrooms but corridors, cafeterias, and washrooms. The problem of maintaining order and safety in these contexts is more severe than in the classroom. The way that the staff deal with it permeates the school, affecting interaction in the classroom along with that in the corridor.

Part III: CORRIDORS

CHAPTER 7

The Problem of Order in the School at Large

THE SCHOOL STAFF are responsible for their students in the halls, cafeteria, yards, and even on the streets leading to and from the school, just as they are in the classroom. Ebullience or hostility can lead to injury in these contexts. And noisy excitement generated there does not necessarily disappear when the students walk through the classroom door.

Adults and students differ over appropriate goals and means in the treatment of decorum and safety within the whole school, just as they differ over issues within the classroom. But in these large and open spaces, larger and more diverse aggregations must accommodate to one another without the prolonged and enforced intimacy of the classroom to motivate and assist them.

The way that relationships in these contexts are worked out is crucial to the character of all of school life. Part III will explore their handling at Chauncey and Hamilton. This chapter will deal with the kinds of difficulty which arise and with the strategies available for coping with them.

THE DIFFICULTY OF MAINTAINING ORDER
IN THE SCHOOL AT LARGE

The most basic problem of order in school is the result of placing large numbers of active young people in very small spaces. Junior high school students are physically active and usually sociably inclined. But from the time the bell rings for classes to start in the morning until the last bell rings in the afternoon students must sit reasonably still and pay attention to planned work for 320 minutes, while they may move about and talk for 75.[1]

When they are free to move and to socialize, the children are naturally in need of exercise for their limbs, their lungs, and their capacity for sociability. While these needs are healthy ones, they create real organizational problems, especially in the physical space typical of schools. In long corridors with little soundproofing young voices talking, calling to distant friends, hooting with delight, or shrieking in mock fear can make a truly deafening racket. This noise makes it difficult for teachers to talk with students after class, wears on adult nerves, and raises yet further the mutual excitement of young persons who within five minutes should be demurely interested scholars. A clump of five or six students stopping in a narrow corridor to share the juicy details of what he said to her and what she said to him creates an impediment to traffic which encourages yet more sociable clumps, until it is difficult for anyone to get through. Many of the children's natural activities also create monumental janitorial tasks. Unless strictly regulated, food and chewing gum tend to appear on floors and ledges everywhere.

The difficulties caused by these problems are relatively minor, although with a very large student body in a very cramped space

1. The exact figures varied by five or ten minutes at the various Canton schools; those given apply at Hamilton. Forty of the 320 minutes are spent in physical education and thus allow at least some physical movement. One could reckon the balance as 280 to 115 except that sociability is not possible during physical education as it is between classes and at lunch.

they can become fairly serious.[2] The worst effects they are likely to cause are wear and tear on the adults and loss of time from class periods if students come in late or bubbling with energy and sociability so that five minutes must be spent in "settling them down."

A second group of innocent activities usually does no harm at all, but once in a great while may have really serious consequences. The chances of problems are few, but the stakes are high. Thus one child running in the hall can slip and cause a broken leg for himself or someone else and with it angry parents at the school board meeting. Boys in the yard competing in accuracy throwing pebbles at a target can hit in the head a fellow student who wanders absent-mindedly into their path.

Every school therefore faces the problem of striking some balance between the healthy needs of the children to use their physical and social capacities and the needs of the organization to move people efficiently from place to place and to protect the health and safety of all persons on the premises.

The spaces of the school outside the classroom also provide opportunities for hostile and predatory activities. Children of junior high school age not infrequently get into physical fights which can result in scars and lost teeth, especially if a group gangs up on one child. Some children threaten smaller children with physical beating to extort small amounts of money. And occasionally boys will molest girls in minor or major ways. These actions, with the exception of some spontaneous fights, are intentional and therefore usually done in less crowded places or at least out of the sight of adults. They therefore present slightly different problems for control.

Finally there is the possibility of collective violence of some kind. In socially and racially diverse schools such as Canton's there is a special problem of group tensions erupting into group attacks. The extent to which this eventuality is a likelihood

2. James Herndon reports that a suburban school in which he taught became increasingly repressive and rigid toward the children as its student body doubled while its facilities remained the same. (See James Herndon, *The Way It Spozed To Be,* pp. 193–96.)

rather than a possibility is a matter of conjecture. But it was a problem of which many school personnel in Canton were keenly aware.

To be sure to prevent a few from engaging in hostile acts, it is necessary severely to restrict the activities of the many. As with innocent activities, school personnel must balance the dangers to the organization and to individuals from possible hostile activities against the needs of all the children for freedom from strict regulation and regimentation. But persons who opt for either side of this dilemma frequently fail to acknowledge any difficulty or need for choice. They either argue that inhibiting rules and procedures are a self-evidently necessary part of school life or they attack them as the creations of small minds and shriveled personalities, quite without practical purpose.

The choice in this dilemma seems to be most frequently weighted toward considerations of maintaining the maximum order possible rather than giving the maximum freedom possible. One important reason lies in the relative visibility and concentration of the costs of the alternative patterns. In the case of disorder which is dangerous or hostile, the mishaps which are prevented are relatively rare, but they are serious and they are highly visible. One child accidentally hit in the head by a thrown rock or one child beaten up by a group of others is himself seriously damaged and will also be the cause of forceful community wrath and pressure on the school. On the other hand, if children are severely restricted in where they may go during the lunch period and closely supervised in their activities during that time, the suffering imposed by this inhibition may involve more "person hours" but is not as acute for any one person or resented so much at any one time. In the long run pent-up energies and resentments may accumulate and have negative consequences for the school as well as the children, but the chain of causes and effects is very elusive in such a situation. Thus the negative effects of erring on the side of caution in preventing disorder are far less tangible than the negative effects which are feared as possible from erring on the side of granting freedom.[3]

3. Sykes discusses a similar dilemma in prisons, particularly in the context of the difficulty and importance of preventing escapes. Only a very small

Further, the location of the costs in the alternative approaches is different. When order is not maintained adults suffer more. Teachers mind noise and disorder far more than most children, and the staff suffer if parents complain or bring pressure on the school (though individual children may suffer too). When restrictions are overdone, children suffer. Children are less aware of and less articulate about their interests, and they are less powerful in asserting them than are adults.

ARRANGEMENTS FOR MAINTAINING ORDER

Rules are a mainstay of schools' strategies for preventing disorderly behavior. They forbid activities which may breed disorder, thus preventing it before it starts. They are a form of arrangement of the situation. Thus, in Canton, children are not allowed inside the school for more than fifteen minutes before and after school unless they are directly supervised by a teacher. They may not be in the hallways during class periods without a pass. During the lunch period they must stay outside the academic buildings in certain designated areas after they leave the cafeteria. These rules are intended to prevent children from being alone or in small groups unsupervised in the school. The purpose is to prevent extortion, sexual molestation, theft, and vandalism, all of which are easiest to perform when there are no witnesses.

Students' activities and possessions are also restricted by rules. Darwin and Chauncey had one-way halls and staircases to facilitate traffic flow. Students may not bring food into the academic buildings or chew gum anywhere in the school; the purpose is to limit janitorial tasks, the danger of slippery spills on the floor, and the number of rodents attracted to the premises. Umbrellas were not to be carried except before and after school

---

proportion of the population would ever try to escape, but when just one man does the community inflicts pressure and disapproval on the prison administration. Therefore, to avoid this unlikely but highly costly danger from the few, the many are subjected to more restraint than they individually require. A consequence is heavy, but less visible, costs in accomplishing rehabilitation and resocialization. (See Gresham Sykes, *The Society of Captives,* Chapter 2.)

because of the danger of their points when carelessly swung about. Anything which could be a weapon was not to be brought to school, nor were radios.

Supervision by adults helps to enforce rules and encourage decorum. Adults are assigned to supervise in crowded areas before and after school, at lunchtime, and between classes. Their task is to keep the amount of noise and roughhousing within limits, to prevent or break up fights, and where relevant to keep traffic moving.

However, rules and supervision are by no means sufficient to keep order in a school without the students' active cooperation. The large size of a school prevents effective patrolling when the halls are supposed to be empty, and the physical character and impersonality of crowds provide a good deal of protection for misdeeds and escape. The students far outnumber the adults, who cannot possibly control them with direct intervention individually addressed.

Order can be maintained only if the vast majority of children in the school *voluntarily* abide by the rules and comport themselves in a reasonably decorous manner. They need not do so gladly or because they understand the reasons for doing so, but do it they must or the adults cannot prevent the school from being a raucous and unsafe place. The methods a school staff uses to induce this voluntary cooperation in the students and the degree of their success are very important ingredients in the life of the school.

TWO CLASSIC METHODS OF OBTAINING ORDER

The majority of older siblings of the children now in the top and bottom tracks had attended Hamilton and the old Lincoln, respectively. According to the descriptions of teachers who had taught at both schools, control was far firmer and more successful in the old days. It was also quite different at the two institutions.

A teacher with long experience at Hamilton describes the pattern of control there in the past:

R: I doubt if we had two children cut class in a year fifteen years ago, ten years ago. It simply wasn't done. Of course, it was an entirely different school atmosphere. It was a college prep high school, a nice little homogeneous academic school. All the emphasis on scholarship. Why it was just unthinkable that a kid would cut a class. The wrath of the gods would have descended on him. He would have been—well, just probably flayed and drawn and hanged from the flag pole, as an example. It was just unthinkable.[4] And now, of course, a kid cuts class anytime he doesn't feel like going, apparently.

I: In the old days would he actually have been flayed and drawn, or was this just the way he felt about it?

R: He'd have been, well, he would probably have been suspended. He would have had a personal conference with the principal. His parents would have been brought to school before he was readmitted. Which is tantamount to being flayed. His teachers would have been shocked beyond measure that he could have done such a thing.

This teacher describes the students' awe before their elders and the construction of a social reality where misdeeds were simply beyond contemplation. He emphasizes their fear of disapproval should they violate social expectations. Other teachers stressed the importance of their not even imagining doing so.

Such a pattern of control requires that students come from a social context in which they and those around them feel a basic harmony with the purposes and style of the school. They must approach the school with trust in its good will toward them and a consequent lack of motivation for more than superficial hostility or rebellion in response to its direction of their lives. They must also arrive at the school sharing its social style and its standards for obedient and decorous behavior in settings directed by adults. They therefore accept its rules as natural, unremarkable.

4. One cannot take such a description entirely literally. The ordinary improvement of events in memory over experience aside, it is important that in the more regimented schools of the "good old days," there were still always individual rebels and classrooms or situations where control broke down. Waller emphasizes that even in the small town schools of the twenties, which he describes in insightful detail, order was a precarious commodity maintained with constant vigilance, which rested in part upon the consent of the governed. (See Willard Waller, *The Sociology of Teaching*, pp. 8–12.)

Such students will be restrained by the same forces that restrain most adults from breaking the fundamental rules of public etiquette. When in public we feel a great hesitation to talk aloud to ourselves, pick our noses, or engage in any of a large number of physically feasible and tangibly harmless activities which are punished only by the disapproval of strangers. We feel that terrible consequences will ensue, though we don't know what they would be.[5] This kind of control depends upon universal success, however. It is awe of the unfamiliar and the fear of shame and stigmatization which restrain. If adult or child sees significant numbers of others breaking rules the practice becomes a possibility which may be considered. The introduction of long hair styles for men is an example of a violation of etiquette which became a change in etiquette.

Students may also be restrained by ignorance and a limited imagination. It simply does not occur to them that one could do anything else but follow expected routines. Seasoned teachers are quite consciously aware of limited experience and ignorance as devices for control. They will take care not to mention some students' infractions to the others, lest they acquire a new idea which would not spontaneously have occurred to them.

Schools which rely heavily upon the students' unreflective acceptance of procedure, their awe of adults, and their fear of disapproval can be said to institutionalize the innocence of the children. I will refer to this pattern of control as the *institutionalization of innocence*.

The students of the old Lincoln came to school with neither the trust nor the innocent ignorance of those who attended the old Hamilton. At Lincoln the pattern of control depended upon swift and consistent use of coercive sanctions. A teacher now at Chancey describes her memories of Lincoln in the mid-fifties.

And then I taught at Lincoln when it was an almost all-Negro school. Eighty some odd percent. And the emphasis on discipline was rather strong, but it was also one of the most efficiently run

5. Erving Goffman is a master at discussing these matters. See his *Behavior in Public Places.*

schools I've ever been in. And the teachers were consistent. They all stuck to the rules and they all enforced the rules. Every teacher in the school was able to teach with the door open. I mean, all the teachers, the principal, everyone was so aware that discipline was important. There was such great consistency in the maintenance of discipline that it was beautiful. There was very little difficulty.

And actually, we sent students down [to the dean] for infractions that practically here all you'd do is [put them in a seat alone in the back.] I mean it was that much more severe. The discipline was tight. But the students didn't rebel and the teachers liked it.

Coercion can very rarely be the routine mainstay of successful control in an organization. However, if coercive sanctions are used consistently and swiftly against all offenders, it soon becomes unnecessary actually to use coercion, for the *threat* of coercion becomes credible and this threat is a far more efficient tool of control than actual use of coercion. In order to maintain the credibility of the threat some actual use of coercion is necessary, but the number of offenders is likely to remain small enough to be manageable.

To establish such a credible threat of coercion in a school, with its constant turnover of students and its fresh start with each new school year, coercion must be used at the beginning of the year, early in the careers of the new and returning students. Since the majority of students are likely to start out somewhat cautiously as they test "reality" in this new situation, the school can respond with swift punishment for even fairly minor infractions and deploy its most extreme sanctions promptly against the few major infractions. This consistent coercive response to all of the first tests by students will create the impression for new students that the school does in fact have strong coercive resources and the willingness to use them on minor and major departures from expected behavior. One of the teachers at Darwin cited an example of this pattern in a high school in the core of a neighboring city which every year expelled up to thirty students in the first month of the school year.

If the students believe that the school has sufficient resources to carry through on all its threats of coercion, it will need to use actual coercion only against a manageably small number of students. This use will reinforce the credibility of its readiness to punish. The school thus creates a myth of unlimited coercive power which the children believe. However, it is important that it *is* a myth, for if the children test it with large scale and prolonged disobedience, the coercive resources of the school will break under the load. The crucial factor in control here, then, is the creation of a state of mind in most of the children in which they believe the cost of disobedience to be too high to be worth paying, and thus they *voluntarily* conform.[6] I will refer to this pattern as the *myth of coercive control.*

The final result bears some similarities to the situation with students who arrive in a state of harmony with the school, and whose innocence of possibilities of deviance is then institutionalized. In both cases, the student considers conformity to the expectations of the school to be the only practicable, perhaps even the only possible, path for him given the nature of the school.

What has happened in both cases is that the school has created out of its fluid variable character and its fragility in the face of student intransigence, a *belief* among its students that schools have a well-defined and forcefully maintained character in which misbehavior by students brings awesome institutional forces to bear upon them. The students are brought to believe it is inherent in the nature of schools that institutional life proceeds unswervingly in its appointed style. Children are creatures far too frail to be able to challenge or deviate significantly from their expected roles without being crushed by the weight of an inevitable institutional response.

Despite these similarities, there are important differences in

6. Richard McCleery makes a compelling analysis of this process in his study of change in a highly authoritarian prison. In this prison a centralized staff system inflicted swift and sharp punishment for the few infractions which occurred. Inmates accepted and cooperated with this system without direct coercion most of the time, for "Inmates regarded authority in the old prison as mean, abusive, and unjust; but, most important, they regarded it as inevitable" (*Policy Change in Prison Management*, p. 13). McCleery indicates that when a liberal administration at the top of the prison disrupted the inevitability of punishment disorder rose sharply.

these two strategies. Where institutionalization of innocence is possible, the children must feel themselves in basic harmony with the school and they must entrust themselves to its wisdom and care. The daily routine need not be regimented as in the other case and there can be a good deal of individual variation in the treatment of students. Rules and procedures are taken for granted and not preoccupying to students or staff, who are thus free to put their primary energies upon academic matters.

But with a myth of coercion, constant regimentation and constant vigilance by the staff are necessary. Situations and individuals must be handled in a standardized predictable manner in order to maintain the illusion of the institution's force. An air of tension and opposition between students and staff pervades the atmosphere. Regimentation and coercion are likely to deepen the hostility of the students toward the institution, thus exacerbating the problem with which they are designed to cope.

The dean of boys from the old Lincoln and those teachers from there who took the least hierarchical role with students reported that order in the halls there had been bought at the cost of considerable disorder and hostility in the classroom.[7] Disorder in the classroom is more manageable than disorder in the halls, but it also conflicts most directly with the academic task. The hostility of students engendered by a coercive regime is likely also to increase their alienation from all of the school's professed goals, including academic ones. To the extent that it is true that a learner must psychically embrace the goal of learning, this method of control is thus directly subversive of educative goals.

---

7. Erving Goffman's treatment of "total institutions" in general supports the common finding in the literature on prisons that when "inmates" are tightly regimented and socially denigrated for the sake of control, they will be under strong psychic pressure to develop an oppositional "underlife" in which they subvert the institution in minor but symbolically important ways. If they do not have this, full-scale open rebellion becomes more likely. (See Erving Goffman, *Asylums.*) Students' lives are not as totally encompassed by the schools as are those of inmates by total institutions, but it may still be that schools which allow students no opportunity for expressive resistance are similarly likely to have increasing levels of hostility and eventual rebellion. For a description of one such school, see James Herndon, *The Way It Spozed to Be,* pp. 165–66.

Canton's schools at the time of the study had relaxed the stern regimentation that obtained in earlier years with the lower class students. They did this with some consciousness of attempting to reduce the psychic pressures upon students and thus encourage more commitment and academic effort. A counselor at Chauncey who was generally a believer in decorum and enforcement of rules argued that the relaxation of hallway discipline had been beneficial:

> Well, I suppose there's an increase in the hallway noise definitely, but I would say, going way back, I can remember some very severe fights with the kids, very explosive in the halls. I don't think we have near that many blow-ups in the hall that we did before. I mean where somebody was really riled up and they just hauled off and beat the heck out of each other, right there. We may occasionally have some kids exchange blows on the grounds.
>
> This is one area where I feel you may have changed a type of expression, where they would harbor much of this, and you would have this undercurrent going on and all of a sudden it would explode. Now maybe many of them get rid of some of this energy by their loudness. I think there is a tremendous excitement among these kids at this level. I don't think you can just keep people restricted all the time, and so I think maybe to release the noise during hallway passing is a healthy situation. Maybe that lets them burn some stuff that would explode in the classroom.

THE EFFECT OF CHANGES IN THE
CANTON SCHOOL DISTRICT

Whether they had wanted to or not, at the time of the study the personnel of the Canton schools would not have been able to continue using either a myth of coercive control or institutionalization of innocence. Influences from the state and the courts, from parents, and from children all converged to undercut essential supports of these patterns of control. In the state as well as the city, public attitudes were coming more and more to support the rights of children over against the school. State directives forbade more than twenty days suspension without expulsion, thus undercutting the most frequent severe coercive sanction used in Canton. And court decisions supported students' rights to dress as they chose, thus undercutting the school's claim to be an arbiter of manners and decorum.

Within the city, a vocal minority of white parents defended their children's civil liberties, broadly construed. Many argued not only their children's right to dress as they pleased, but their right not to pledge allegiance to the flag, or to stay away from school for a day when a student strike for peace was called. Some went further and objected to any tangible punishment on the grounds that "misbehavior" ought to be talked through, not simply punished. And a few even held that children ought not to have to attend classes if they judged they did not need them. These attitudes of the parents, along with the other factors described in discussing the high track children's ideals for the classroom, prevented the children from believing the school's ways to be inevitable, an assumption which is a fundamental necessity for institutionalized innocence.

Black parents also were an active force. Their concern was expressed in the very fact of integration and the pressure that it brought upon the schools not to subject black children to a more regimented or coercive overall regime than white children and their parents would be willing to tolerate. Though leading black parents accepted punishment more readily than vocal white parents, they kept an eye upon the extent and equity of its use. They were ready to complain if black children were suspended or expelled in too large numbers, especially if white children were not. And they were also ready to complain about insults or peremptory handling of black children. At both Chauncey and Hamilton there was at least one incident in the course of the year over which black parents became collectively angry. The black children followed not only their parents but militant older teenagers and young adults. Many were suspicious of any kind of control by whites and carefully scrutinized the fairness of school practice.

The school board and the district administration were responsive to resistance to traditional controls from both sets of parents

and children. They advised principals, informally, to be as
sparing as possible in their use of punishment when parents objected to the occasion or form of its use. Two of the three
principals mentioned in their interviews that the central office
had explicitly overruled them and offered more lenient treatment
for specific offenders. In the district's appointment of disciplinary
deans, choice of new teachers, and style of rhetoric, it de-empha-
sized rules and punishment for infractions. Under such conditions, punishment can no longer be considered inevitable and
children will grow increasingly willing to test the school's power
over them.

Similarly, the school board reviewed policy on such matters as
the pledge of allegiance to the flag and students' absence from
school to attend anti-war rallies or observe a student strike for
peace. They listened to students argue their position in favor of
permissive policies on these matters. The school board's recognition of the possibility of moral argument on these subjects gave
official support to students' questioning of the fundamental
practices of both the school and the society. Innocent acceptance
of both as immutable givens of existence cannot survive under
such conditions.

Beyond these matters of attitude and policy, there were
processes within the daily operation of the schools which
militated against both institutionalized innocence and a myth of
coercive control. The diversity of the student body undercut
both. Each depends upon an appearance of inevitability so that
students do not question it. But all the schools contained
alienated lower class black students who would never offer the
school the trust required for institutionalized innocence and
upper middle class white students who would never stand for the
regimentation of coercive control. If one group of students will
not accept a form of control, its necessity will be destroyed in the
eyes of the other.

The absence of these forms of control led to rising levels of
disorder in all the schools. The very presence of such disorder
undercut control further, creating a spiraling effect. A student
who sees his peers subjected to opprobrium or punishment yet

survive will be less awed by these processes. Increasing familiarity with the processes as they are applied to himself will also decrease their sting. Thus students lose their awe of disapproval and of punishment and begin to calculate costs and benefits, the pleasure of nonconformity versus the price of chastisement.

In such a situation, the school must actually lessen its use of scowling disapproval and of tangible punishment. For if it uses its stronger sanctions on burgeoning minor problems, students will become habituated to them, and it will be left with few punishments that still deter to apply to really serious offenses. But when students find that little or nothing happens to them for violating minor rules, they come to suspect the school's vulnerability to determined resistance, and they are emboldened to violate more important rules when they have reason or desire.

LEVELS OF DISORDER IN CANTON'S SCHOOLS

Despite the impossibility of controlling the students through fully developed versions of the classic methods used in earlier days, the Canton schools were not the scenes of unbridled disorder. The adults all agreed that the schools had at least "some" problem in maintaining order and that the matter was a difficult one requiring considerable attention. But they did not agree in assessing the amount of disorder or in comparing it to schools in other districts.

And indeed such comparative judgments are very difficult to make. A school may have loud boisterous halls but few fights, few fires set in bathrooms, and few incidents of extortion of money from smaller children. Or it may have precisely the reverse pattern with quiet halls and orderly crowds, but all the other problems flourishing. Adults may disagree about the point when a shoving match between two boys should be defined as a fight and considered a serious problem.

It was clear to an observer that the noise level between classes in Canton's halls was high, and that there were traffic jams, semiserious scuffles between children, and occasional headlong chases. But two substitutes who worked both in Canton and one of the two larger urban districts in the area were impressed by a lack of tension and hostility in the atmosphere of Canton's halls.

All of the schools had a problem with students cutting classes. The deans' (disciplinary officers') waiting rooms were always well populated with students sent from the halls or from class, but all the deans agreed that the seriousness of these students' infractions varied over an extremely wide range. Teachers had sole discretion over sending them; some sent students very quickly and others sent them only in the most severe circumstances.

There were at least a few cases at all the schools of extortion of lunch money from smaller children and of impertinent advances made by boys to girls. It was very difficult to get an estimation of the frequency of these events because they were not always reported by the children and not systematically recorded by the school. A systematic inspection of all formal referrals to the dean at Chauncey and at Hamilton from the opening of school until January 15 of the year of the study showed that the vast majority of offenses recorded were less serious than fighting. Cases more serious than fighting, such as extortion or advances to girls, were even rarer. However, the presence of notes in the files on incidents of the latter two kinds suggested that they were not always written up on formal referral forms and so did not all appear in the figures for comparison. According to one of the boys' deans many fights outside the classroom also are never written up on referral forms because the dean is called to the fight or the fighters brought directly to him. Still, in over a year in the halls and classrooms of the schools, I never saw a really angry fight.

The Canton schools were vulnerable to the special problem of racial conflict between students. However, there were few overt problems on a daily basis. With the exception of a few students, the races segregated themselves in the cafeteria and on the playground, dealing with their differences by avoidance. The dean at Hamilton reported keeping a tally of every incident of student conflict which came to his attention for one week. He found the overwhelming majority occurred between black students, followed by some between white students, with a tiny minority occurring across racial lines. There were some reports, especially from white parents and some teachers, of black students jostling white students to spill their food in the cafeteria or muttering comments to them and moving on.[8] No sustained contact was involved and the incidents were generally not reported.

In two years, there were two collective disturbances in the schools which involved black students indiscriminately attacking white students. Both occurred during significant racial turmoil in one of the neighboring cities. One was at Darwin in the fall preceding the pilot study. The other was at Hamilton after the deaths of Martin Luther King and a local teenager. It occurred during the study at Hamilton and will be discussed at some length below.

Teachers who believed in proto-authority within the classroom saw coercion as appropriate in the school at large. Those who believed in an incorporative approach expected institutionalized innocence to be workable in the school at large. Most of both groups were baffled and angered by the failure of the central and school administrations to push these forms of control. But teachers favoring a developmental approach considered coercion repressive and institutionalized innocence stultifying. They were pleased with their absence, if not with the resulting disorder. They saw the more hostile and harmful forms of this disorder as a symptom of the students' lack of sympathy with the school; so they tried to attack the problem by increasing students' commitment to the organization. In general they sought to institute order by inducing the children to cooperate out of their attachment to the school and their desire for a safe and productive social life for all who were part of it.

---

8. Though I probed for it, I could find evidence of few overt verbal attacks and essentially no physical attacks on blacks by whites. However, the overall social context made the whites clearly dominant. In a different study of two junior high schools in a conservative area with substantial proportions of working and lower class whites, sometimes with poorer social and academic resources than the majority of blacks in the school, it was clear that whites initiated hostile actions between the races as often or oftener than blacks. (See Mary Haywood Metz, "The Exercise of Control in Two Midwestern Junior High Schools.")

THE DEVELOPMENTAL APPROACH TO ORDER

The teachers who hoped to establish order through the positive cooperation of the children found the alienation of many of the children in the bottom tracks to be their first and largest stumbling block. So long as these children felt estranged from both the personnel and purposes of the school, they were likely to engage in boisterous disruption and hostile acts toward the building, other children, and each other.

The developmental teachers had a great deal of difficulty winning these children to commitment to the school's goals even within the classroom. That setting provided support for their efforts through the possibility of building an extended and positive personal relationship and through the students' ambivalent interest in learning. But outside the classroom most settings did not include personal relationships with adults and there were no academic benefits to hold out. In this context, the task of winning these children's commitment to the school and to good order within it was truly a difficult one. However, if it could be accomplished it seemed that the serious anti-social acts could be curbed, for these children did not turn destructive or hostile behavior on individuals and institutions with which they were on friendly terms.

Even with the children in high tracks who felt at home in the school, developmental patterns of control through the students' accepting shared responsibility presented special problems outside the classroom. The personal relationship and the clear academic goals of the classroom were lacking. And these students could often not see any important purpose behind school rules, or any relationship between them and school goals as they understood them.

Cutting was the most serious problem with these students. Some of the ablest students claimed that they did not need to go to classes in some subjects. Study halls were an especial bone of contention; students argued that if they could work better at home and got their work done regularly they did not need to go to study hall. Since the students making these arguments were often the ablest, teachers had to grant that there was merit in their arguments. On the other hand, student judgment in such matters is fallible. And more important, there was no provision in the school structure for students who were not in class. They were left to linger in the lonely crannies of the school or to adventure upon the streets, both situations likely sooner or later to bring someone to harm for which the school would be responsible.

Teachers who gave this approach to control serious consideration concluded that it could not be workably practiced without rearranging the schedule and curriculum of the school to a more flexible pattern. The pattern of classes of standardized length meeting five days a week needed to be broken up into time spans and group sizes more appropriate to the nature of each subject and the working style of given kinds of students. There needed to be legitimate pleasant spaces available to students who had no work to do at that time and who wished to be sociable.[9]

Similarly, it was hard for students of this age to believe that any important harm could be done by noisiness or traffic jams in the halls. They could not understand any barriers to allowing students access to the halls during classtime. Their ears and nerves were more resistant than adults' to noise levels; they were not responsible for getting classes into a working mood or integrating late comers into a task already explained and started. The likelihood of injury from running in the hall or from attack in a lonely spot was too remote to seem real.

Teachers who hoped to get students voluntarily to maintain order argued again for structural changes that would reduce many of these problems. Breaking schools up into smaller physical and social units would do away both with long, crowded, echoing halls and with the impersonality which makes hostile attack more likely. Smaller details were also expected to help. For example, carpets on the floors would reduce noise and create a more intimate atmosphere and library centers within easy reach of classrooms would allow more flexible activity with less danger.

9. Many schools have recently been making changes of just these kinds.

The principal at Hamilton probably had the best analytic insight into the problems the schools face of any informant in the study. He felt very keenly that there was inconsistency in the district's expectations. Sympathy toward students' claims of conscience and expectations for room to experiment was combined with an expectation that order be kept in a temporal, physical, and curricular structure which demanded that everyone do the same things together at the same time, a structure designed for a standardized, hierarchical approach to school process. Not inherently an advocate of the developmental approach, he recognized the problems it was trying to address. But above all he felt the need for a policy which would allow a consistent method of control, whatever it might be. In the research interview, he addressed the problem of attendance, which he considered the most severe problem with children in the top tracks. Parents of this group of children had gone to the school board twice during the year asking permission for their children to be excused for skipping school on days when there had been large scale protests against the Vietnam War which called for participation by high school students. In anticipation of the second event, the principal asked for direction from the board:

> Well, I've asked many times for more clearly defined expectations. Just as an example, I went to the Board not too long ago and asked that they indicate clearly to us what the District's expectations are as far as attendance is concerned, so far as cutting and absences of various natures. And it came to kind of a head when the Board indicated a rather liberal approach to students who left campus because of conscience. The Board indicated to us as principals through the chief administrators that we were to be relatively lenient in these cases.
>
> I think this is the general feeling that the principals have in the District, that you go through the book work, you keep track of absences and so forth, but you don't do very much in a punitive way to correct it. You look for other avenues, and I certainly am sympathetic to looking for other avenues. . . . But I still have a feeling that there's a real understanding, almost, amongst the students

that the District is *not* going to deal with truancy in a very severe manner. And it's not just a District problem; the courts have given the District very little support in these areas. . . .

And I would say that the general lock-step, period-after-period structure of our schools' program is *not* compatible to [relaxed] attendance rules. And if expectations are going to be high in the sense of attendance, then there have to be more strict ways of handling it. If expectations are going to be minimized in terms of attendance, then something has to be done to the school structure to allow for it.

Despite the lack of structural adjustments a sizable contingent of developmental teachers in Canton along with some of the counselors and deans, tried to get students to support school order out of their own commitment. They explained to them the reasons for the importance of orderly behavior and obedience to many of the school rules. They tried to support this strategy through less direct methods, giving students responsibility for themselves and treating them as persons capable of independent trustworthy action. They hoped thereby to increase their commitment to the school and its goals and their sense of responsibility for maintaining minimal cooperative order.

These teachers were more numerous and had more impact at Hamilton than at Chauncey, where more effort went into attempts to restore attenuated forms of the classic methods of control. In the remaining chapters of Part III, I will analyze the differences in the approach of the staffs of Hamilton and Chauncey to their matched student bodies and the differences in those student bodies which resulted.

CHAPTER **8**

Faculty Culture
and Student Order

THE STUDENTS at Chauncey and Hamilton acted quite differ-, ently. Because the student bodies were closely matched in racial and social characteristics,[1] we have the rare opportunity of studying the effects of the school upon the behavior of children

1. According to a visual census by teachers in 1967–68, Hamilton's student body was 53 percent white and Chauncey's 48 percent. Hamilton was 38 percent black and 9 percent "Oriental and other," while Chauncey was 48 percent black and 5 percent "Oriental and other." There is a fluctuation in racial percentages from year to year. Thus the difference between the schools in the percentage of the student body which was black was 10 percent in 1967–68, but 6 percent in 1966–67 and 8 percent in 1968–69.

The two schools were even more similar in social characteristics than in racial ones. The census tracts for the city are nearly coterminous with boundaries of the districts for the junior highs. A comparison of the 1960 census figures (using three categories for education, all the census categories for occupation, and four categories for income) revealed only two categories in which the schools differed by more than five percent. These two differences (both of eight percent) showed Chauncey to have more persons with at least some college education and with family incomes under $4,000. However these differences reflected high proportions of persons with high education and low income in tracts adjacent to the University where large numbers of its students lived. These tracts fell into Chauncey's district, but had only a minor impact on its population because there were few children of students old enough to attend junior high school.

without having to turn to the presumption that differences between schools are caused primarily by differences students bring with them from home and community.

There were both obvious and subtle differences in the character of the faculties and the administrations of Hamilton and Chauncey which affected the behavior of the students. They differed in the kind of educational goals and technological approaches to which they gave priority. They also differed over the importance of order as a goal and over methods of maintaining it.

This chapter describes the different behavior of the children with respect to order. It discusses the possible sources of these differences in the differing plants and histories of the schools, but especially in the differing cultures of the faculties. Because these all pushed in the same direction in their effect on order at each school—and in a direction opposite to that at the other school—the weight of each factor is difficult to assess.

DIFFERENCES IN ORDER AT HAMILTON
AND CHAUNCEY

The differences in order between the two schools were striking. During the times when students moved from class to class, Hamilton experienced more noise, boisterousness, and running in the halls than did Chauncey. Further, students were not as prompt in reaching their classes. At Chauncey the halls were nearly empty during the last thirty to ninety seconds of the four-minute passing period, while at Hamilton they were well populated right up to the end of the five-minute one. More students were tardy to class at Hamilton, and after the bell one could often hear the sounds of stragglers wending a jovially sonorous path through the halls. At Chauncey those children still about in the halls even in the last minute *before* the bell walked briskly and quietly.

Both schools had lunch in two shifts, and both forbade students to enter the corridors of the classroom buildings during their lunch period. At Chauncey this rule was generally well observed, though some supervision and enforcement were necessary. At Hamilton it was widely violated. Whether as a result of this difference or not, there was considerably more litter in the halls of Hamilton than those of Chauncey.

The student bodies differed in the tone in which students spoke to adults they encountered in the public areas of the school. At Hamilton it was commonplace to hear a child reply to an adult who questioned him in the hall in a hostile voice with defiant words. At Chauncey this occurred rarely indeed.

Finally, Hamilton was plagued with some actually or potentially really serious problems of order which did not occur at Chauncey. At Hamilton fires were set in washbasins and waste cans on a fairly regular basis. While these caused little real danger and were usually promptly extinguished, they occasionally engendered considerable smoke. During the spring a series of false fire alarms automatically emptied the school and summoned city fire equipment. In some weeks there were two or three of these alarms, though in others there were none. Finally there was a collective disturbance on one day in April. Three false fire alarms were rung. A growing number of black students—eventually one to two hundred—stayed out of classes and badgered white students. They spilled white students' food in their laps in the cafeteria, and they grabbed purses or other belongings and threw them out of reach on top of lockers in the hall. They drew a dozen or so white students into fights, sometimes setting upon them in groups. Nothing of this kind occurred during the year at Chauncey.

It is difficult to say precisely how much more disorder there was at Hamilton than at Chauncey because of the difficulty of defining a universe of opportunities and then counting the comparative incidence of various practices. More important, both adults and students may go to some lengths to hide the occurrence of forbidden events from one another. The adults wish to maintain the students' ignorance of others' misdeeds so that they will not take them as examples. The students hide their own misdeeds to escape punishment. It was very clear that both adults and students were more careful to hide such occurrences at Chauncey than at Hamilton. Most of the serious incidents I became aware of at Chauncey I found out about either by being on or near the scene or by being told about them in confidence in an interview with someone who had been on the scene. Even other teachers were not told about these events. At Hamilton on the other hand, a teacher would think nothing of announcing to everyone present in the faculty lounge that he had just put out a fire in a washbasin.

At Hamilton teachers and students agreed that cutting was widespread, and some students made little attempt to hide the fact that they cut. At Chauncey teachers held that cutting existed but was uncommon, while students in their interviews almost universally described it as common. But—unlike the Hamilton children—they were a little wary in discussing the matter with an adult, even an outsider. When they did talk about it, they described elaborate strategies used to hide it from teachers.

Consequently, it is not only difficult for an observer to know just how much more cutting and how many more serious incidents took place at Hamilton than at Chauncey, but it is much more difficult for the *participants* to know. They will act upon their impressions, and these are affected by the presence or absence of strategies of concealment.[2]

THE PLANT AND THE HISTORY OF
HAMILTON AND CHAUNCEY

Hamilton had a plant and a history which made it more vulnerable to disorder than Chauncey. Hamilton has a considerably larger student body. Its plant is far larger and more rambling than Chauncey's. It occupies an irregular piece of land approximately two square blocks in size. The main building is a long

2. An additional difficulty of comparison, peculiar to this study, lies in the fact that the study at Chauncey took place during the fall semester of 1967 – 68 and that at Hamilton during the spring semester, an unusually turbulent time. That spring contained the currents of disillusionment and anger over the Vietnamese War which led to President Johnson's dramatic March 30 withdrawal from presidential candidacy. The students in the top tracks, at least, were articulately aware of these events. Martin Luther King and then Robert Kennedy were assassinated during that spring, and the whole student body at Hamilton visibly responded to both events, though less dramatically to the latter. Reports from substitutes indicated that problems of order at Chauncey did increase during this tumultuous time, but that they never reached the level, or the open style, of Hamilton's.

two story one with two wings fit together at an angle. Extending from either end are a separate science building and a chain of "temporary" bungalows containing twenty-seven classrooms and a set of administrative offices. The buildings face on two sides of the lot and sit on a slight ridge from which the land rolls downward past old and new gymnasia and out of sight to a fence along the far streets. Such a plant abounds in places to play hooky and places to waylay unsuspecting peers. Chauncey, on the other hand, is built on a single modest block with a flat terrain. The buildings are compact with a courtyard in the middle and playing fields set beside them. It is far more easily supervised.

Hamilton's plant is also more formidable and more depressing to the spirit than Chauncey's. If such subtle influences matter, it would make the students feel less at one with the school. Both plants are old, predating the Second World War at least, with a scattering of new buildings or additions in each. Hamilton's main building is more expensive and imposing, with an attractive facade at the front. But the dark stained wood paneling and dark stained chairs make the classrooms sombre while the halls are long, dark, and oppressively institutional. The play yard where the children go at lunch time is covered with asphalt and located outside the basement cafeteria. It is in every sense at the backside of the building. Chauncey, by contrast, has buildings which are well lit and decorated with light paneling or painted in light colors. The courtyard where the children go at lunchtime is aesthetically paved and decorated.

Hamilton had weaker resources for supervision. Despite its larger student body, it had no more principals or disciplinary deans than Chauncey. Further, at Hamilton the principals, deans, and attendance keeper and the counselors for the eighth grade were new at their jobs and still learning by their mistakes at the time of the study. Of this group, only one counselor for the eighth grade had been in the position since before desegregation four years earlier. At Chauncey, by contrast, all of these officers[3] had been in their posts a minimum of five years and most con-

3. The dean of boys was a partial exception since he had moved from counseling to the dean's position two years before the study.

siderably longer. They had worked out smooth routines of handling physical supervision, and they had a common rhetoric and pattern of mutual support in talking with the children.

Finally, the history of the schools created far more turmoil and instability among both faculty and students at Hamilton than at Chauncey. Before desegregation Hamilton had had a very different student body. It had been 85 percent white and essentially all middle class. It had included six of the eight census tracts in the city with a median education of sixteen years or more. Its area included the largest concentration of conservative oldtimers who had previously dominated city and school affairs. Many parents and teachers had developed a close relationship and a fierce pride in Hamilton's reputation as the highly academic junior high school which produced a preponderance of student leaders in the high school. The teachers were a cohesive group, warmly attached to a paternal principal of twenty years' tenure who retired in the spring of 1963. When a drive to recall the school board for ordering desegregation was mounted in 1964, this newly retired principal ran on the slate opposing the incumbents.

At the time of desegregation the district hierarchy was most worried about difficulties at Darwin, where sheltered upper middle class white children would be attending school on the "wrong side of the tracks."[4] Therefore the redrawing of district lines was done in stages, so that Darwin's enrollment was decreased during the first year of transition. But this was arranged at the cost of giving Hamilton, perceived to be the strongest school, a sudden increase of 200 students. With them came an influx of new teachers, many of them unwilling transfers from the old Lincoln.

Many of the children who had to leave their familiar surroundings in the Valley to attend Hamilton in the strange territory of the Heights were angry. They let the school feel the force of their discomfort. Teachers from the old Hamilton were not only

4. Canton's physical and social topography provide a classic match. The railroad tracks bisect the city, roughly separating the poorest areas from others. And the lower the altitude of the land, the lower is the social class of the residents.

disgruntled with the changes but unprepared for them. The principal was new in his position and not experienced with the kind of children newly entering the school. Every teacher or administrator who had been in the school that year spoke of it with a look heavenward.

Overenrollment was temporary. The teachers gradually acquired minimal skill in coping with the new students. Students who expected to come to Hamilton from mid-elementary school on, along with their elementary school classmates, were less hostile to the school than those removed from an already composed junior high school class. The central district personnel realized that Hamilton was the school experiencing the most problems overall and the most difficulty with the black children in particular. It started assigning to Hamilton the most experienced and skillful new teachers and those most concerned with teaching black or poor children. Nonetheless, the strains of the change were still a part of the present character of the school in the year of the study, four years after desegregation.

Chauncey had become desegregated "naturally" with the slow changes in the demographic composition of the city. Except for the loss of the ninth grade, it experienced little change in the rearrangements following desegregation of the system's schools in 1964. The proportion of races in its student body changed by only a few percentage points as it gained some children from the Valley who would previously have attended Lincoln, balanced by a group of children from census tracts with median education of sixteen years or more formerly assigned to Hamilton. In the process the school enrollment decreased by 100. Further, the rest of the district and the central administration rapidly became more sympathetic to the problems Chauncey had been experiencing in coping with a diverse student body.

FACULTY CULTURE

The most important condition creating the differences in order between the two schools seemed to be the attitudes and practices of the faculty at each. There was an unmistakable difference in the teachers' approach to the children. At each school the teachers came to share ideas about the character of children, teaching, and schools. A faculty culture grew up. New recruits to the school were socialized into it and continuing members reinforced one another in their adherence to common beliefs. As in any cultural setting there was variance in the degree of individuals' attachment to the culture and some variation in the content of beliefs. But the leaders in the faculty were the most active exemplars of the generally shared beliefs, and those who were out of sympathy remained on the fringes of collective life, having little effect upon their fellows, or upon students other than those they encountered directly in the classroom.

However, there need not be just one culture in a school. And at Hamilton there was not. Instead there were two very sharply opposed points of view each forming a rallying point for a faction which defined itself partly in opposition to the other. In the last chapter, the point was made that the classic methods of controlling student bodies through a myth of coercion or through institutionalized innocence, depend upon the students' belief that the school's routine and its response to them are inevitable and unshakable. Such a belief will not persist when the teachers treat the children in quite different ways. Consequently deep disagreement among the faculty destroys these methods of control.

Faculty Culture at Hamilton

Faculty culture at Hamilton was divided into two bitterly opposed factions. One group was composed of teachers with a developmental teaching philosophy, most of whom had joined the faculty during the four years following desegregation. The other faction was led by teachers with an incorporative teaching philosophy who had been at Hamilton for many years.

The position of the developmental teachers is fairly well described by the exposition of that position in Chapter Four. The incorporative teachers followed the philosophy described in that chapter, but they also shared some other common beliefs and attitudes. These teachers identified solely with the academic aspects of the teaching process. They were strict in their standards for behavior, but they considered enforcing these standards to be none of their job. They had nothing but praise for the former dean of boys who had used coercion effectively on the children they sent him. But this man, who was now vice-principal, shook his head despairingly over them in the privacy of the interview:

> Some teachers if the youngster bats his eye or chews gum or coughs loud or what have you, then he's misbehaving. Another teacher won't have any problem with that at all. . . . But some teachers . . . every instance of what they call misbehavior is just referred out. It's the dean's job or it's the counselor's job or it's the vice-principal's job. And those are the teachers that as a rule have most of the trouble.

These teachers had enjoyed teaching at the old Hamilton because—at least as they remembered it—they had to concern themselves with little but academic teaching of receptive students. They were able as well to enjoy some reflected glory from those students' backgrounds and accomplishments. They still spoke with obvious pride of both of these. They expressed anger and hostility toward the lower class black students who allowed them none of the former pleasures of teaching. They were nearly as angry at the children in the top tracks who challenged, questioned, and often refused to perform well in response to the highly structured curriculum and tasks these teachers liked.

All of the incorporative teachers from the old Hamilton did not follow this pattern. Some were more flexible in their teaching methods; and they were generally also more successful in keeping order and inducing learning. They were less hostile toward the students, who were in turn more cooperative toward them. They therefore had fewer incitements to direct anger in class. A better circular relationship between student and teacher developed.

But these flexible teachers were not the leaders of the incorporative faction. Rather the least flexible and most hostile were. Although these teachers were still angry about the changes made in their school with desegregation, the temper of the times forbade expression of these feelings. They consequently directed much of their explicit anger against developmentally oriented teachers, whose nonenforcement of some school rules, departures from ordinary curricular style, and encouragement of students' self-assertion were, they argued, largely the cause of the students' resistance to their own teaching. The developmental teachers responded with resentment toward the incorporative oldtimers, whom they argued made no genuine effort to teach the children, put them under undue pressure, and insulted them so that they arrived in the developmental teachers' classes in no mood for learning.

The sharply defined character of the cleavage between these groups was heightened by the fact that both felt defensive about their educational position. The teachers who regretted the passing of the old Hamilton and its style of teaching felt that the district clearly rejected their philosophy. The children also seemed to reject both their personal style and their teaching goals, at least those in the bottom tracks and the more vocal ones in the top tracks did. Further, for those who were most genuinely interested in academic progress with the children—and these did tend to be the more flexible and less hostile toward the children—the developmental teachers' claims and occasional evidences of greater academic progress created self-doubt.[5]

The developmental teachers also felt defensive. The district did not always support them in their innovations, as it moved slowly in contemplating changes in teaching style or school structure. Further, these teachers were inventing and experimenting with methods in an effort to get cooperation from the resistant students. As they moved away from standard curricular materials, they had little objective evidence of the success of their efforts. Most were fairly thoroughly prepared in an academic subject and had an identification with it. They were sensitive to their opponents' cry for "subject matter," and would say that "of course subject matter is important, but . . ." while their opponents rarely said, "of course using the children's interests is important, but . . ."

5. One of the teachers in this group read a set of students' poems dittoed by one of the developmental teachers and sighed, "I wish I could get something like this from the students." Others, less frank, must have shared her feelings on occasion.

The cleavages between these two groups, defined by educational philosophy, happened to coincide with other cleavages as well. These social differences increased the distance and the acid character of relations across factional lines. The primary differences were ones of age and dress style. The leaders and the numerical preponderance of both factions were women. The tensions which commonly exist between older and younger women were compounded by the fact that at the time bright colors and short skirts were newly in fashion. The younger teachers adopted them and the older did not. Consequently, the older teachers appeared staid and out of touch to the younger ones, while the older ones found the younger to be gaudy and indecent, attempting to deny their adulthood.[6]

The groups also differed over politics. The younger developmental group were in open opposition to the Vietnam War, which the older group seemed generally to support. And the more militant of the younger group also went so far as to wear buttons advocating the release from prison of a local black militant whose case had become a cause célèbre. The older teachers considered this practice open flouting of the due process of law in front of the students.

Resentment between the factions was so strong that they rarely talked with one another. Each group had staked out a territory in the faculty lounge and the cafeteria—which happened to be architecturally suited to such separation—and a member of one opposing camp rarely invaded the other's territory. Neutrals avoided the lounge and occupied a small unclaimed territory in the cafeteria. This separation provided fertile soil for rumors and atrocity stories about the other group's practices, which flourished in abundance.

The clannishness was explicit, even among the "younger" teachers. A new teacher was assessed for his loyalty to one side or the other. To socialize with the older teachers was to show sym-

6. Interestingly, dress corresponded even more exactly with educational philosophy than with age. I guessed two teachers' ages wrong by twenty years because one in her twenties and one in her forties dressed like the other age group and also shared their educational convictions.

pathy for their approaches and a lack of solidarity with the younger teachers. A young first-year teacher told in her interview of being approached by a member of the younger faction and queried about her indiscriminate socializing with young and old alike:

> When I first came here I just thought I was one of the big happy family. . . . And my first experience was when one of the teachers, younger teachers, came over to me and said, "I've really wondered about you—we've been wondering about you."
>
> And I said, "What are you talking about?"
>
> And she said, "Whenever I've come into the lounge you're sitting with . . ." you know so-and-so and so-and-so, meaning the older teachers. Because I just sit down and talk to anybody; I don't look at who I'm sitting down and talking to unless they're someone specific. And she really [was upset with me]. This was my first awareness of what was going on around here.

The fact of division in the Hamilton faculty served to perpetuate itself in a circular process. Each group honed its pedagogical position in opposition to what it believed to be the approach of its opponents. Since they rarely talked across group lines and never saw one another in the classroom, they remained unaware of substantial areas of theoretical and pragmatic agreement. This agreement was at its greatest in actual classroom practice, where each had to bend his ideals to the pragmatic requirements of the physical setting, the students' activities, and the broadest requirements of the teacher's role.

The polarizing effects of the debate were evident in teachers' responses to the research interview. There were striking discrepancies between the teachers' reports of their practical activities and general philosophy in the early part of the interview and their discussion of their philosophy at the end in the context of a question concerning the issues dividing the faculty. The later discussion simplified the situation, ignoring practical difficulties recognized earlier. In the context of division, teachers tended to present their own position as further out on the continuum of incorporative and developmental styles than they had earlier; practices or attitudes mentioned earlier which included elements of the opposing view were ignored in this context. The same kind of discrepancy could be noted between conversations among members of only one faction and discussions in a setting such as faculty meeting where opposing factions faced one another.[7]

Faculty Culture at Chauncey

At Chauncey the faculty culture was far more unitary. The leaders were teachers of middling tenure, mostly somewhere around ten years. Unlike the older teachers at the other schools they had chosen to stay in a socially and racially diverse school. And they had experienced no sudden change in the character of the school.

Like the oldtimers from Hamilton, the leaders of Chauncey's faculty culture expressed an incorporative philosophy and placed

7. Since my study of Darwin was only an introductory pilot study, I do not have enough data to analyze it with as much confidence or thoroughness as I can the other two schools. On the other hand, it provides some instructive parallels and contrasts with the others, especially with Hamilton. Order at Darwin was better than at Hamilton, but not so good as at Chauncey. Darwin had a faculty culture split between oldtimers at the school and developmental teachers, most of whom were recently hired. But at Darwin there was less acrimony and more cooperation among the teachers than at Hamilton.

Both sides at Darwin felt less on the defensive. The most extreme in the oldtimers' faction took a position of proto-authority and valued control of their classes above academic progress. They were able to attain this control to their satisfaction and so, despite a lack of harmony with the wider district, felt they were adequately doing their job. The younger teachers thought control a secondary goal, and that control in the older teachers' style might even be counterproductive. They therefore had none of the Hamilton developmental teachers' ambivalent attraction to their opponents' goals. These teachers were also generally less radical in their innovations and so not in conflict with the district office.

The social characteristics of the leaders of each side at Darwin were different from those at Hamilton. They were men in both factions, and while they differed in age and dress, these issues were less important. The architecture did not lend itself to separated groups, and in the lounge two of the leaders often engaged in open debate. They grew most heated on the safer ground of politics over which they also differed in ways consistent with their educational philosophies. But even on educational issues, they would disagree vigorously. Other teachers, gathered around the single coffee table, would joke, "Here they go again," but would listen intently and throw in comments which sometimes expressed crosscutting positions. Direct debate and the visibility of middle positions served to lower the emotional pitch of the conflict at Darwin.

a strong emphasis on academic teaching. But they displayed far more flexibility in their approach than did the leaders of Hamilton's incorporative faction, or even most of its more flexible members. They expected to have some difficulty in obtaining the degree of order necessary to teach. They expected to have to put in effort to obtain sufficient punctuality, neatness and decorous classroom demeanor for academic tasks to go smoothly.

These teachers openly preferred their high track classes and openly exhibited some generalized frustration and discouragement about the task of coping with the lower track ones. They also displayed unveiled hostility and anger toward individual disruptive children in these groups. But they did not exhibit either covertly or overtly the level of generalized anger and hostility toward the groups as a whole that the oldtimers at Hamilton did, and they did not place blame for their difficulties in dealing with these children on other adults in the school or on its arrangements.

These dominant teachers were so moderate in their style and flexible in their approach that they did not seem utterly alien to newer teachers whose approach was predominantly developmental. Many of the older teachers used developmental methods in a generally incorporative context, and there was visible variation among them around this central tendency.

The newer teachers consequently did not form a faction or culture of their own, but became assimilated to the dominant one of the experienced teachers. Recruitment policies had an effect as well. For as it became clear that Chauncey was the most smoothly operating school, the district assigned to it the least experienced and most traditional of the new teachers.[8] These teachers had fewer resources or less motivation to initiate their own faction than the newer teachers at other schools.

At Chauncey personal characteristics and practices did not supply fuel for factional division. A considerable proportion of

8. The principals were allowed to express preferences among the new teachers hired, though they did not always get their wishes. Chauncey's principal would have been the most likely to choose the group which Chauncey in fact received.

the older and the incorporatively inclined teachers wore the bright informal clothes which set the developmental teachers off from others at Hamilton. Further, the Chauncey teachers mixed freely with one another in the public spaces of the school. They did not use the two tables in their section of the cafeteria as a setting for cliques, but rather followed an informal rule to fill up first one table then the other in a solid row as they came from the steam table.

But Chauncey teachers also carefully avoided the subjects of education and politics in their conversations. Less than half the conversation in the cafeteria and lounge concerned school matters, compared to the overwhelming preponderance of the conversation at both other schools. Also in contrast to the other schools, where problems and policies were warmly discussed, what conversation about the school did take place centered upon safe subjects, the foibles of individual students or noncontroversial procedural matters.

They sensed that their broad consensus on educational philosophy was fragile, and they treated it gently. Some of the teachers were quite explicit in individual interviews about the presence of divergent views which could create rather sharp conflict among the faculty. Most wanted to avoid such conflict, partly for the sake of smooth social relations and partly for the sake of smooth school functioning.[9]

Nonetheless, though practice diverged more than rhetoric at Chauncey and private thinking more than public, the very existence of public consensus exerted a socializing influence on all the teachers, especially the inexperienced ones. It operated to create more actual unity than would otherwise have existed.

At each school, the difficulties of teaching provided an impetus for faculty division as different persons thought of different responses to the failures of current practice. At each, the

9. In the previous year, a number of factors, foremost among them the presence of two vocally dissident teachers, had threatened to break up this consensus. A process of polarization had started. But with the apparently voluntary departure of these teachers and some changes in the policies of the principal, the teachers had re-established the common culture—with a little more awareness of its fragility.

pragmatic limits of the physical setting, the students' activities, and the broadest definitions of the teacher's role placed limits on variety in classroom practice. At Hamilton, the possibilities for philosophical division were realized to their fullest and the reality of considerable pragmatic convergence unrecognized. At Chauncey the possibilities for philosophical division were muffled, and considerable variety in private thought and private practice publicly unrecognized.

THE EFFECT OF FACULTY CULTURE
ON STUDENT ORDER

In a sense both factions at Hamilton were right in blaming upon the other faction their problems in getting cooperation in the classroom and order outside it. For the clear presence of disagreement and even bitter conflict between members of the faculty shattered the picture of a school with a unitary and inevitable character which might under other circumstances have been presented to the students.

Even when teachers did not directly criticize one another to, or in front of, the students, it was clear in their diverse actions and their responses to students' mentions of other teachers' practices that there were deep differences among the adults in the school.

This lack of a unitary definition of the school situation made an effective myth of coercion or the institutionalization of innocence out of the question as methods of control at Hamilton. It also made both the incorporative and developmental approaches seem to be matters of personal choice, and the students as well as the teachers were therefore free to have their own preferences about them. The student had no reason to think of one approach or the other as inherently part of all schools, and therefore it could occur to him to try to influence a given teacher's pattern or to try to locate himself in the classroom of a teacher whose pattern he preferred. [10]

10. Because of the high incidence of really severe conflict in some of Hamilton's classes, counselors there were quicker than at the other two schools to transfer a student to another teacher's class when the conflict became serious.

Students quickly perceived that neither covert nor overt rebellion would be met with a consistent response. It was possible to disobey without fearing universal stigmatization and, if one were careful about detection or about which adults became involved, perhaps even without receiving punishment. Much rebellion without principled cause was encouraged by the division on principles among the adults. Once this disobedience occurred on a fairly large scale the limited resources of the school to deal with deviance were revealed to the students and the cycle of increasing disorder and retreating sanctions discussed in Chapter Seven ensued.

The existence of sharply felt conflict between the factions at Hamilton probably also contributed directly to student disorder. The emotional tone of the conflict between the teachers was at fever pitch in March when the study began. The students were taken on an interracial retreat during which there were several direct and emotional confrontations between teachers of the two camps. At a faculty meeting in the school one teacher spoke on an issue which touched closely upon the split in the faculty, made a defiant personal defense of her methods, and then dissolved in tears before she could finish. It is unlikely that feelings this strong were not communicated to the students at least at an intuitive level. They must have played some part in the high level of collective excitement among the students.[11]

At Chauncey, by contrast, the relative agreement and harmony among the teachers made it possible for them to present a unified front to the students. Though they might differ fairly widely in their individual practices in the classroom, they shared much of the same rhetoric and the same basic definition of the school

---

While this practice solved some difficult situations, it undermined control and acceptance of teachers in general by destroying students'—and teachers'—resigned acceptance of an inevitable year together during which they would have to learn to get along.

11. Stanton and Schwartz discuss just this kind of phenomenon in a mental hospital. They document in far more detail than is given here a connection between covert disagreements among staff members on a ward and the appearance of collective excitement among patients. (See Alfred H. Stanton and Morris S. Schwartz, *The Mental Hospital,* Chapter 15.)

situation. They were nearly all essentially incorporative in their approach, but with varying admixtures of developmental elements. They were generally benign but firm, not hostile, yet not yielding to counterdefinitions of the situation. The lack of direct hostility toward the students and of tension among the adults kept the general emotional tone cool. And the unity of the adults made the students see the character of the school as unitary and inevitable. Whether they liked it or rejected it, few were likely to defy it openly or to try to change it.

THE EFFECT OF STUDENT ORDER ON
FACULTY CULTURE

These different levels of order also had an effect on the character of faculty culture at each school. There was a circular interaction between faculty culture and student order. At Hamilton it was clear to each teacher that there was difficulty in maintaining order in the school as a whole, not just in his particular classroom. If the students were noisy and boisterous throughout the school and if cutting and false fire alarms were common occurrences, then his problems in teaching were probably not solely the result of his own inadequacies. Presumably his problems in the classroom were part of a broader problem in the school.

Hamilton teachers were thus prodded by the visible disorder in the whole school into reflection on the sources of the resistance they encountered in the classroom. The widespread and serious character of student disaffection suggested that more than a few clever mechanisms aimed at particular difficulties would be needed. Some fundamental changes would have to occur. As a result, these teachers were far more reflective, explicit, and consistent about their own philosophies of teaching and about what they thought the approach of the school as a whole should be than were the teachers at Chauncey.

Amidst an atmosphere defined as good order at Chauncey, teachers felt themselves individually at fault when their classes did not behave in an orderly manner. Other teachers' classes apparently were orderly, so the fault must lie with themselves.

Given this atmosphere, teachers were very hesitant to speak publicly of their difficulties in maintaining order either inside or outside the classroom. Problems caused by individual difficult children were the one exception to this rule. Teachers did publicly compare notes, and sometimes with obvious relief, on their difficulties in keeping the same particular students from being disruptive forces. Discussion of these students' activities provided a vent for general frustration and a focus for considerable attention at Chauncey.

As a consequence of this reluctance to speak of problems in maintaining order, teachers, especially the less experienced, lived in ignorance of their shared difficulties. Some of the newer teachers I observed were very apologetic about the amount of disorder in their lower track classes, even though these classes were about average for the school. They were surprised when I assured them that their problems were a familiar story to me.

Because of the relatively good hall order and the lack of public discussion of classroom noncooperation, Chauncey teachers did not see disorder as a fundamental problem calling for basic changes in the school. Rather they saw it as a pragmatic problem for each teacher to solve in his classroom. Consequently they did not turn for solutions to reflection on the fundamental goals and relationships involved in their task as the Hamilton teachers did, but turned rather to pragmatic methods available for solving their daily problems. They sought eagerly for more effective means of presenting ideas or developing skills, for better books and other materials, and they looked for effective mechanisms for dealing with particular problems such as the child who chronically forgets to bring a pencil to class.

In the interview with teachers there was a question asking for devices a teacher might have worked out on his own to deal with such situational problems as a child who could not remember a pencil or one who was feeling generally negative toward anything he was asked to do on a given day. Chauncey teachers replied to this question with interest and at length, though inexperienced ones answered for the most part only that they were in desperate search of such devices. The Hamilton teachers, on the other hand, tended to brush this question aside with, "No, I don't have anything like that," a statement that "gimmicks" did not solve the real problem, or a longer discussion of their general philosophical approach to the classroom as a whole. The Chauncey teachers had little to say in answer to questions designed to elicit their general philosophical approach to teaching, their fundamental goals, or their understanding of appropriate student—teacher relationships in the classroom. But the Hamilton teachers responded to *these* questions with interest and at length.

The Hamilton teachers, therefore, were driven to fundamental questioning about the discontents which motivated the children by the troubles which obviously beset the school as well as their own classrooms. But the Chauncey teachers, in the absence of obvious problems besetting the whole school, met the problems in their own classrooms with small pragmatic adjustments which did not question their broad agreement about the school's proper overall character. Disorder encouraged the Hamilton teachers' questioning, and fed each faction's belief that the other was the root of the school's problems. The disorder among the students which was encouraged by their quarrels operated to sharpen those quarrels. At Chauncey the relatively smooth functioning of the school in the visible spaces outside the classroom seemed to confirm the value of the school's approach, which an individual teacher experienced as a matter of faculty consensus. The apparent viability of this current general practice discouraged him from thinking through, or practicing, an alternative, and thus from threatening that consensus.

The fundamental questions asked by the Hamilton teachers and the acceptance of a benign but firmly incorporative approach to education by the Chauncey teachers had consequences for the behavior of the children aside from their disobedience and obedience. But before discussing these effects it is important to ask about the impact of the principal upon the faculty and the students. It is the principal who bears formal responsibility for the conduct and achievement of both the students and the faculty. Many of the teachers thought the principal's role to be the key to the character of the whole school. The next chapter will analyze the very different ways in which the two principals played their formally identical roles.

CHAPTER 9

The Principals' Impact on the Schools

THE POSITION of principal stands where the schools' organizational needs and imperatives most forcefully conflict. The principal is formally accountable to his superiors in the district hierarchy for all that happens in a school. Yet the teachers who have direct contact with the children, who have the most to do with what happens, do most of their work out of his sight and hearing and with at least a minimal formal claim to autonomy. The principal has direct responsibility without direct control over the events for which he must answer.

In Canton, the central district officers formally expected principals to support and encourage diversity, experimentation, and independence among both teachers and students. And they were consistent in granting the principals the freedom which would encourage them also to experiment and develop independence as administrators. Principals had wide ranging autonomy in running each school.

But the district still expected good order, while all its policies did very little to support that end. If a school was the scene of continued or dramatic disorder, whatever its other strengths, district officers would be required to take action and the formally appropriate action would be to hold the principal responsible.

The principals thus were keenly aware that they were responsible both for imaginative academic education and for safety and order in every part of the school. They were also aware that this double responsibility entailed practical contradictions and the necessity for choice.

At Chauncey the principal, Mr. Brandt, responded to the contradictory demands upon his office by choosing to fulfill one and to screen the other out of the school's awareness. He made his choice for order and safety. He interpreted autonomy for students and teachers as an expectation of courtesy, consultation, or the offering of alternatives. He put his own responsibility for the school first, and he ran it as he thought it should be run, accepting opposition or serious alteration from no one. Mr. Brandt's successful accomplishment of this kind of control was a remarkable feat in the exercise of power. However, he was able to follow the style he did in part because the history of the school and the recruitment of teachers, discussed in the last chapter, kept it on a fairly even keel.

It would not have been possible for Mr. Brandt to still the demands of students and teachers for diversity and autonomy in the context of Hamilton as he did at Chauncey. Mr. Henley—who took over at Hamilton in the year of desegregation—did not try. He believed in delegating responsibility to teachers. And once this pattern was started at Hamilton, there was no way it could be reversed. Almost any administrative decision came to be interpreted as a choice for one or the other of the opposing camps of teachers. Mr. Henley tried to deal with this problem by allowing the teachers to feel the force of the contradictory pressures for autonomy and for order, so that they would begin individually and collectively to take responsibility for reconciling them. However, the teachers for the most part accepted their autonomy but left the maintenance of order beyond the classroom to someone else. It was easy to blame the other camp for the general problems of order which resulted.

Mr. Henley could delegate his responsibility. He could not delegate his accountability. He bore the burden of the blame for student disorder and finally resigned under pressure.

CHAUNCEY: MR. BRANDT'S ADMINISTRATION

Mr. Brandt imposed his choice for the priority of order over autonomy by never admitting that he made it. He was catholic in claiming allegiance to the importance of all generally accepted school goals and the validity of all accepted relationships. He refused to rank goals in importance. He avowed his firm belief in consultation and discussion with subordinates, whether faculty or students; but stood equally clearly for firm insistence upon behavior appropriate to a school as he defined it.

Mr. Brandt's readiness to admit the validity of almost any common value in education disarmed those who opposed his practical choices. Teachers who objected to one of his practices were greeted with warm agreement in some form of the statement, "Now I see your point of view, you've heard me say that is important, but. . . ."

The consequence was a subtlety in Mr. Brandt's style of running the school which made it hard to define. It resembled an impressionist painting. Seen from up close, where the faculty and students were, his style had a soft, diffuse, blurred appearance. But seen from the distant perspective of comparison with Hamilton it was sharp, clear, and vivid. Like an impressionist painting too, it was made up of a myriad of little touches, each seemingly meaningless, but taken together forming a sharp image.

Mr. Brandt's emphasis upon order was visible directly in his choice to commit much more of the teachers' and counselors' time to supervisory duties than did the principals at the other schools. Teachers sometimes objected that these duties took time needed for academic purposes. They claimed that they needed the time between classes when they were assigned to supervise in the halls to rearrange their papers and their thoughts for the next class. They argued that a student could take roll so that they could start the class briskly upon its major activity without allowing attention to dissipate during roll.

Mr. Brandt denied any conflict between goals here. He claimed the objecting teachers simply displayed a lack of logistical imagination. If teachers would simply assign a written task at the opening of the period, the students would be starting the class while the teacher rearranged papers and took roll. But, if such tasks are to be meaningfully integrated into the class's work they severely limit the possible academic activities for the whole forty-minute class. The tension between supervisory and academic tasks remains, and Mr. Brandt gives the supervisory task primacy.

In practice Mr. Brandt operated much like an incorporatively oriented teacher in dealing with teachers as well as students. His role was primarily bureaucratic and parental.[1] But he did not perceive himself as simply giving orders to be followed. Rather, he always emphasized suggestion and persuasion as the appropriate modes of superordination. Still, a suggestion refused became a command. The following passage from his comments in the research interview illustrates both his behavior and his style of expression:

I: What you said about [all the teachers taking extracurricular] clubs leads into my next question. When people are reluctant, what is your mechanism for getting cooperation?

R: Kill 'em with enthusiasm. I really don't think you drive people who are intelligent and well educated. You try to lead them, and you try to encourage. But I try not to get into a position that I'm adamant, that [I say] "You've got to do this." And I think the easiest way to do it is to give people alternatives. After all, you and I are going to get along a lot better if I say, "Well, would you like to do this or this or this? We think everybody should carry something. Or

1. Comparison of the relationship of authority between a principal and his teachers and between those teachers and their students is instructive. It would be interesting to study the consequences of consistency or inconsistency in goals and role conceptions claimed by a principal with his subordinate teachers and the claims each makes as a superordinate with his students. Schlecty has developed a complex typology of schools based on four aspects of control relations extending from administrators through teachers to children. After identifying thirty-six possible types, he weaves together a variety of smaller studies in informed speculation about the impact of various types on selected problematic aspects of school life. (See Phillip C. Schlecty, *Teaching and Social Behavior*.)

can you suggest something that you would like to do?" And ninety percent of the time they'll go along with it.

I: And what happens the other ten?

R: Then I think we have to push people. I've pushed people into doing things which I felt they ought to do, and they were very reluctant. And afterwards they thanked me for it. They'd never tried this before, and they had avoided it studiously. They found out it's something they liked to do. . . . And I think this is the best technique. I try to avoid putting a teacher in a position where they're going to say, "I ain't a'goin to do it, and you try and make me." Because a teacher can be transferred; a teacher can be forced to assume responsibilities.[2]

Despite his initial approach of suggestion, and the offering of alternatives, Mr. Brandt never wavers in his determination that every teacher will take extracurricular activities, whether he believes he should or not. (At other schools many did not.) At the same time, he denies the existence of genuine conflict, claiming that even those teachers he coerces "thank me for it." His actual style was sometimes less open-ended than his description suggested. He made a frequent practice of announcing the establishment and composition of a committee in faculty meeting without so much as prior notification to its members. And he would assign major responsibilities by note without including a question as to the teacher's willingness to undertake them.

The discrepancy between Mr. Brandt's rhetoric and his practice in matters such as this annoyed his teachers. But it did not lead to rebellion. He succeeded in controlling them and in getting their compliance without much objection primarily by controlling their definition of the character of the school. He created an impression that the way he asked them to conduct themselves and to direct the children at Chauncey was inherent in the inevitable character of public schools. It was not a matter of his personal decision but simply given in the nature of things. Teachers accepted this definition of the situation. Yet practices

2. Mr. Brandt admitted elsewhere that it was very difficult to transfer teachers in Canton though he claimed it could be done.

which not only he, but teachers talking in the privacy of the interview, described as simply necessary were poles apart from practices at Hamilton just across town with a matched student body.

Mr. Brandt created his clear picture of the character of school out of many little strokes. Important among them was his emphasis upon the school's placement in a larger system of state laws and district directives which specify activities and narrow discretion. The faculty handbook which he developed is double the length of the ones at the other two junior high schools and filled with quotations from state laws and district directives—while the others have few. Many of these statements are vague or diffuse. But when Mr. Brandt cited "the law" or "district policy" in support of his directions teachers usually accepted his statements without further discussion.

Mr. Brandt saw to it that communication within the school flowed hierarchically wherever possible. He used various devices to underscore his own position as the source of authoritative statements. Unlike the other principals, he issued all faculty and student bulletins over his signature as communications from him, though the bulk of notices were contributed by other staff members. Faculty meetings took place in a regular classroom, but a lectern and microphone were specially installed for the occasion. Mr. Brandt stood behind the lectern in a formal setting, occasionally calling upon someone else to give a report. He called attention to his practice of limiting these meetings to an hour's duration, using this reason to forestall and occasionally to cut off extended questions or debate. Yet in every meeting during the study there were agenda items of at least fifteen minutes duration which were not matters of immediate business. There were, for example, concerts by a student quintet and a humorous movie unrelated to teaching. At Hamilton and Darwin, the principal sat at, or on, a table among the faculty, and faculty discussion and decision making formed a substantial part of the meeting.

As Mr. Brandt underscored the principal's formal and symbolic position at the head of the school, he made his own vision of

the school part of its inherent character. Teachers whose disagreement with that vision was serious nonetheless accepted it as
the only possible basis for action at Chauncey Junior High
School, and they voluntarily left. Mr. Brandt described his
conscious use of this strategy in an indirect way in his interview:

> I: If somebody is really unwilling, what kinds of pressure can you
> bring besides saying, "Do it."
>
> R: The technique I try to use with people is to kill them with en-
> thusiasm. And this works on many people. They can't stand anybody
> being so enthusiastic about working with kids, and they leave.
>
> I: You mean leave the school?
>
> R: Yes. This has probably been my most effective weapon.

Mr. Brandt co-opted the teachers' innovative energies. He did
this for the faculty as a whole by creating a plethora of
committees. Most of these had only modest tasks, but enough
meetings so that teachers generally attended about one meeting a
week, a much higher load than existed at Hamilton. All
committees of any kind reported ultimately to the principal. At
least twice during the year he established committees on controversial problems, then overruled their decisions.

He appointed as department chairmen the most energetic
teachers who were informal leaders among the faculty. He gave
this position heavier responsibilities than at the other schools,
thus keeping these teachers busy at tasks of his own choosing.
They also had high levels of contact with him personally and with
the administrative problems of running the school, experiences
which might be expected to increase their sympathy with the
principal's definition of the situation.

Mr. Brandt also quieted restlessness with plans for schoolwide
innovation. He had the faculty as a body explore the possibility of
putting the school on flexible scheduling. Two respected teachers
were even given reduced teaching loads to study the matter.
There were visits by teams to schools elsewhere in the state
already on such plans. Several times when teachers would
mention one of their frustrations to me, they would comfort

themselves with the thought that flexible scheduling might alleviate it. But the planning bore no fruit, at least in the two years following the study.

Mr. Brandt was extraordinarily successful in creating a definition of the inherent character of schools which his teachers adopted as an assumption of their working lives. He kept them in a state of considerable innocence about the pressures for autonomy and diversity issuing from the community, supported by the central district, and put into practice at Hamilton. But he could not block out from their daily experience the students' restlessness.

Mr. Brandt met this challenge by individualizing both the students' resistance to school procedures and the teachers' experience of it. His ideal for teachers' treatment of students resembled his own approach to the teachers. He believed that the values to be served and, beyond a certain point, the behavior to be tolerated were fixed and immovable. But he argued that good management can smooth out any difficulty.

The following comments from his interview suggest the style in which he talked with teachers about their handling of the students. Asked about the "really difficult kids" he said:

> Any kid that has any guts and gumption, you can back him into a corner and finally he will tell you off unless he's a beaten whipped kid. So I think what a teacher has to do is to be fairly skillful. . . . And I think part of it is in the way you approach the kid. I try to be completely polite to a kid, the way I like to be treated, no matter what he's doing. If that doesn't work, I can scream and holler and be as rough as the next guy. But that's my approach. That's the way I think kids like to be treated. And most of them respond. The toughest kid will respond, because this gives him a feeling of status and all the other things which he needs, for his own ego. I think this is true of your hard core kids. They need politeness. And some of them will come around to this.
>
> I think also you have to be flexible enough so that you don't push them into a corner. I saw this done beautifully in a classroom with the kids. "I ain't going to study today, 'cause I don't feel like it." And the teacher just grinned at him. And she said, "Well, I'm

going to give you a book just in case you change your mind." In five minutes he was studying. She could have kicked him out, sent him to the dean, because he told her he wasn't about to study. But she just grinned at him and said, "Here's your book. Come on, you'll feel like it," and went on to the next kid. And this takes a little expertise.

The hard core kids, I think they need to be handled firmly, and they need to be handled with love and affection. And with a certain amount of rigidity. That there does come a point where it's either fish or cut bait. You've got to make a choice. You do it or you're gone. And most of them will shape up, and the ones that won't shape up then have to go.

Mr. Brandt sees problems of order as arising from the nature of *individual* children, not from any fundamental conflict between the school's assumptions and the situations of whole categories of children. And he sees classroom problems as normally minor ripples, amenable to simple principles of courtesy and firmness. Teachers mentioned again and again his love of anecdotes like the one in the quotation, as he talked with them about their troubles. This anecdote with its homey simplicity and happy ending suggests that any teacher who will muster good humor and patience will have classes whose members cooperate and work all of the time.

In approaching the teachers' problems with the children in this style Mr. Brandt suggested that any serious problems of order that might exist in their classrooms probably resulted from their own failure to display patience, imagination, or firmness—from a lack of skill as adults dealing with children. He made them feel guilty and inept. These feelings sent them back to their classrooms determined to find a way to cope. He motivated them to use their own resources to the limit. These feelings also led teachers to hide their problems lest they display their own shortcomings to other teachers. The teachers' reluctance to talk about their classroom difficulties mentioned in the discussion of faculty culture thus arose in part from the principal's definition of those problems as a badge of the teacher's ineptitude.

The Chauncey teachers were genuinely ignorant of their

common problems because of this practice. The principal directly encouraged this ignorance with a pervasive policy of confidentiality about problems of order vis-à-vis teachers as well as students. Even a group walkout of black students from an after-school dance was not openly discussed and not known to many of the faculty. When an incident between a student and one of the deans blew up into a cause célèbre in the black community, the teachers were told none of the facts in the case. This policy ostensibly protected the student's right to confidentiality, but it also kept the faculty from polarizing over the behavior of the dean.

Mr. Brandt emphasized the existence of individual children who were "hard core" or "kooks" who could really disrupt a classroom despite a teacher's best efforts. His emphasis upon these students was not simply rhetorical. In a committee meeting I attended, he stated very firmly that students with repeated disciplinary problems should be placed in special programs in the school, and if that were not possible, expelled. In fact, the state-funded "EH" or "educationally handicapped" program, established for children with learning disabilities, was thought by most Chauncey teachers to be "emotionally handicapped," because it was filled to capacity with children all but one or two of whom had been referred for being discipline problems. At Hamilton the program had low visibility, was known by its right name, and included less than a full complement of children, all of whom had learning disabilities which were not primarily emotional.

Mr. Brandt's attitude toward rebellious children gave the teachers permission to talk about their troubles with them without fearing stigma. Consequently, most of the discourse among the teachers about difficulties in teaching centered on individual troublesome students. Teachers were highly aware of EH and some even lobbied for the establishment of another section for children who created discipline problems which would not entail EH's certification by experts. (Such a section had been discontinued some time previously under pressure from the central office.)

In many cases, Chauncey teachers' private ideas about alleviating classroom difficulties gave the management of difficult individuals first priority. At Hamilton teachers of all persuasions generally believed the most disruptive children in a class to be simply exaggerating a much more common lack of harmony with the school's functioning. Because of the Chauncey teachers' ignorance of the extent of students' resistance to the school, and because of their absorption with the idiosyncracies of colorful individuals, they did not ask themselves individually or collectively whether the overall character of the school was at odds with the world view or the needs of large numbers of students. Such questions at Hamilton led teachers to the diverse answers which so polarized them. Chauncey's faculty harmony depended upon their belief in the principal's construction of reality.

Nonetheless, their daily dealings with the students in the classroom made the Chauncey teachers restive with Mr. Brandt's bland assumption of the curative powers of good humor and good management. Yet such was his success in defining the school for them that they had difficulty in naming the source of their uneasiness with him. There was nearly universal tension in teachers' relations with the principal, but they experienced and expressed their discontent as a matter of "little things," a question of personality. They were embarrassed and apologetic at the degree of their anger over issues which when articulated seemed to be personal peccadilloes.

In the previous year, several miscalculations by the principal and the presence of two outspoken teachers had galvanized the faculty into organizing a "faculty senate" to express the desires of teachers to the administration. But the only concrete reforms they suggested had to do with faculty supervisorial loads and the establishment of procedures making it easier to remove troublesome individuals from the classroom. Even in rebellion, they thought in the principal's categories.

When their reforms were quickly granted the fire died out of their movement. In the year of the study, after the apparently voluntary departure of the two outspoken teachers, the faculty senate never functioned.

HAMILTON: MR. HENLEY'S ADMINISTRATION

Mr. Brandt did not admit the contradiction between arrangements required to maintain order and those required to meet the expectations of restive children for participation on their own terms. He dealt with the dilemma he faced by denying one half of it.

At Hamilton Mr. Henley made many choices opposite to those of Mr. Brandt. He freely admitted the contradictory demands being made upon the school in expectations for good order and for responsiveness to the styles of diverse and demanding children. Instead of responding to these contradictions by emphasizing the principal's responsibility for the whole school, as Mr. Brandt did, he responded by delegating as much of that responsibility as possible to those who were asking for freedom and autonomy. He recognized the inappropriateness of existing school structures for the style of activity expected by students and parents, and by the district. He thought individual good will to be a frail tool with which to cope. He hoped by passing on responsibility to the faculty—and to a limited degree to the students—to get them to see the need for concerted collective action to maintain good order alongside individual initiative. Finally, he believed that the appropriate mode of leadership in a school is one which emphasizes academic goals above others and which grants teachers formal—as well as de facto—autonomy in their pursuit.

The following excerpt from his discussion of the role of principal in the research interview illustrates the differences in concept and in style between him and Mr. Brandt.

I: What are the main activities, as you see it, of the principal's job?

R: Well, I think the one word is organization. That's the main responsibility, to provide organization. This would certainly encompass a number of interpretations, and in this particular situation at Hamilton, I would say I spend most of my time putting out fires,

figuratively.[3] There are so many factions within the faculty; there are
so many factions within the community; there are so many stimulating, exciting experiences that our children are involved in in this
day and age—and particularly in Canton—that these are the pressures that seem to come out in the school situation. And I would say
that I spend most of my day involved in mediation, or explanation,
or working more at an almost crisis level.

In his specific relationship with teachers, he was puzzled about
what was appropriate, feeling that he should respond to their
needs and desires as well as to those of the nature of the
organization and its work:

I think the authoritarian approach of the past probably does not
apply now with the organizations that the teachers have developed,
competing professional groups,[4] and the awareness and the desire
for involvement that so many of the teachers have. I feel that a principal who uses a strict authoritarian approach is probably going to encounter many, many problems.

And yet, I can sense that the teachers want direction in a way, and
it becomes a dilemma in that respect. They would feel much more
secure—they, I mean the majority or probably the average teacher
would feel much more secure—if the principal or someone on the
staff made it very, very clear which way he turns at each corner.

I think this could be an extreme in the authoritarian direction or
it could be an extreme in the opposite direction. So we have to find
that middle ground where the principal is astute enough to
determine just how much direction he can give without some sort of
rebellion. And it *is* an academic environment, and I think a princi-

3. At the close of a detailed descriptive case study, Wolcott uses the same
metaphor to summarize the character of the work of the elementary principal.
(See Harry Wolcott, *The Man in the Principal's Office*, pp. 314–15.)

4. Mr. Henley made reference here to two competing teachers' organizations, a union chapter and a local branch of the National Education Association.
Teachers and administrators alike were aware of the presence of both organizations, but neither was in the forefront of their thoughts. Teachers especially
considered the organizations to have little direct influence on the schools.
Principals felt their impact mainly in the possibility of having to justify any
dismissal to them, a fact which made the principals more ready than previously
to get written documentation of staff problems and slower to dismiss marginally
competent or cooperative teachers.

pal must give leeway to the teachers to develop a program that they feel is prudent.

At the same time that Mr. Henley allowed teachers considerable latitude for diversity and initiative, he could be firm when he thought they were acting outside responsible bounds. He dismissed a tenured teacher in the middle of the year[5] and had some very strongly worded talks with others at both ends of Hamilton's philosophical spectrum whom he thought were behaving irresponsibly.

But he had more regard for the rights of individuals than for sources of effective control of the faculty in these matters; he kept his reprimands confidential. Unless the teacher told on himself, it seemed to other teachers that the extreme behavior went unsanctioned. Thus teachers at each extreme were able to become indignant at the principal's sympathy with teachers of the other extreme and to interpret his disapproval of themselves as a sign of bias in favor of their opponents. Reprimands to themselves could thus be dismissed as the words of someone whose definition of the character of the school, and whose claim to authority based on this definition, they did not accept as legitimate.

Mr. Henley's belief in delegating responsibility to the faculty served to give the divisive forces among them, described in the last chapter, their full play. It quickly became difficult for him to take stands without appearing to take sides. He consequently maintained a low profile most of the time. Where at Chauncey Mr. Brandt was the single dominating force in the school, at Hamilton the teachers collectively were the dominant element, while the principal merely mediated.[6]

Mr. Henley tried conscientiously to follow the district's formal-

5. The teacher—mentioned earlier—had publicly used physical force on a student, after repeated warnings not to do so.

6. In a study of twenty-eight high schools Corwin found that staff conflict was affected by a variety of complex constellations of factors, rather than by a set of additively contributing conditions. However, other things being equal, where faculties were more professional in their orientation, conflict among the staff tended to be higher than where they were not. (See Ronald G. Corwin, *Militant Professionalism.*) In summarizing the character of the discordant schools, Corwin draws a picture reminiscent of Hamilton (ibid., p. 348).

ly announced style of procedure. In so doing he expected those
beneath him in the organizational structure to act with a sense of
responsibility as they exercised their autonomy. Many among
both the teachers and students did so. But many did not. As
difficulties with order born of the many sources described in the
last chapter rose, the district officers looked to the person
formally responsible. On April 2 Mr. Henley resigned, effective
in June.

AN INFORMATIVE ISSUE: THE PLEDGE OF ALLEGIANCE

The contrasting styles of the principals became graphically
clear in their handling of a single issue which arose at both
schools. This issue—the school's appropriate response to students' increasing refusal to recite the pledge of allegiance—
also illustrates students' collective pressure for a part in defining
the moral order of the school. At both schools students had been
expected to pledge the flag in their first-period class each
morning. At first scattered children in the upper tracks objected
to doing so, but the objection spread until in most of the
first-period classes I observed at Chauncey only the teacher's
voice could be clearly heard, accompanied by a faint mumble
from a few students.

Even some of the teachers had come to object to the requirement. One of Chauncey's more developmental teachers summarized the major objections of both students and teachers in an
interview:

> I think it's meaningless to have these kids say it every day.
> Absolutely meaningless. A period is forty minutes long, and if you're
> going to prepare the kids for the pledge, and then have them recite
> it, and then have a follow-up, there goes forty minutes.
>
> I think the patriotic mimicking business is ridiculous. The pledge
> would mean something to these kids if—for instance, two years ago
> we had a big row in my history class, and we sat down for forty
> minutes to talk about what is the pledge all about. Why do some of
> you kids object to saying it? And the kids would come up with,
> "Well, there isn't freedom and justice for all." I said, "That's true.

But are we saying that 'with liberty and justice for all' now, or is the pledge for something that we want the country to become?"

You see nobody explains it this way. They ram the stuff down the kids' throats and I don't blame them for objecting. I mean look at the whole society. . . . (trails off)

I could see saying the pledge if the kid understands that this is a pledge for what we hope America will *become* some day, rather than saying it is a lie because it's not that way today.

Also this "under God." I, personally I suppose, believe in God in my own way, but what about the kids who don't? I don't think that should be in the pledge. I think it's a violation of the separation of church and state. And I'm surprised that this hasn't gotten to the Supreme Court.

Given resistance to the pledge of allegiance by a majority of the children and some of the teachers, Canton High School instituted a flag-raising ceremony in the courtyard before school each day in which all children could participate. Those who did not wish to did not have to. In the fall of the year of the study Darwin and Hamilton also adopted this solution to the problem. With these examples elsewhere and increasing expressive aliena-tion by the children, pressure built for a change in the practice at Chauncey.

Mr. Brandt met this by putting together a committee to study what change might be made. He announced the formation of the committee at a faculty meeting (without prior notification to the members). The explanation of this agenda item incited the only attempt at debate in faculty meeting in my five months at Chauncey. Mr. Brandt firmly cut it off:

They moved on to the pledge of allegiance. Mr. Brandt said that several people have felt that this policy should be reviewed, that per-haps the spirit of it was not being maintained. "So I have appointed a committee to study the matter and report to us."

He went on to say that state law requires that they have the pledge every day and that it be interpreted to the children and put in such a context that it remains meaningful and does not become ritual. Further he said we have not been abiding by state law which says that we should have at least two periods in a year when the meaning of the flag and respect for it are discussed.

Then he added that state law did leave some flexibility. The flag need not be saluted every day in every classroom as it now is, but some other plan may be possible. But Mr. Brandt made it clear that the pledge would have to be given every day to every child. So where the flexibility came from was not entirely clear. He did suggest that the words are not given in state law, and the children might be able to write and recite their own pledge.

Someone asked, what about those of our students who "fancy themselves conscientious objectors? What should we do with them?" Mr. Brandt replied that the law makes no allowance for that.

The voice persisted, in an incredulous tone, "Are we supposed to *force* them to pledge?" Someone else asked, "What about *teachers* who fancy themselves conscientious objectors?" Mr. Brandt replied that the law makes no allowance for teachers either. "If you will read the code, it is quoted in your teacher's handbook."

Someone said, "Frank, when you say the law makes no allowances, does that mean—" Mr. Brandt interrupted, saying that all the relevant parts of the law are included in the teacher's handbook and the speaker should read it before they discuss it. The committee will report.

Someone else asked a question and again he quelled it saying to read the handbook. There was some anger in these last questions. Mr. Brandt said he did not mean to be unreasonable, but the law is quite clear and they should not take time to discuss it until they have read it. He sounded impatient.

Someone said, "But what if the law is unenforceable?" He retorted with anger and impatience, "No state law is unenforceable." And in fact, he continued, "Most of these have a little hooker in them so that the superintendent is responsible to carry them out and his agents are to do their part. And not to do this is to commit a misdemeanor and can be prosecuted if the state wants to."

On the morning after this faculty meeting I interviewed the teacher whose objections to the pledge of allegiance were quoted above. Her comments suggest the probable course of the meeting had the principal been less brusque. They also indicate the faculty's acceptance of Mr. Brandt's claims for the inevitability of his definition of reality.

I: Yesterday in the faculty meeting there seemed to be a lot of anger.

R: There is a lot of anger! We have a very interesting staff. (Laughs) We're split just like society's split. There are groups of us that feel the pledge is meaningless, that it would be better to have a discussion in the history class; and if a kid conscientiously objects to saying it, I'm not going to make a big thing out of it. Why make a martyr of the kid for that? I think that the teachers who are angry about it—as you saw there was a lot of anger—feel somewhat the way I do.

And then you have the teachers, the more—what should I say— the older teachers, plus the more conservative teachers who feel this is a state law and therefore it must be obeyed and the kids should say it every day because that's the way it's in the book. And the kid's being un-American if he doesn't say it every day. And this sort of business. So the faculty is split. And there is a lot of anger on this issue.

I: Well, was any of that anger directed at the principal or the way he was handling it or . . .

R: Ah . . . somewhat. No. I think, well not really at the principal, because in a sense he's in a situation where he has to enforce the state law. He's in charge of the school. I don't envy his job. He's got a very hard job. (Laughs) No, I think there was some resentment of his saying essentially it's state law and it's tough if you don't like it, that sort of thing.

Had the principal allowed an open discussion of this issue, the division among the faculty would have become evident and the debate probably would have been heated. Thus the carefully nurtured public unity of the faculty would have been threatened. Further, by insisting on the futility of debate in the light of clear regulation by law, the principal kept his own position as the definer of the situation. He simultaneously won sympathetic understanding even from those, like the teacher quoted, who might oppose the policy. That the principal's actions were a policy to keep the definition unitary rather than a straightforward reflection of the compulsion of law is demonstrated when one reads the section of the faculty handbook to which the principal referred the teachers for an answer. The entry opens with an account of a resolution passed by the Canton Board of Education which prescribes the wording of the pledge precisely and requires the participants to stand at attention. Thus the elements Mr. Brandt described as flexible were in fact rigidly determined from above. The state law requiring the daily recital of the pledge which he considered precise was, on the other hand, vague in its requirements. The faculty handbook quotes it:

> There shall be a daily pledge of allegiance to the Flag of the United States in each public school, conducted in accordance with regulations which shall be adopted by each governing board.

The entry in the handbook closes with a paragraph which implies that the time and place of the pledge are in fact within the jurisdiction of the staff of each school:

> At Chauncey we stand and give the Pledge to the Flag during [the first class period]. We also begin all our assemblies with the Pledge to the Flag.

The committee to consider the pledge of allegiance met under the chairmanship of the vice-principal and came to the conclusion that Chauncey should join the other schools in having a flag-raising ceremony outdoors which would provide every child with an opportunity to join in the pledge of allegiance every day. A member of the committee describes their reasoning:

> R: Now the dissension is first around the content of the pledge, secondly about the necessity of saying it to express one's loyalty to the country.
>
> I think these were the two primary forces working on change. But then the kids were so [unwilling] that the saying of the pledge was becoming not even neutral. But it was becoming increasingly negative as an enforced thing that one had to do. One either didn't believe in it, didn't like it, or just simply didn't want to do it and was being forced to. He would then barely get out of his seat and just barely, you know, hold himself above it. Turn his back to the flag while it was being said. And so on.
>
> I: Was the committee fairly evenly balanced of people for and against the pledge?
>
> R: Let's see. There was a very staunch Republican, an extremely conservative person, and a person that considers himself to be

extremely liberal and neo-politics oriented. And, three or four of us, I guess were sort of in the middle, concerned not primarily about the ideology of the pledge itself, what it meant, but about what was happening within the school setting to the kids that were saying it.

I think the report of the committee indicated that . . . they would like to see further done to encourage persons to express their loyalty or to have greater appreciation for the heritage that we have. But at the same time, the vehicle of following the state code as we have was not meeting this end.

I: How did the staunch Republican feel about your final recommendations?

R: They were quite acceptable to him. Through the discussion, I think, his primary concern was that we encourage loyalty and that the present method of giving the pledge was certainly not encouraging loyalty. And he was much in favor of finding another way of meeting the state law requirement, which would allow for greater possibilities.

But in the next faculty meeting Mr. Brandt made the following report to the faculty on the recommendations of the committee and their implementation. The record is from field notes:

The pledge committee wanted the pledge to be said at the flag raising each morning and then for the bulletin to contain ideas about our democratic society for the teachers to discuss in class if they want to. But, says Mr. Brandt, the state code is very explicit that the pledge shall be said every morning in every classroom . . . so they have referred this up to the board and asked the district attorney for an opinion. The committee report will be held pending that decision. He added that it may be that Canton High School, Darwin, and Hamilton are actually not obeying the law and that we will be the only school which is abiding by the proper procedure. (His tone implied that the Chauncey staff should feel proud over this.)

The district attorney ruled that the spirit of the law was that the pledge of allegiance must be said by every child in the classroom every day. The matter was then taken to the school board which required that the pledge of allegiance, or equivalent patriotic reading, be recited in every class in every school during the first period of the day. Children must recite it unless they had a parental letter permitting them not to. By this time I had moved to Hamilton where I heard the ruling at the March faculty meeting. But I encountered a Chauncey teacher shortly afterwards and asked what had been said:

> I asked him about the flag. What had been said at the March faculty meeting after the board made its ruling? He replied that it was announced that now the children don't have to say the pledge if they can get a permission slip from their parents. (Note that his first response is to say now things are looser, the children don't have to say it.) . . . I asked if there were any discussion at the faculty meeting. No, he said, it was just more of the same, "the law's the law and that's it."[7]

It is significant that Mr. Brandt reported in his interview that it was at his behest that the state law was brought to the district attorney for decision. Mr. Brandt thus took a very active part in seeing to it that the practice of saying the pledge of allegiance in every first-period class, every day, was maintained. Whatever Mr. Brandt's explicit motives for this act may have been, its consequence was to support his right to be the definer of the school's procedure and the representative of awesome higher authority within the school. To have changed policy on a matter of symbolic significance because of students' objections would be to lend legitimacy to their desire to share in defining the character of a school, of its educational goals and appropriate procedures.

Of course to refuse to make a change and to require the students to pledge allegiance—even with carefully regulated individual exceptions—was to go against their grain in ways which Chauncey's teachers articulated in the quotations above. But the strains created were likely to be expressed in the classroom, where Chauncey's teachers would have to deal with

7. The tone of this reply is unusual. The respondent had just come to Chauncey after teaching at Hamilton for some time. He found himself radically out of sympathy with Mr. Brandt's style and asked to be transferred back to Hamilton after one year at Chauncey.

them in isolation. While there would be consequences in the students' overall attitude to the school, they would include reinforcement of the students' perception that the character of Chauncey was given and immutable, however they might feel about it.

The faculty meeting at Hamilton at which Mr. Henley announced the new board policy stood in striking contrast to the proceedings at Chauncey. It provided a telling picture of the relationship between Mr. Henley and his faculty. At the outset Mr. Henley passed out copies of the new policy. He explained to the teachers that the school's general flag-raising ceremony would no longer suffice, that they would have to return to saying the pledge (or a patriotic reading) in each first period class. In explaining the clause which allowed children to be excused with parental permission he suggested that teachers send them to the main office for forms, since handing them out in class might increase the number of applicants through the power of suggestion. However, teachers who wished to hand them out might do so. At this point many hands went up and the first teacher recognized asked if children who were excused were required to stand.

"Hmmm," said Mr. Henley, studying the document, "there's nothing said about that."

A long and acrimonious debate among the teachers ensued. Some defended requiring all students to stand out of respect for the flag and for the sentiments of those saying the pledge, while others claimed that to remain seated was part of an act of principled objection to the proceedings. Yet others brought up pragmatic considerations. Some pointed out that if those who remained silent sat it would be easier for teachers to tell whether they really had permission, while others emphasized the problems that could arise in enforcing a rule for standing. Despite the heated and prolonged character of this debate, it was occasionally laced with humor which evoked widespread spontaneous laughter.

Then a teacher addressed a new problem to Mr. Henley. What constituted a "patriotic reading"? She supposed an enthusiastic

Chicagoan would probably be satisfied with Sandburg's "Fog."
Would the school board be satisfied as well? Field notes suggest
the tone of the further proceedings:

> Mr. Henley said dryly, "I am sure we are going to get some com-
> plaints to the board on some of our patriotic readings." Someone
> suggested he make a list of approved ones. "Not on your life," he
> replied.
>
> Mr. Henley had explained that *district attorneys in nearby counties
> had ruled that a flag-raising ceremony does satisfy the law*, but that this
> county's had ruled that it does not. And the school board felt bound
> to follow the ruling of their own county's district attorney. Mrs.
> Fimwright now asked if it might be appropriate for someone,
> probably a parent, to test this ruling in the courts. "Perhaps so,"
> said Mr. Henley in a noncommittal tone. [Emphasis mine]
>
> In the debate surrounding whether students should stand, two or
> three people said that the principal should determine what the school
> policy will be and then the teachers should all follow it. The princi-
> pal demurred. He said that the school board's statement is extreme-
> ly vague and he thinks if the board wants to make it more explicit
> they can do so. But as it stands there is a great deal of latitude, so
> that it is difficult to say just what is and is not allowed. His tone
> was critical toward the vagueness. . . .
>
> [Following more debate among the teachers] the head of the
> language department moved that there be a pledge or a patriotic
> reading in each class and that those who objected to saying it be
> allowed to remain seated. . . . After some more talk they took a
> vote. The tally was thirty-two for and thirty-two against, a tie. There
> was some discussion of the appropriate parliamentary procedure. Had
> it failed since it did not get a majority? Should the abstainers be
> asked to vote? Someone said the chairman should break the tie.
> Mr. Henley replied humorously, "I wouldn't do it. I'd pay Mr. Gore
> [the vice-principal] to do it for me!" (Humorous though the tone
> was, it was clear Mr. Henley would have nothing to do with
> breaking the tie.) Finally someone who claimed to be a parliamen-
> tarian ruled that the motion had failed.
>
> After some more debate, a man with a booming voice made a
> motion that they follow the words of board policy allowing teachers
> to use their best judgment in its interpretation. . . . [Yet more
> debate ensued before] the motion was put to a vote. It carried
> easily, perhaps two-thirds voting for it.

Faced with almost the same situation, the two principals define it and handle it very differently. Mr. Brandt refers to the solid rock of state law, Mr. Henley to the ambiguity of competing legal opinions. Mr. Brandt refused at the earlier meeting to let the faculty discuss the issue, claiming that the clarity of the law put it beyond question; Mr. Henley refuses to clarify an ambiguous edict from above even when asked to, allows the faculty to vote on their interpretation of it, and recoils from breaking a tie in the vote.

Hamilton's spirited and at times emotional debate, only part of which is set down here, represents just the revelation and sharpening of faculty differences that Mr. Brandt seemed to want to avoid. Mr. Henley not only did not quell it but refused to take sides or offer opinions, and above all backed away from deciding its outcome. The existing clarity of opposition made any stand he might take a partisan act, alienating one faction.

In dealing with the pledge of allegiance, each school denied a part of reality. At Chauncey Mr. Brandt denied the reality not only of students' moral sincerity but of their simple unwillingness to comply. He then forced the teachers to manage the denied aspects of reality in their separate classrooms. At Hamilton, the faculty refused to acknowledge the need to settle on some common practice if any policy were to be effectively carried out.

OVERALL STAFF TREATMENT OF STUDENTS AT THE TWO SCHOOLS

As principals, Mr. Brandt and Mr. Henley stood at the point where conflicting demands upon the schools met with palpable force. Everyone else connected with the schools held them ultimately responsible for order, decorum, and routine, on the one hand, and for freedom, autonomy, and quality education, on the other. But the skeptical students made order difficult to maintain and the structures of the school were never designed for freedom or autonomy. Faced with an irresolvable dilemma, the two principals chose to deal with it by grasping one horn. Mr. Brandt opted for order and routine while reaching for as much autonomy and education as courtesy and skill could salvage. Mr. Henley opted—less voluntarily—for autonomy and education while reaching for as much order and routine as teachers' and students' senses of commitment and responsibility could obtain. Mr. Brandt set the context within which faculty culture and its interaction with student order and student culture took shape. Mr. Henley faced a historical and social situation which left him less power to shape events. He responded to his faculty in large part, though he had some independence in defining the school for the students directly.[8]

Essentially, Mr. Brandt succeeded in creating and maintaining a pattern of institutionalized innocence among the faculty and through them—to a lesser degree—among the students. He fashioned a definition of the character of the school and the character of the students to which the staff offered broad assent. With close supervision and swift, sure—though not biting—treatment of clear offenses, Mr. Brandt also established an attenuated myth of coercive control among the students. He had probably done as good a job as was possible of restoring classic methods of control—and with them relatively good order—to the school.

Fundamental in Mr. Brandt's—and his faculty's—definition of the character of the school was the belief that students not only should, but would, accept the values and education offered by the school in an incorporative fashion. Difficult individuals might be beyond reach, but with skillful handling the rest would prosper and respond to a traditional curriculum and flexible but clearly hierarchical adult roles. The challenging white children in the top tracks were merely going through some transitory adolescent rebellion. The resistant black students in the bottom tracks merely lacked academic skills and perhaps habits of scholarly diligence taught in middle class homes. There were no

8. In his study of ten junior high schools, Anderson found a complex set of factors affecting teachers' individual and collective responses to authority from above. The socioeconomic characteristics of the student body were one of the most important factors affecting the structure of authority among adults as well as between adults and children. (See James Anderson, *Bureaucracy in Education*, Chapters 4 and 5.)

matters of principle, value or world view dividing teachers and students. Some of the more experienced and sensitive teachers suspected that the differences between adults and students were more fundamental, but even they believed with the others that the students *should* share the generally accepted values and relationships which Chauncey promoted. They were only perplexed about how to bring the children to agree.

In order to maintain their picture of the students—and to persuade the students to accept it as well—the Chauncey teachers had to deny the moral seriousness of students' challenges to their definition of the proper conduct of the school. They had also to deny that racial and social class differences created significantly different perspectives on life or significantly different educational needs. For if the students' challenges were serious or if racial and social differences had important educational implications, then students should rightfully have a part in defining the character and goals of the school. As a consequence the incorporative teaching mode—and more important the institutionalization of innocence in the school at large—would be undermined.

The teachers at Chauncey maintained considerable social distance from the students in order to protect the awesomeness of their adulthood in the students' eyes and with it the validity of the school's incorporative approach. But this social distance also helped them not to see too clearly the skepticism and alienation which they generally sensed among their students. Avoiding discussion of their daily activities and overall strategies with one another not only protected them from admitting failure to someone more successful but also protected them from admitting the enormity and intractability of the pedagogical problems they faced.

They expressed their half awareness that their activities did not quite fit reality in their response to the research. They were collectively more self-conscious about the presence of a sociologist in their midst than the staff of either Hamilton or Darwin. And they were surprised and fascinated at the end of the field work when told I was interviewing children. Yet though they made comments such as *"That* must be interesting," they did not inquire—even in general terms—what I was learning. The staff at Hamilton discussed their quarrels and activities in my presence without inhibition from the very beginning of the study. They took the student interviews for granted as a part of studying what happens in the classroom and displayed little curiosity about them—because they communicated far more openly, though not necessarily more amicably, with students than the Chauncey teachers did.

At Hamilton, the adults did not hold a common view of the students. Mr. Henley not only allowed but encouraged diversity in the teachers' approaches with his stress upon professional autonomy and the primacy of the academic task. The teachers used their freedom to concentrate upon the classroom, working in their separate and often inconsistent styles. In that context, their responsibility for the children's learning and safety encouraged considerable pragmatic adjustment to the need to maintain order. At the same time, many developmental teachers engaged in imaginative and dedicated teaching which went far to meet the students' subjective and objective needs. They also thought and talked perceptively about changes in school structures which would facilitate the learning process. But most of these efforts were individualistic. They did not go beyond small groups of friends to create collective endeavors in the school.

As the teachers concentrated on their separate classrooms, everyone was responsible in the school at large and no one was responsible. Each faction blamed the other for growing disorder in the corridors, while only scattered individuals felt compelled to take active steps to counteract it. While the needs of both high and low track students were relatively well met in many classrooms and the students became more at home and more committed to the school's endeavors than those at Chauncey, problems of order and even of safety beyond the classroom door became increasingly serious.

There was no possibility of maintaining control through the institutionalization of innocence or through a myth of coercive control. Adults of all persuasions agreed that children in both the top and bottom tracks were offering fundamental challenges to the basic premises upon which a school with an incorporative approach is run. But they evaluated these challenges differently. The incorporative teachers, the oldtimers, believed these fundamental challenges to have a superficial origin. They saw them as the result of discontented adults "stirring up" the children. They blamed developmental teachers and influential people in the community. Without intervention from these adults they believed the children would not question traditional incorporative school styles. The institutionalization of innocence would be workable. The black children would respond to the school no differently from white children, except that they were "a little slower."

But though these teachers believed that unified adult insistence upon traditional educational goals and school decorum was the appropriate and effective path to take, they saw no chance of taking it in the current context of Hamilton or even of Canton. Their dominant feeling toward the running of the school as a whole was one of impotent anger and ambivalent withdrawal. While their sense of frustration and often of hostility was communicated to the students, they took little positive initiative, and so left the field open for the developmentally oriented teachers to attempt active definition of the character of the school for the students.

Consequently, the dominant voices speaking for the school represented it to the students as an institution which sought their commitment to its goals in a developmental mode and asked for their autonomous responsibility in maintaining order and safety. However, the voices the students heard lacked coherence not only because of the disagreement of the incorporatively oriented faculty, but because the developmental teachers followed their individual ideals and developed few common strategies and little common rhetoric with which to address the students as a body. Further, the principal's approach in dealing directly with the students was a combination of a flexibly incorporative approach and a developmental one. Hamilton thus provides an example— but a complex and partial one—of the effects of a staff's use of a developmental approach in the school at large within the context of traditional physical, social, and temporal structures.

If a school attempts to maintain cooperation and order through student responsibility, there must be extensive communication and discussion between faculty and students—quite in contrast to the need for social distance and awe to maintain a myth of institutionalized innocence.

There was far more formal communication to and from the students as a body about the affairs and practices of the school at Hamilton than at Chauncey. In December and March Hamilton scheduled "talkout" sessions during school hours, for students to meet in groups with teachers who did not grade them for a discussion of opinions, suggestions, and grievances about the life of the school. Chauncey had nothing of the kind during the year of the study until late in the spring when a teacher organized "Operation Breakthrough," a set of such sessions—but held after school and chaired by parents and other outsiders.[9]

Hamilton gave more attention to the weekend interracial retreat which had become a tradition at all the secondary schools. A whole assembly was devoted to slides and accounts by students. The teachers who had staffed it held a follow-up meeting for themselves to discuss issues which had arisen during its course. At Chauncey it was simply announced, held, and then ignored.

In March at Hamilton, Mr. Henley responded to restlessness among students over several issues by calling an assembly for a "state of the campus" address. He detailed progress on various student complaints running from the condition of some dilapidated buildings through the dress code to the newly compulsory pledge of allegiance. He announced student committees to discuss action on some of these matters. He also announced that he had obtained the Board's consent to listen to a delegation of students who wanted to protest the requirement for saying the pledge of allegiance. (They did appear before the Board which

9. In response to the restlessness of the previous year Mr. Brandt had established a series of meetings for himself with small groups of children, chosen alphabetically. These had been highly formalized, with each child in turn given a chance to state three ideas before yielding the floor to his neighbor. Mr. Brandt carefully controlled communication from the students to him and its availability to any other adult. These meetings were not reinstituted the following fall, during the study.

praised the quality of their presentations, but did not change the policy.) Nothing of this kind occurred at Chauncey.

Finally, there was far more discussion of students' feelings and activities in both faculty and student bulletins at Hamilton than at Chauncey. And faculty discussed students' statements, activities, and apparent inner states at far more length with one another.

At Hamilton, while the incorporative teachers thought racial differences should be ignored, the developmental teachers argued that they were important and should be recognized. They argued that to ignore them was to deny the values and life situation of the black students who were the minority. Many of these teachers used the term "black," which was just beginning to gain general currency in place of "Negro." And a sizable group of both black and white teachers sponsored activities, assemblies, exhibitions, and clubs which emphasized the history and artistic expression of an African and black American heritage. These efforts culminated in a formally proclaimed black culture week during which the students wore African costumes they had made, performed programs of music and dance, exhibited arts and crafts, and cooked an African meal available to all at lunchtime.

At Chauncey only one black teacher pushed for such assemblies, exhibitions, etc., and there were consequently few. The staff as a whole minimized the fact of race as much as possible. They were embarrassed by the correlation of race and academic achievement, and avoided discussing it unless asked about it directly. Their effort to minimize race was graphically expressed in the nearly universal adoption of the term "Caucasian" as well as their failure to adopt the term "black" over "Negro."

The face which Chauncey's adults together presented to its students was one emphasizing conforming behavior. They encouraged unexamined cooperation and held up a single standard of praiseworthy goals. The adults seemed unified and there was a clear hierarchical distance between them and the children.

Hamilton's adults created a far more complex and disjunctive context for their students. The structure of the school and its routines were also hierarchical and standardized in formal outline, but less so in practice. Discussion of rules and student participation in their reformulation were more often formally instituted. And students were allowed and sometimes encouraged to express their feelings about the school in contexts which signified formal attention from adults. Finally, and significantly, violation of rules became so widespread that it was informally accepted in the lack of a serious attempt to enforce many minor rules, while some teachers made no secret of the fact they thought these rules unimportant.

The way that the staffs of the schools as wholes defined the character of the student body and the way they treated them in their interactions in the corridors, in assemblies, and in informal encounters had a considerable impact upon the students' attitude toward the school and their behavior both outside and inside the classroom. The next chapter attempts to define the different character of the matched student bodies of Hamilton and Chauncey.

CHAPTER 10

Differences in Student Culture at Chauncey and Hamilton

DIFFERENCES in the behavior, attitudes, and social relationships of the students at Chauncey and Hamilton were palpable. Each student body accepted the adults' definition of the character of their school, and they responded to the schools accordingly, and therefore differently.

These different definitions of the character of a school created for the students different relationships with the school and with each other.[1] Social structure among the students was minimal

1. There is very little research on the effects of the total gestalt presented by the adults of a school upon the student body. Research using survey techniques finds that relationships are complex and interactive. James Coleman's large-scale study, *Equality of Educational Opportunity,* is the most ambitious attempt. See also Simon Wittes, *People and Power,* a study of power relations, and Carl Nordstrom, Edgar Z. Friedenberg, and Hilary A. Gold, *Society's Children.* The latter study uses observations to interpret the survey results and thus takes into account more idiosyncratic constellations. Friedenberg's and Henry's essays based on observations in high schools also deal with the way many factors in adults' words and actions form a whole to which students respond. (See Edgar Z. Friedenberg, *Coming of Age in America,* and Jules Henry, *Culture Against Man,* Chapters 6 and 7.)

since there was little opportunity during the day for activities which were not closely directed by adults and since students stayed together only two years. Nonetheless, there did exist a roughly defined social structure among students which differed between the schools. Similarly, each school generated collectively shared attitudes and styles of behavior in the student body as a whole and in definable subgroups of it, a student culture and subcultures.

STUDENT SOCIAL STRUCTURE

To discuss social structure among the students of these schools, one must consider the races separately. At Chauncey, the white students who dominated the social structure were capable and conforming ones who dressed conventionally. These were the students whose names were mentioned by the faculty, and these were the students elected to the student council. At Hamilton by contrast it was students with aggressively liberal pedagogical and political beliefs and with offbeat clothing and hair styles who drew the faculty's attention and won elections. At each school the dominating group seemed more numerous to the eye. There seemed to be more children who dressed and acted in conventional ways at Chauncey, more with offbeat styles at Hamilton. But it is difficult to know whether these impressions reflect actual numbers or the greater social activity and so greater visibility of each group at the school where it dominated.

At Chauncey there was no group of black students with prominence in the school as a whole. There were one or two who held elected positions among the students, but their social ties were with white students; they were not part of the black social structure.[2] Except for these, the black students whose names were mentioned by the faculty were the most rebellious "discipline problems" from lower tracks.

2. This was a striking fact, since at both schools the races segregated themselves virtually totally in the cafeteria and the yards. A black student who associated with whites in these contexts (or vice versa) was unusual indeed. This was especially the case at Chauncey, but even at Hamilton there were only a small number of children who moved easily across racial lines.

At Hamilton, by contrast, there was a small, but relatively numerous, group of black students who were elected and informal leaders among all the students and visible to the faculty along with the leading white students. These students usually had at least some classes as high as Track Two. They might have some classes in Track Three or have some in Track One. Many (not all) of them had middle class backgrounds and came from nearly all-white neighborhoods and elementary schools. But they identified with the other black students and took on styles of dress and speech to express that identification.

Interestingly, the black students in the lower tracks who were in the most disciplinary difficulty did not receive the notice among the faculty that their counterparts at Chauncey received. At Chauncey such students stood out in a generally conforming context. At Hamilton there was enough generalized resistance and disorder so that individuals expressing these feelings did not gain as much visibility.[3]

Differences in the status of the racial groups as wholes in the two schools were reflected in physical visibility, just as were those within the white group. Though there was actually a larger proportion of black students at Chauncey than at Hamilton, the impression one received was the reverse. At Chauncey black students seemed a clear minority though they in fact constituted just under half the student body. At Hamilton they appeared a majority, though they were in fact slightly over a third.

These different impressions were fostered by tangibly different behavior. Even though the black children at Chauncey were more vocal and expressive in the corridors and play yards than the white ones, they were considerably less so than their counterparts at Hamilton. Further, large numbers of the black students at Hamilton had developed a social ritual to express their claim upon the school as their territory. Each morning they gathered by a corner store at a bus stop a block from the school and moved up

---

3. At each school there were a few highly rebellious upper track white students who were the topic of frequent faculty discussion. Perhaps they were visible because of the general expectation that capable children from the middle class will find themselves in harmony with the school, or failing that, that they will be socialized not to rebel directly.

the street toward the school in large groups throughout the twenty minutes before school opened. Once arrived, they gathered on the front steps in clusters leaving only a narrow passage through which others might enter the school. There were several side entrances to the school and most of the white children used these, even though they would not be the nearest to their homes or bus stops. At Chauncey both black and white children entered the school singly and in small groups as soon as they arrived by foot or bus.[4]

A more vivid indicator of the social structure of the two student bodies can be found in the person and the attitudes of the students elected president of the student council. At Chauncey the president was elected for a year's term. The students chose one of the two black students in Honors classes, this one an A student even in that select company. He was light skinned, had closely cropped hair, wore glasses. His dress and speech were indistinguishable from those of his white classmates. He skied in winter, played in a violin quintet, and otherwise acted in the style of the privileged Honors children. His father was listed on his registration card as in an occupation which is clearly white collar but not managerial or professional. In a research interview the boy, Duncan Taylor, seemed tense and anxious to answer the questions correctly. He relaxed only during a clear digression from the written questions. His record of unmixed A's from Honors mathematics to gym and shop indicated strong desire (as well as ability) to do well in all school situations.

Duncan seemed, in other words, to be the very model of the boy from an ethnic minority who has set out to make good. In the atmosphere of Chauncey where middle class manners and mores and academic achievement were stressed, but where the white

4. The roughly six percent of the students who were neither black nor white, almost all Oriental, lacked both social and physical visibility in both schools. They were quiet in classes and the halls. They behaved like the more conventional white students—and associated with them more than did the blacks. A few of them were elected leaders. Nonetheless, though they made no public expressions of ethnic consciousness, they formed their own informal groups in the cafeteria.

children as well as the teachers were anxious to be as liberal and equalitarian as possible, he was the natural electoral choice of the white children. And as a black running against a (longhaired) white boy he was also the obvious choice for the black students.

At Hamilton the student council was elected by the semester. A longhaired white boy in Track One and Honors classes was elected the first term. Though having some sympathy with the teachers' dilemmas, he in general shared the values of the dissident but academically able white children.

He did not run the second term and was replaced by a black, Warren Young, who was in Track Three math and Track Two in the verbal subjects of English and history. This boy spoke in the dialect of the majority of black children and came from the ghetto, as he himself called it. His grades were erratic, ranging over two marking periods from A (in English) to F (in history). One of his teachers described him as sometimes her best and sometimes her worst student, saying that he was imaginative and inventive whether he set his mind to being helpful or obstructive. In the research interview he spoke volubly and with feeling of his experiences and opinions, including his disagreements with adults and refusals to obey them on principle. Many of the attitudes he expressed were similar to those of the questioning white students.

The two student body presidents were thus both capable black students, yet each displayed many of the characteristics of the leading white students at his school. Duncan was adult centered, obedient, and achievement oriented. Warren was skeptical and challenging in his attitude to adults and erratic in his achievement. He worked where he felt in sympathy with a teacher and a task and did not work when he came in conflict with a teacher or the subject matter.

These two student body presidents also each reflected the attitude of the school as a whole toward the black students in the lower tracks. Duncan portrayed his attitude toward these students both directly and indirectly as he answered a question in the interview about the tracking system. He had just described a situation where a teacher did not discipline for a clear infraction of school rules. For the second time in the interview he explained that such lenience occurred only in the high tracks:

> R: Oh, and this was because it was in an Honors class. I don't know if this might of happened in a Three or Four Track.
>
> I: Do you get the feeling that things like this are very different in Honors classes and Three and Four?
>
> R: Well, one of the reasons why there is tracking, as far as I can see, is that some kids need more discipline than others. I mean everybody, I guess, could need more discipline than somebody else. But then sometimes this really gets [to be] a serious condition. And in this case, if they continually disrupt the class, then that means they learn slower; and if they learn slower, that means they're farther behind, they don't know as much. And then as soon as you get into junior high school and this has gone on for six years in school, then they put you in a different class because the people that didn't have these discipline problems were smarter because they learned more. And the ones that did were less smart. And so in order to try to keep everybody at their level and help them advance more, than if they were, you know, all put in one happy jumble, then they divide them up into tracks. And so I think that it sort of all ties in.
>
> And, of course, there are those people who don't have any problem of discipline and are just dumb. They're in Three and Four. They don't put them up in One and Two because they don't have a discipline problem. But in general, it's tied in.
>
> I: One thing I wondered about with Three and Four was how much it was people who were discipline problems and how much of it was people who were dumb. I mean whether it's fifty—fifty or seventy-five—twenty-five or what. Do you have any idea?
>
> R: Well, most of the people, as I said before, most of the people who are dumb do have discipline problems and vice versa. Excluding those I guess you could say that there are, I don't know, maybe five or ten per cent. Five or ten per cent who are just plain dumb and don't have a discipline problem.
>
> I: And what about some kids who are really bright, they could do it if they wanted to, but they just don't?

R: Well, I know this guy who was put down in Track Two and Track Three. He's in all Honors this year. But last year he just didn't try at all. He didn't want to try. He was sort of running away from the world and he was in Track Three in history and Two in math and, you know, really way down there low. And, so it doesn't really mean that there's any—he was just in there because he had a discipline problem. He wasn't trying so they just put him down.

Duncan professes to know little of life in the lower tracks. For him even Track Two is "really way down there low." His statement implies that the unfortunate souls who exist in these nether regions do so because of their own failings. Despite his race, Duncan was neither a representative of, nor a spokesman for, the majority of black students in the school. He exhibits no sense of kinship with students who are not orderly and hard-working in response to the school's expectations.

Warren, on the other hand, had warm ties with black students in the bottom tracks. And he identified himself psychologically with them, despite some sense that he was moving away from them. He described his relationship with these other students in the interview as he explained why he did not like a black man on the school staff whom he encounters at lunchtime in the yard:

One thing I don't like him for—when I'm in a group of kids, a group of my friends—like a lot of people come from the Heights and the good schools and the homes and everything, you know? I came out of the ghetto, that's where we come from. And I grew up with all those boys and girls down there, the real rowdy kids. And when we're standing around in the yard, he'll go by and he'll call me out of the group and he'll say, "You shouldn't hang around with those kids because it makes you look bad."

I said, "Well, they're my *friends*." I'm not going to switch my friends because of what somebody else thinks. Like a lot of them are dirty, and they dress, you know. And he's always calling me out of stuff. . . . [Emphasis the speaker's]

Warren knows that despite his loyalty to his friends, he is no longer one with them. He describes them as "the real rowdy kids" and acknowledges that their standards of cleanliness and dress are unacceptable to middle class adults. But most telling of all, he speaks of the ghetto as "where we come from," even though his address is still there. Just the same, in both active social ties and psychological identification Warren was to an appreciable extent a representative of, as well as a spokesman for, the black children in the lower tracks. He stands for their legitimate participation in the school.

Each of these two student body presidents exemplifies the style expected and exhibited among the students at his school. Duncan accepts the arrangements of the school and the adults' justifications for them as self-evident, inevitable, right. His race is a part of his consciousness only as it requires him to try even harder and excel even more than his peers. He identifies with the adults' perspectives and seems in the process rather prematurely old, careful and staid. His statements about tracking could have come from the mouth of an administrator carefully justifying the tracking system to an outsider.

Warren, by contrast, is self-conscious in his effort to become his own man. He throws off the advice of a successful black adult (though perhaps ambivalently) to shun his old associates as he climbs upward. Yet he knows he *is* moving upward and leaving them in another way of life. He is self-consciously black, yet he tries to integrate that fact with friendships with whites and the desire to participate in a predominantly white world. He is inwardly reflective and outwardly challenging as he tries to come to terms with his inner journey and his outward context. He is also—according to at least two of his teachers—capable and willing to bring a class to a halt out of his own mood or for his own purposes.[5]

At Chauncey neither the teachers nor any of the student leaders gave expression to the realities of the lives and perspectives of the black students in the lower tracks. While they were treated with reasonable courtesy and with little overt hostility, they had no

5. After our interview, which stretched beyond the study hall for which it was scheduled, I observed Warren—who was supposed to return to class—on his hands and knees under the open window of the dean's office, upon business of his own devising. He knew how to turn an opportunity to his use whether his purpose was highly serious or puckishly playful.

positive place or role in the school unless they were able to participate in the school as at least modestly achieving scholars, behaving like the conforming white students. At Hamilton there was a small cadre of student leaders like Warren who had ties of friendship and identification with the students in the lower tracks. Further, many developmental teachers and a group of self-consciously black teachers of several pedagogical persuasions all acknowledged their right to participate in the school in their own style.

STUDENT CULTURE

Differences in the style of behavior and attitude of the students at Chauncey and at Hamilton were even more marked than differences in the social structure of the student bodies. There were distinctive styles in the way the students comported themselves within the school and in the kinds of feelings they expressed toward it.

Substitutes are particularly good informants about the character of schools as wholes. They have close contact with many groups of children within one school; so they can see characteristics which are shared by the students of many different teachers. And they have experience at several different schools simultaneously; so they can see the variety of premises and practices which are quickly taken for granted by the teachers in one school.

Substitutes who worked in Canton seemed in close agreement as they described the differences between Chauncey and Hamilton. Most had pronounced preferences for one school over the other as a place to work, but they differed over which they preferred, depending on their own priorities. They found the children at Chauncey politer and more cooperative. It was easier to get through the lesson planned for the day before the period ended. But they were also more passive and less engaged with the material. They found the children at Hamilton more alert and more actively involved in the class. But they introduced questions and digressions which made it difficult to finish the planned lesson. And they were often rude.

Observations of classes for this study led to the same conclusions. Chauncey students seemed more manageable and diligent, but also less mature and less reflective about the substance and form of their education. The Hamilton students seemed more independent, reflective and insightful about their education, in many cases more directly responsive to the activities and conditions which support the fulfillment of the school's educational goals. But they also seemed more self-centered and arrogant.

There were similar differences in the way the students at the two schools responded to the research interview. At Chauncey even the children in the top tracks and those on the student council gave brief answers then waited for the next question. At Hamilton the children, especially those in the top tracks, were comfortably voluble. They talked about their own concerns about the school, sometimes seizing the initiative and the floor to go on at length whether or not their answer had much relationship to the question. It seemed the Chauncey students expected an adult to direct and dominate a conversation while the Hamilton students expected to have considerable opportunity for self-direction and self-expression.

While the differences in the students' styles applied to some degree to all the students, they applied most directly to the students in higher tracks. The students in lower tracks at Chauncey did not have the same kind of acceptance of the adults' models of the school that the others did. Although they were relatively polite and compliant compared to their counterparts at Hamilton, they were compliant out of alienation, not out of acceptance of the school's pattern for social life. They responded with mental withdrawal to the fact of being invisible unless they accepted social mobility, ethnic self-denial, and the style of the conforming white students. They tolerated life in the school. Most did not attempt serious conflict with it. But they withheld psychic engagement.

This withdrawal was markedly noticeable in their responses to the research interview. In response to a question about how they would change the school if given the power of a dictator or wizard the primary theme was their own release. Two could give no reply but that they themselves would leave. Others gave the same kind of reply indirectly, saying for example that attendance should be voluntary. Further, despite the fact their behavior was more orderly than that of the Hamilton students, in this private context they displayed noticeably more bitterness both toward the school as a whole and toward individual adults than did students at Hamilton. And it was at Chauncey, not Hamilton, that two different students chosen for the sample because they had no disciplinary referrals responded—hesitantly—to the question giving them a wizard's powers by saying they would do away with all the "hate" in the school. A third spoke of wanting to improve relations between teachers and students and observed that most of her fellow students automatically have negative expectations of a white teacher and feel immediately negative toward him.

Lower track students at Hamilton were far less hostile and withdrawn in their interview responses. And, though they might not like many parts of the school and many of its teachers, they did feel that at least some of the teachers and the student leaders were open to their participation. In their daily behavior they responded to the school's ambivalent openness with ambivalently active participation, as they took over the front steps, were noisy in the public spaces of the school and challenged teachers in the classroom. They were louder and more overtly hostile than the Chauncey students, but they were also more engaged in the life of the school.

THE SCHOOLS RESPOND TO CRISIS

The interaction of the adults' style of running the school and the student culture of each school was especially clearly revealed when both schools were presented with a sudden crisis generated by the surrounding society. They had to respond immediately with little time for planning, and each responded in its characteristic style.

The crisis was the assassination of Martin Luther King and the rioting which broke out in several major cities almost as soon as the news was received. The assassination occurred on Thursday, April 4. The following day was the last school day before spring vacation in Canton. A meeting of persons from all district schools was called for Thursday evening. Two leading black students from the high school made a plea that the schools remain open for education in a tribute to the man who had died but that each school hold some kind of formal memorial observance. Their suggestion was adopted and those persons who had gathered from each school met to make plans for their own school.

In planning for the day there were two needs to be met. One was the maintenance of order, the need to cope with disruption and possible violence from angered black students. The other need was that of giving expression to a sense of loss and an affirmation of racial unity.

The Plan of the Day at Each School

At Chauncey much effort was poured into maintaining adult control.[6] The usual method of friendly supervision was used but in multiplied force. Substitutes were hired for the day not to take classes but to patrol the halls and to take extra "cooling off rooms."[7] Parents and friends of the school were also brought in for hall and yard supervision. As one of the substitutes described the scene, whenever she looked down a hall she could see four or five other adults. Some children who seemed upset were sent to the front office and their parents called to come and take them home. As usual the most difficult children were eliminated from the regular setting as a means of control.

The memorial assembly at Chauncey, the major vehicle for meeting the need to express a sense of loss and unity, was short, lasting ten or fifteen minutes. The children attended in four shifts instead of the usual two, as a measure to cut down the possibility of collective excitement. As with most events at

6. The description of events at Chauncey is based on accounts given me by three substitutes and one regular teacher who were present that day.

7. These were rooms supervised by a teacher where children who were upset or disruptive but not engaging in behavior warranting a visit to the dean could be sent to get them out of the classroom.

Chauncey the major initiative came from a teacher, the drama teacher. He planned a presentation together with some students from his drama classes, classes which were officially heterogeneous but elective and drawn almost exclusively from the top tracks. The presentation consisted of the persons on stage giving speeches and readings, and the audience joined only in singing "We Shall Overcome."

The two informants in the study who attended the service, both teachers primarily concerned with lower track students, described it as a dramatic presentation from the stage rather than a service in which the audience participated. And they both pointed out that the students on stage were not only mostly white but almost exclusively in high tracks even if black.[8] The children chosen to perform on this occasion were the usual leaders of the school. This event simply underscored the fact that those leaders were all either white children or black members of high track classes similar to the white children.

Although the staff at Chauncey were probably unaware of their choice, they had in practice chosen to emphasize the maintenance of order over the need to express loss and unity. This choice was pointed up by the contrasting way in which the same day passed at Hamilton.

Hamilton did not hire extra substitutes. Children were not sent home.[9] And the memorial assembly was held in the usual two shifts instead of four as at Chauncey. Thus Hamilton did not take the steps Chauncey did to keep order through adult control.

The plans for the assembly at Hamilton were turned over

8. The school had invited some students from the Black Students' Union at the high school to join in walking the halls, although repeated previous efforts by students to have them visit the school had, so some informants said, failed. According to one informant, at the urging of these black high school students some of the white children were removed from the program and black children from lower tracks substituted for them between the first and the last performance of the assembly.

9. Some students walked out of Darwin and the high school and walked through the center of the city engaging in minor vandalism. Upon hearing of this on the radio some parents came to both Chauncey and Hamilton on their own initiative and took their children home early.

primarily to the students. The student body president took the lead. Because he and the student council as well as the informal leaders of the school were a more diverse group with broader contacts in the school than the leaders at Chauncey, it is not surprising that they chose leaders for the assembly more representative than those at Chauncey. The program they planned was longer than that at Chauncey and provided for more audience participation. It was universally praised as a moving experience, even by the "old guard" teachers. The usually restless and noisy assembly audience was attentive and quiet even through a period of silent meditation.

It is not clear that the adults at Hamilton had made a conscious choice to de-emphasize control, to emphasize a cathartic expression of grief and unity, or to give leadership to a cross section of students who might serve as a symbol of that unity. As at Chauncey, administrators, staff, and students simply responded to this crisis as they responded to most other events. And the students displayed their best side.

The Student Body's Response

The day passed at Chauncey without any unusual events. One of the substitutes reported that the children in fact behaved better on this day than on most, but that the extraordinary supervisory provisions created considerable tension:

> [He said] there were all these extra adults patroling and all the students were tense. They all walked around more or less rigid; no one would have dared try a thing. In the lunch line, which he often has to monitor as a substitute there, no one cut in front of someone else. On other days someone always tries. By the end of the day the kids and the teachers were all nervous wrecks. But there was no trouble.

Another substitute gave a similar report, but a third had a different impression:

> She said if you looked down the hall you could always see four or five adults posted. I asked if this made the children nervous. She said no, she thought rather the reverse. Many of those super-

vising . . . knew some of the children. They acted friendly; she didn't feel any tension.

One might conclude from these accounts that, like the adults, some of the children were made tense by these measures and others were not. A careful reading of the teachers' comments suggests that it was the students who sometimes get into disciplinary difficulties who were most tense. These predominantly black children were the ones who were potential targets of control while the majority of white children were targets of protection.

One of the substitutes who remarked upon the high level of tension also said that the students most given to making trouble in the school, the hard core discipline problems, either never came to school at all or left early in the day. He credited part of the peacefulness of the day to their absence.

The response of the students can be seen as, like the plan of the day, an exaggerated reflection of the normal pattern of the school. On this day of crisis, the common psychological withdrawal among the lower track black students was outwardly expressed in the physical withdrawal of the most resentful. This physical withdrawal allowed events in the rest of the school to proceed reasonably smoothly, just as their psychological withdrawal did under more ordinary circumstances.

The day at Hamilton unfolded in a different manner. According to some of the students interviewed there had been talk of fights and a skirmish or two before school opened, but the assembly changed the student mood. Many of the black students were still upset and angry, however. The student body president and some of the other leaders stayed out of class and talked with them. Accounts differ somewhat here, but apparently they decided they ought to accomplish something, and their discontent focused upon the tracking system. [10]

A growing, and in time an integrated, group of students decided, possibly at the suggestion of a teacher, possibly only

10. There had been talk of changing it for over a year, and several proposals had been made. But little concrete had happened.

with his concurrence, to visit classes of other tracks than their own, thus integrating them for that day. They did so for the rest of the day. Their manner was peaceful and polite, but their actions nonetheless flew in the face of routine, attendance rules, and teachers' expectations.

In the meantime, a group of black students had circulated a petition to rename the school after Martin Luther King and had gotten the signatures of approximately half the student body. School was dismissed two periods early. An integrated group of one to two hundred students went to a church led by a black central district staff member visiting the school for the day. There they had another memorial service and a "talkout." And then they went home.

But that was not the end of the crisis at Hamilton. During spring vacation the teachers were active. A group of black teachers succeeded with the principal's cooperation in having the matter of tracking put on the school board agenda for the Tuesday after school reopened. And another group of teachers succeeded with the principal's cooperation in having a policy made that there was to be no more spontaneous heterogeneity of classes. In the meantime, a local teen-aged black militant was killed by a policeman under hotly disputed circumstances. Some black adults said later that this event was far more inflammatory for the children than the killing of Martin Luther King.

On the Monday following spring vacation the black students returned to Hamilton with considerable anger arising from outside events, and with the expectation that something would happen to change tracking practices. Some of the teachers argued for an assembly to inform them of the plans to make a presentation before the board, but the principal held fast to the theory that school routine should be firmly re-established. A terse notice was put in the student bulletin:

> Committees are working on the possibility of regrouping classes. No arrangements for group changes have been made yet. Every student must attend his regular classes.

Mr. Henley met with the executive committee of the student council at the opening of school to explain that there would be a presentation to the school board the next evening and that there would be a student meeting after school Tuesday to make suggestions to be included in that presentation.

But this was not enough for the impatient students. They were angry and they wanted visible action. As the student body president told the story in an interview later, some felt they had been betrayed by promises on Friday that "something will be done" and now with (so it seemed to the adults) the danger of their fighting gone, they were being told to go back to the old routine. Anger was high among those who felt they had been sold out on the particular issue of tracking and among those who were generally angry at the adult white world. The student body president felt violence was going to erupt, so he and some other students wrote out a bulletin and, with the cooperation at various points of three teachers, circulated it. It called for a meeting during the fourth class period of students interested in changing grouping. The principal learned of it and tried to countermand it, but it had already been announced in most classes and a large number of students attended anyway.

According to the student body president the meeting did cool tempers somewhat. There had been threats—which he took seriously—to "get" two of the most disliked adults, to break windows, and to do other serious damage. Still, when the meeting adjourned just before the beginning of the first lunch period a group of black students ran through the halls and cafeteria taking out their anger on whatever white students happened to be in their path. They grabbed girls' purses and threw them out of reach on top of lockers, knocked cafeteria trays out of hands and off tables, and attacked about a dozen children with fists. Even though no one was seriously injured, the school was facing collective disturbance.

The student body president and his associates had lost control to what some teachers called the "fringe kids," the black students in the deepest academic and disciplinary difficulty, those with the least hope and the most anger toward the school and the society it represented.[11]

At Hamilton as at Chauncey the adults and students were true to their usual styles. The mixed nature of the students' response to the school was made dramatically clear. On the first day, a large number of students used initiative and responsibility in making an assassination an occasion for interracial solidarity. On the second day, a large number of different students acted out their anger, frustration, and disappointment with the school in physical hostility.

It seems that the principal and the teachers who tried to draw all the children, including the black and lower track ones, into the life of the school had significant success. The black students came to feel that the school was there for their needs as well as those of the white students. They had some stake in it. The more able, successful, and easily sociable of these students learned to participate constructively—if not always conventionally or

11. The reader will be curious how this crisis was resolved. The students' rebellious mood did not cool overnight. The next day opened with a special assembly concerning the incidents. While the principal, the dean of boys, the student body president, and other black student leaders spoke, a large and visible contingent of black children were noisy and restless. But then six students from the Black Students' Union at the high school, invited by the faculty, came on to the stage from the side of the auditorium where they had been waiting. Their carriage and dress bespoke all the symbols of black pride. They commanded the attention of their younger colleagues with their presence. Then they administered them a fierce tongue lashing. They called them "cowards," "dogs and cats not fit to come in with the people." They told them that if they wanted to get anywhere at all in a world dominated by the white man, let alone have any power in facing him, they had better get right down to the business of learning what the school had to teach. The noisy children grew quiet. There were no more incidents that day.

In our formal terms, the high school students, wrapping themselves in symbols of values the students' espoused over against those of the school, restored legitimacy to the school's goals. They did so by making them instrumental in a transitory fashion to the goal of black self-assertion. But nonetheless they emphasized the importance of pursuing these goals wholeheartedly.

Hamilton's teachers recognized that their capacity to control a significant minority of the students had been restored to them by a group of militant black teenagers. After these events, they made more effort to cooperate in maintaining order and took concrete steps toward accommodating their differences. Order improved.

obediently—in the life of the school. But the students who were most alienated from the white world or less able to cope with academic tasks could not operate comfortably in what was still a mainstream school. These students also received the majority of the hostility expressed by the most disaffected teachers. They only had hopes raised and then dashed. They were disappointed, insulted, frustrated. Their anger was not far below the surface. And the school's very openness to other students left it vulnerable to attack from those whom it did not successfully reach.

CONCLUSION

Outside the classroom, in the school at large, the participants' perspective on school goals changes somewhat, and especially so in a context like Canton's. When the adults think of the aspects of school life beyond the classroom they think primarily of students' activities in crowds placed in large spaces. It is student life in the corridors, cafeterias, and play yards which dominates consciousness. Here academic goals are not being directly sought, and in any case the difficulty of maintaining order in these spaces overwhelms all other immediate considerations. In the corridors the question is not one of competition among educational goals but one of order in competition with everything else.

Yet what happens in the corridors cannot be divorced from what happens in the classrooms. And the pronouncements and definitions of the adults which define the character of the school as a coherent social situation affect corridor and classroom alike. So there are intimate interdependencies between the strategies chosen to maintain hall order and the ends and means which can be sought in the classrooms adjoining. The reverse is also the case, ideas and attitudes absorbed in the classroom leave with the students and affect their behavior elsewhere in the school.

Just as Canton's white and black parents in their different ways insisted that the school seriously pursue academic goals, they also insisted that it limit its disciplinary sanctions.

Canton school board meetings were commonly filled to

capacity, ran long, and included heated floor debate when it was allowed. These were schools under outside pressure. And yet the dominant factions pushed goals, technology, and structure which were in opposition to the centralization, hierarchy, and standardization which organizations commonly use as a defense against external intrusion. The very nature of the external pressure prevented the usual defense.

While the parents, board, and central administration stressed academic goals, especially developmental ones, and the technology and structure to go with them, they expected reasonable order to be maintained. They were consistent to the point of toleration of a good deal of noise and even minor aggressive activity, which other communities would not have countenanced. But while the most vocal parents may have accepted quite a bit of disorder, others did not. The board and central administration bore final responsibility as well as political accountability for order as well as for academic education. When serious or repetitive disorder occurred, they made it very clear they would take steps against responsible adults in the schools.

The principals were primarily accountable for all that happened within the schools. Formally they stood in a traditional bureaucratic relationship of hierarchy with the district officers above them. They were not protected by ideas of academic freedom or by tenure. Because they were given a good deal of autonomy in running their schools, their individual judgment and administrative skill were expected to be primary tools for their task. They were thus given maximal personal responsibility, as well as autonomy, in overseeing a set of conflicting social forces acted out by others.

Mr. Henley attempted to follow formal district policy. He delegated, persuaded, and inspired, while he stressed academic matters before order. His personal skills were less than outstanding in a task in which it is questionable that even the most extraordinary of persons could have succeeded. The district chose to deal with the situation by encouraging his resignation. In this context, Mr. Brandt's decision to violate the spirit of explicit district policy and to make order the school's primary working consideration—though not its primary rhetorical one—becomes very understandable.

However, the principals' decisions and their personal skill in implementing them were only one of the cluster of factors which gave each school its direction as well as its resulting complex character. Because the schools operated as units within a larger decentralized organization, and because they were similar in most of their formal characteristics, as well as their student bodies, it is easy to see the operation of a range of other factors which made a difference.

In the most proximate sense, personnel were the deciding factor. At Hamilton, the personal beliefs and characteristics of the faculty as a collectivity operated to deepen schism among the adults along not only professional but personal and political lines. However, the characteristics of the personnel were in part a reflection of the history of the school, the school district, and the city and country.

At Chauncey personnel seemed an even more important factor. Mr. Brandt occasionally resembled the lonely boy with his finger in the dike as he tried to hold away from the school the contradictory demands of the times, the community, the central administration, and even the students. He seemed almost single-handed to create the character of the school. And yet, while one can easily imagine Chauncey having come to resemble Hamilton in significant degree, if not in toto, were Mr. Henley to have been its principal, one cannot imagine Hamilton resembling Chauncey even under the hand of the redoubtable Mr. Brandt. At Chauncey, also, history and recruitment were important.

The contrasting actions of the principals and teachers at the two schools set up answering currents among the students, which tended to accentuate rather than to lessen the differences in adults' patterns. Each school developed deepening unmet needs of opposite sorts. The distinctive characteristics of adults and students in both schools resulted from a cluster of idiosyncratic influences. The scope given these influences was in turn a result of the character and the policies of the school district as a whole.

On the other hand, despite the unique constellation of

pressures which decided the detailed character of each school, in broad outline they exemplified the consequences of a choice between educational commitment and reliable order which many schools must make. The single most important characteristic of the Canton schools was the challenging, skeptical character of the students—compounded by the significantly different kinds of challenge from the affluent white and poor black students. Hamilton was organized to win the students' commitment to the school and its purposes, hoping thus to use their informed efforts for both academic accomplishment and orderly procedure. Chauncey was organized to maintain what was possible of students' unreflective awe of the school, hoping to use their docile cooperation for the same two goals. Hamilton overcame some of the students' alienation, and won higher levels of commitment, but left itself open to significant disorder. Chauncey kept a reasonably orderly, safe school, but one which failed to engage the skeptical students.

Part IV: CONCLUSION

CHAPTER 11

Beyond Canton

THE PARADOX OF THE SCHOOLS' MISSION

Public schools have a paradox at their very heart. They exist to educate children, but they must also keep order. Unless the children themselves are independently dedicated to both these goals, the school will find that arrangements helpful for one may subvert the other. Yet to sacrifice either for the other is to default upon a school's most fundamental responsibilities to both the children and the society.

If a child is to learn, he must embrace the goal of learning as his own. The more complex and subtle the learning, the more thoroughly must he embrace it. But in general, a child must believe there is some purpose for himself in learning what is presented him in school or he will not learn it. There are many purposes which will suffice. He may learn to satisfy disinterested curiosity, to better his status in adult life, or to please a teacher whom he likes. He may not even reflect upon his purpose, but simply trust the adults around him to set him tasks which will be valuable to him as he grows up. Still, if no reason is compelling for him, if he cannot see some reward in learning, he will passively or actively resist the efforts required of him toward that end.

The tension between order and learning is muted if the vast majority of the children who attend a school arrive wanting to learn what it normally teaches. The school does not have to make special efforts to win their commitment to learning goals. The adult staff can then maintain a broad unity of definition and style which will lead students to accept the school's mode of operation as natural and inevitable. Without undue regimentation or harsh coercive methods, it can establish order in the corridors through the institutionalization of innocence. Within the classroom, teachers can work in an incorporative style, yet bend flexibly to the passing requirements of individuals and groups without fear that the students will unduly exploit departure from routine. If they choose, they can use a developmental style instead, within limits. The economies of effort in such a situation are enormous. They free a great deal of the teachers' and students' energies for attention to the substantive material of education.

What such a school must not do is to call into question—or allow the students to call into question—the fundamental worth of what it teaches and the rules and routines which support its good order. There are serious psychological and pedagogical costs to preventing students from questioning their surroundings. The tension of learning and order is not resolved in this situation, only brought to a balance or compromise.

But, as in Canton, when students arrive questioning and even radically doubting the value of what a school teaches, or when some students induce the rest to do so, innocence is lost. The tension between order and learning easily becomes acute and pre-occupying. Students who do not see any point for themselves in learning what the school has to teach not only will not learn. They also will not behave in an orderly fashion while they put in six hours a day in a compulsory, and for them useless, occupation. The school must therefore persuade them both to value its educational agenda and to behave in a reasonably quiet and cooperative fashion.

The simplest way to get unwilling persons to act in an orderly manner is to regiment their activities and swiftly punish small offenses from the outset to create a myth of coercive control. The school must be run in a unified way which standardizes behavior and allows few exceptions or deviations. But success in this endeavor creates a relationship of opposition and alienates the students yet further from the school and its educative purposes.

In contrast the most effective ways to persuade skeptical students to learn are for the school either to find links between their studies and their existing values and goals or to take as its first task persuading the students to share the goals the school normally has. In other words, the school must first win their commitment to the organization or its activities and use that commitment as a motivation to learn. With either method, the appropriate technological process implies flexible, diverse, and open-ended activities and relationships. But these will destroy the students' sense of the school as a unitary and immutable context. Such a sense is necessary to either institutionalization of innocence or a myth of coercive control.

Activities which lure the unwilling to become involved in learning thus undermine the most important support for traditional methods of keeping order in the school at large. Where a school effectively entices skeptical or alienated students to learn, order is likely to become precarious unless the school is so successful that it creates in *all* the students sufficient commitment to the school as a social entity so that they preserve order out of a sense of responsibility.

To put this argument in the formal terms used in Chapter Two, a school in an environment of students who do not share its educational goals is faced with contradictory imperatives. Opposing technological processes and opposing structures are required for reaching the formal goal of education and for supporting the instrumental goal of order. The fundamental organizational character of the public school creates opposing requirements as it deals with unwilling students.

Some of the common changes which schools have instituted in the last decade, in response to the pressures of unwilling students among the affluent as well as the poor, can be seen as efforts to soften the opposition in requirements for education and order. One large category of changes consists of efforts to reduce the difficulty of maintaining order by making the physical and social setting less fragile in the face of students' energetic activity. New and remodeled buildings use sound absorbent and aesthetic materials. They have shorter and wider corridors or do away with them altogether, using architectural plans which lessen the amount of traffic in one place and avoid isolated spaces where unwary students can be set upon. Similarly, staggered and more flexible schedules ease the problem of surging noisy crowds giving way to deserted passages, playgrounds, and bathrooms. The provision of physical locations and blocks of time in which students may comfortably and legitimately socialize with their fellows may help to lessen their excitability in other parts of the school and the day.

Similarly, efforts to increase students' attachment to the academic curriculum through the introduction of more choice may increase their educational commitment without undermining the unity of the faculty. Specialized courses have been added to the curriculum and required courses have been divided into sections with varying emphases. Magnet schools, specializing in one educational style or one curricular area, have been instituted largely in the hope of inducing middle class white students to attend inner city schools, but they have also been designed to appear either practically useful or intrinsically interesting to ethnic minorities in the hope of increasing their academic commitment.

These steps will help to mute the tensions the schools experience in dealing with unwilling students. They may reduce unintentional or casually motivated disorder and they may transform some unwilling students into willing ones. But they do not by themselves solve the problem of the school's vulnerability to disorderly or aggressive actions from a few. Nor do they generate reliable academic commitment from students whom the larger society gives reason to be skeptical of the worth of their schooling.[1]

1. Illich, in his *Deschooling Society,* is only the most extreme of those who argue that the fundamental form of compulsory public education creates so many problems that it should simply be abolished. But to disestablish public school systems and to create private alternatives to replace them completely

Further, unless the gradual spread of court ordered urban desegregation comes to a halt, more and more schools will have to deal with racially and socially diverse student bodies. Lower class students are least amenable to methods of control based on institutionalized innocence, and children and parents from the middle class will not submit to a myth of coercive control. Traditional methods of maintaining order developed with homogeneous student bodies will be placed under severe strain simply by the nature of diverse student bodies, and may very well have to be abandoned. Breaking up schools' reliance on a myth of coercive control is an important part of the agenda of persons supporting desegregation as an educational improvement for poor black children.[2] Faculties used to homogeneous student bodies will have to make some significant readjustments.

AUTHORITY IN EDUCATION

Much of the impulse of current theoretical debates and alternative practices in education has taken the form of an attack upon authority. If the argument of this book is correct, then that impulse has misstated its target. An attack directed at authority takes specific excesses among superordinates in authority to stand for the phenomenon itself. The terms of the attack vary somewhat, depending upon whether the spokesmen or the students involved are members of the disaffected upper middle class or members of economically disadvantaged ethnic minorities.

Let us consider the objections of the affluent first. Descriptions of authority by educators and students who wish to do away with

would be a gargantuan undertaking. In 1974, children five to seventeen years old enrolled in day schools constituted over twenty-two percent of the United States population. In other words, nearly one person in four is enrolled in elementary or secondary school. More than one out of every twenty-five employed persons is part of the instructional staff of such schools. (More are involved as secretaries, janitors, cooks, etc.) See *Statistical Abstract of the United States: 1974*, 95th ed. (Washington, D.C.: Bureau of the Census, 1974), pp. 121, 351.

2. Where schools attempt unsuccessfully to maintain a myth of coercive control the very worst educational results may occur. (See Mary Haywood Metz, "Order in the Secondary School.")

it, stress its character as a relationship of power between un-
equals. The typical style of authority for them is either proto-
authority or incorporative authority where a teacher (or administrator) takes a parental role with a traditional view of the moral
order. In other words, these opponents of authority think of the
case where the moral order remains unarticulated and the superordinate has broad rights to arbitrary personal discretion. In fact,
these critics usually do not acknowledge the relevance of any
moral order at all. They consider authority to be based primarily
upon the traditionally powerful status of the superordinate supported by little else. The vision of authority against which they
react is thus a caricature which leaves out the crucial element of
the relationship.

It is difficult to know how much this vision of authority
reflects an association of authority and authoritarianism. The
verbal association of the two was striking not only among the
staffs of the Canton schools but in the university's School of
Education, where I established some contacts. Time and again
when I introduced my study as one of authority in the school in
either setting, my conversational partner would refer to it as one
of authoritarianism. (I soon ceased to introduce the study in this
way and spoke of it rather as one of the school as an organization.)
But the misunderstanding was telling of the depth of the association of the two terms in educators' minds, or at least in the minds
of educators like those in Canton.

If one returns to the source of the term authoritarianism in the
study of *The Authoritarian Personality* by Adorno and his colleagues[3] it is very clear that authority, as the word is used by
most social scientists, is distinct from authoritarianism. The
term authoritarianism was first coined to describe a personality
type, but that type was formed, so the psychologist authors

3. T. W. Adorno et al., *The Authoritarian Personality*. The authors of this
seminal work encourage the association of authority with authoritarianism, for
while they never define authority, they implicitly equate it with the form of
control used by the parents of authoritarian subjects. They identify what they
call "external authority" (as contrasted to "inner authority" or a self-regulating
conscience) with the ability to dictate subordinates' values as well as their
actions. See for example p. 230 and p. 598.

argue, by a particular style of parental control. That style is very close to what I have called proto-authority. It stresses the wishes of the powerful parent with little other justification. Adorno and his colleagues contrast it with the control exerted by parents of persons scoring low in authoritarianism. These parents stressed the teaching of general principles guiding behavior. In our terms, the parents made explicit reference to a comprehensible moral order in guiding their children. Roughly then, to identify authority with authoritarianism is to confuse proto-authority with authority.

One can consistently support, and enforce, authority, without any taint of authoritarianism. Indeed, both the majority of leaders among the high track students in Canton and the developmental teachers seemed to understand this principle perfectly well. They sought a consistent and explicit moral order and an acknowledgement of students' rights to scrutinize both it and a teacher's faithfulness to it. But they did not seek the elimination of authority.

Some alternative schools do reject authority altogether. They perceive it as a symbol of regimentation and of unlimited power of adults over children by virtue of nothing but the simple fact of age. The most dogmatic hold that students have a store of educational wisdom equal to that of adults. Such a position obliterates the claims of a society and its smaller social units upon the individual. It denies the existence of a cultural and technical heritage of any current worth. And it similarly denies that experience bestows skill, knowledge, or wisdom which can be imparted to others. It makes every child a Robinson Crusoe while surrounded with potential companions and teachers.

There are similar problems in the less extreme case where a school goes to great lengths to allow students the right to define—and redefine—its moral order. In attempting to take highly intelligent and articulate young people seriously, it is easy for adults to find themselves abdicating altogether from responsibility for the definition of educational goals and the transmission of information. When the impulse behind these students' claims is given free rein, it can result in endless discussion and redefinition of goals with every passing interest. And it is easy for a class or a student body to become preoccupied with process to the near exclusion of substantive learning.

Adults who persevere in such a situation in pursuing substantive, impersonal learning, not directly relevant to the students' interests, cannot rely upon students' trust in response to either the office of teacher or demonstrated academic competence. If the fundamental worth of the academic endeavor is repeatedly at issue then good faith and competence in serving it are no longer legitimate grounds for the right to command. In such a situation, teachers must muster forms of power other than authority—especially personal influence—if they want their students to cooperate in academic learning. But generating the resources for these forms of power without a core of authority distracts from the task at hand and exhausts the teacher's psychic resources before the actual teaching task is begun.[4]

Such overreactions have begun to breed counter-reactions, schools designed with rigid curricula and discipline. This ping-pong of reaction and counterreaction misses the point which the best of Canton's experienced developmental teachers grasped and expressed without apology. While it is necessary to have educational goals which students can embrace, and often necessary to let them participate in defining them, the adult retains responsibility for setting major educational directions. It is not only his right but his duty to remind the students—peremptorily if need be—of their responsibility to put forth effort in *some* form of legitimate intellectual endeavor. And in choosing that form they will have to accede, on occasion, to the wisdom of their elders.

Open classrooms and non-directive learning have flourished best at the primary level, where students are learning fundamental verbal and mathematical skills, and substantive content is of minor importance. A child can learn perfectly adequately by reading, writing or calculating only about matters which interest him.

4. For a cogent study of control in alternative secondary schools which explicitly reject "authority" see Ann Swidler, "Organization Without Authority."

But at the secondary level, students must be expected to learn skills requiring more structured sequences. And they should not be allowed to graduate from high school in ignorance of a wide variety of very specific kinds of information in which they may have absolutely no spontaneous interest. Among other things, they should have mastered the complexities of advanced arithmetic and elementary algebra. They should know the rudiments of the major natural sciences, and have some acquaintance with the history and geography of all the sections of the globe. They should have advanced reading skills, including not only comprehension but speed and critical ability. And they should be able to express themselves cogently in writing. These fundamental goals, so simply stated, are difficult accomplishments. They are not attained without the focused attention of both students and teachers.

There are enormous savings in time and in psychic and intellectual energy if a class will take the word of adults that some of these subjects which are not inherently appealing will in fact be of use to them later. This principle applies with particular force in those subjects which have an orderly and progressive structure, for example mathematics and elementary foreign language. The difference in attitude of Canton's top track students toward mathematics classes and toward those in more vaguely defined subjects indicates some recognition of this fact. And the conduct of these mathematics classes by competent incorporative teachers who took the role of expert professional demonstrates the possibility of a viable relationship of this kind with generally skeptical students.

The pedagogical point to be made here is that the worth of a teaching style or strategy cannot be judged without reference to both the character of the students and the character of the subject. If the children do not embrace a given educative goal, simple insistence is often a poor strategy of persuasion. In this circumstance, the teacher must work first upon their desire to learn. It is helpful if—in developmental fashion—he makes his goals more general and more various, while spending much of his energy in experimenting with strategies to lure the students into interest in the undertaking. The definition of the relationship must be quite open-ended. Until students become committed to learning, encouraging that commitment is the overriding pedagogical task. Once it is accomplished other issues come into play.

If the subject matter involves the teaching of critical or creative capacities, a teacher must operate in a relatively developmental style, allowing the students to set goals and devise strategies upon which he comments. But where the subject matter has a clear structure which needs to be acquired as a tool, then a teacher can more appropriately proceed in an incorporative fashion, following orderly approaches worked out by experts.

The crucial issue in choosing a pedagogical strategy thus is not a general decision about the amount of structure or freedom, or about basic skills and information transferral as opposed to generalized skills and discovery. Rather the first concern is whether the students believe in the worth of what they are learning. Until they do, methods must be designed primarily to encourage that belief. Once students are caught by the desire— or necessity—to learn, it is important that they develop the capacity to operate in both structure and freedom. They will need to acquire highly structured skills of computation and grammar and highly generalized ones of mathematical reasoning and creative expression. They will need to learn the rudiments of traditional subjects and the capacity to ask independent questions about them.

Where students are both poor and members of racial minorities, the impulse to reject authority revolves less around the issue of individual freedom and more around those of curricular substance and cultural style. However, this is difficult territory, for what passes for cultural style is frequently a complex system of defenses against rejection by the larger society. Some well-meaning high status whites who have argued for the integrity of minority cultures have failed to grasp this point when they maintain that there is no need for such students to master literacy or fundamental mathematical skills. Few persons who share the students' background hold this position. If the children of the poor are to have a chance at economic survival, let alone comfort, they simply must master these skills and use them as effectively as whites with whom they will be in competition for even modest jobs.[5]

Of course the teaching of non-western history, literature, and current affairs are quite a different matter. But these change the substance, not the form of the school's endeavors. They may have implications for the style of authority, but by no means require its absence, rather the reverse as the student learns to share in a common tradition. The same applies to direct and indirect methods for instilling ethnic pride in students.

If the analysis of the attitudes of lower track black students in Canton given in this book is correct, such children hold tightly to the conventional goals and values of the society, but with great ambivalence. It is very important to them that teachers try to teach them their conception of an ordinary school curriculum and expect them to exhibit ordinary courtesy and honesty. At the same time, they reject these expectations with their actual behavior because they think they cannot live up to them, or that they will not be conventionally rewarded for doing so.

Much has been written about the cultural differences and cognitive lacks eventuating from the short pasts of poor children as they enter school. Considerably less attention has been paid to the shadow thrown by their futures, or their perceptions of their futures. These children expect no future reward—and possibly even the punishment of disappointed hopes—if they conform to the school's expectations. Poor children living in enclaves have only to look around them at the adults they see every day to conclude that people of their social background stay on the bottom of the social heap. Racial divisions make this hopelessness especially

5. Jonathan Kozol, himself an affluent white, writes passionately but convincingly on this topic. (See his *Free Schools*.) Elliot Liebow gives one of the most sensitive and incisive analyses available of the ways in which the distinctive subculture of lower class black men is in fact fashioned as a defense against rejection by the larger society. He claims they actually share mainstream values but cannot enact them because of their economically marginal situations. (See his *Tally's Corner*.)

sharp when minority persons fear that if they do succeed in acquiring academic credentials and conforming to middle class styles of life they will not reap the fruits of their labors.

It is not surprising if many poor and non-white children feel they have failed before they start. For psychological safety they reject the system which rejects them and remain impervious to the enticements and the threats exerted by the school. Here authority is rejected in the school not for itself but because the children cannot embrace the moral order which the adults present as its foundation.

The schools may ameliorate these problems by recruiting staffs whose beliefs and whose racial, social, and personal characteristics will refute the children's despair as much as possible. They can design their curricula to counteract the children's attitudes. They can change the recruitment of student bodies so that these children will not be segregated.

But the schools affect social structure and social stratification in the society at large far less than they are affected by them. So long as the society appears stratified on a largely ascriptive basis while preaching equality of opportunity, the students who think they are bound to lose will not embrace its representatives in the public schools. Not only will they fail to learn, they will act out their alienation in expressive disorder within the school. And the schools will be faced with the sharp opposition of steps which will encourage what commitment and learning is possible and those which will maintain order and safety in the immediate situation.

Sources of Data

INTERVIEW SAMPLES AND SETTINGS

The samples of administrators interviewed at both Chauncey and Hamilton consisted of all persons in the relevant categories. All principals, vice-principals, deans and counselors working with eighth graders were interviewed. I chose the sixteen teachers at Chauncey and fifteen at Hamilton whom I both observed for a day and interviewed by selecting all teachers in a set of departments who taught predominantly eighth grade classes. I used this method of sampling to avoid either my own or an advisor's bias. It also assured teachers that they had been chosen on an impersonal and unthreatening basis. It further indirectly required their participation, as I explained that I was asking "all teachers of eighth grade ____" to participate. The departments were selected to offer variety in the structure of the material to be taught and in the appropriate mechanical processes of running the class. At Chauncey the sample included all teachers of eighth grade math, English, social studies, family living, shop, and homemaking. At Hamilton, where departments are larger, it included all teachers of eighth grade math, English, and family living, plus one social studies teacher.

Neither teachers nor others were required by the principals to participate. I requested each to participate individually in a face to face encounter somewhere in the school—usually in privacy. Only one slot in the sample was refused and filled with a replacement.

The children to be interviewed were chosen through a quota sample. Four children were chosen from each academic track.[1] Of these four two were boys and two were girls. In each pair of one sex, one child was chosen who had no "referrals" in his counselor's file indicating that he had been sent out of class for discipline during the eighth grade year. The other had at least one.

Within this framework where possible I chose children whom I had seen in classes so that I knew something about their actual classroom behavior. This practice introduced a bias toward students who were visible in class for one reason or another. However, such a small sample could not be strictly representative, and it is the students visible to an observer who are visible to their classmates and teachers and actually set the tone of the class. To balance this bias I also purposely picked some students whose names I knew from some activity not requiring spontaneous initiative whom I intended as examples of the "quiet" students. I included a few students I did not know in categories which were hard to fill. One of the serendipitous findings of the study was the fact that it was nearly impossible to find a student in the bottom track in either school (and in the bottom *two* tracks at Hamilton) who had not been sent out of class for disciplinary reasons at least once during the eighth grade. It was also hard to find girls in the top track who *had* been sent out.

Interviews with adults were conducted in the privacy of administrative offices or empty classrooms. Most with teachers took place after school but some were in unscheduled "preparation periods." The latter occasionally had to be done in two

1. A child need not be at the same level in each subject; so respondents were categorized by the level of at least two of their tracked subjects. At Chauncey the two Honors groups in each subject contained a larger percentage of the roughly 425 children in the eighth grade than did the two at Hamilton for roughly 725. Therefore Honors was treated as a separate track for sampling at Chauncey but mixed with Track One for a group of eight at Hamilton where fewer children had more than one class at this level.

segments. Interviews with teachers lasted from forty minutes to two hours, usually about an hour at Chauncey and an hour and twenty minutes at Hamilton. Administrative interviews averaged about an hour, except the ones with principals, which approached two.

Interviews with children at Chauncey were conducted in an office used by a part-time guidance worker in the complex with the counselors' offices. At Hamilton most were conducted in a small storeroom off the library, which contained a table and chairs. A few were conducted in a small classroom converted for use by the part-time guidance worker. The interviews were conducted during the students' study hall period. The shortest lasted fifteen minutes. One at Chauncey and four at Hamilton ran significantly over forty minutes into the next class period. Most approximated forty minutes.

PARTICIPANT OBSERVATION

Since even the best efforts of an observer cannot eliminate completely the impact of his or her own person on the setting, the reader deserves some discussion of the observer, the process of observation, and their effects on the situation.

People respond to the presence of others in terms of a number of standard statuses. In this case it was important that I was young, a student, and a woman. Each is a low status not ordinarily perceived as wielding much power. These characteristics thus made me less threatening to the adults than a man in the middle of his academic career doing an identical study. My personal style is normally mild mannered, and I made a conscious decision to use that style together with my unalterable statuses as a research strategy. At each school I managed to fit into the round of teachers' informal association fairly smoothly.

I also had the status of a sociologist. Here it was more important that I *lacked* certain other statuses. I had never taught in elementary or secondary school, and I was not in the field of education. I also was not (yet) a parent. All of these non-statuses made me credible as someone who came without an ax to grind.

Since I genuinely needed a good deal of basic information about the functioning of schools, I embraced the role of learner. In my observing classes and interviewing teachers more than one person who was initially wary grew comfortable in undertaking to inform me.

Organizational research differs from research in many other settings because the respondents are in contact with one another. Thus the impression the researcher makes upon one will be communicated to others. One has to be very careful in such a setting not to displease influential persons, for their reaction can color that of every one subsequently contacted. Similarly a positive reputation can smooth the later path of the research.

My initial days at each school following students to classes gave me an acquaintance with teachers so that I could ask the most cordial among those in the departments designated for the study to participate first. I found that this strategy worked. My relations with the staffs generally grew smoother as time went along.

The setting of the study in a network of relationships restrains and affects the respondent as well as the researcher. Because I was present in the schools, observing and talking to many people, my respondents knew that I had access to a great many facts about the school. They were thus less likely to be reticent about matters that they might not normally reveal to outsiders than they would otherwise have been. In interviews I often referred to my knowledge of an event or to an assessment by another unnamed person and asked the person being interviewed to verify, explain, etc. Where factions existed teachers sometimes talked to me at length because they wanted to be sure that their position and their version of certain practices or events were recorded.

In informal settings with adults, especially in the teachers' lounge and at lunch, where I engaged in prolonged participant observation, I carefully alternated my location and companions so as not to seem to prefer the company of any group or individual. I never volunteered comments on controversial or school-related topics. I replied to questions with other questions, carefully bland statements, or agreement that such-and-such was indeed a

puzzling problem. The staffs respected my independent status
and rarely pressed me for commitments. When they did, I pled
my learner's status.

On the other hand, when topics irrelevant to the school's
business arose—such as the difficulties of getting a car fixed or of
losing ten pounds—I made an effort to participate in the conversation in order to build up a sense of rapport and shared humanity
and to make my relationships less asymmetrical. I think this
participation made my presence less intrusive than it would have
been if I had been consistently uncommunicative. I took thought
to my non-verbal communications, making an effort, as in class,
to keep my body posture and facial expressions expressing
interest but not approval or disapproval. In dress, I balanced my
visible youth with a formal style; I consistently wore my long
hair up and I continued to wear the quieter styles which the
younger teachers were forsaking.

I felt fairly successful in becoming an accepted neutral part of
the social landscape among the adults. Among the students I had
few problems in the classroom, but considerably more in the
interviews. In classes I always sat in the back. Experience at
Darwin taught me that it affected the class least if the teacher
introduced me or not according to his own predilections. I soon
learned that the best introduction was a simple identification as a
university student, come to observe, and I thereafter suggested
this to teachers. They generally followed it. Because of the
proximity of the university, it was common for student teachers
to observe classes. I looked like one of these, and students thus
generally assumed I was one and lost interest almost immediately. However, this was more true of the upper track students
than the lower track ones.

The lower track students were used to the occasional presence
of social workers, court workers, and other representatives of
officialdom who took a part in shaping their lives. My appearance also fit these categories. While students in the upper tracks
who questioned me almost always asked "Are you going to be a
teacher?", students in these tracks also sometimes asked if I were
a "psychologist" or from Juvenile Hall.

The students in the top tracks ignored me except for an occasional glance at a boring juncture or under very special circumstances such as those described in the Track One math class in Chapter Six. Children in the lower tracks ignored me most of the time, but would fairly often check to see my response when a member of the class entered a serious clash with the teacher. Sometimes children who initiated humorous hijinks would look around frequently for my response. I quickly learned to ignore the latter pattern so that it did not last long. During clashes of student and teacher I put down my pen and put on as blank an expression as I could.

I always asked teachers afterwards how typical each class was. The teachers rarely described those classes where students referred to me for an audience in a case of clowning or conflict as especially excitable or conflictful. So while I doubtless had some impact, on lower track classes especially, the effect was not so great as to make them behave outside their normal range of activity.

The structure of the schools made the arrangements for interviews with children extremely formal. Except at Darwin the principals asked that I send letters to parents asking for permission and follow up with telephone calls if the parent did not reply. To get students to the interview I had to send a student messenger with a slip of paper which became the student's hall pass to get to the counselors' offices at Chauncey or the library at Hamilton. (Calling them out myself at Darwin turned out to make them conspicuous and uncomfortable; so I resorted to the school's usual routine.) When the student arrived I explained what I was doing and gave him a chance to refuse. However, it is difficult for a student to say no to a strange adult and only one—who was to have his picture taken that hour as I later learned—refused. Once in privacy inside the spare counselor's office or the library storeroom, I gave a longer explanation of what I was doing and invited questions.

For the children in the higher tracks the interview was an assimilable situation. Most parents had forewarned them. Some were easily familiar with the idea of research; others got a good enough idea when told I was writing a long paper about schools.

These children were pleased to have their opinions solicited. Some children in the bottom tracks also adjusted easily, but others seemed embarrassed. They probably once more confused me with probing psychologists, if not court workers.

Even when the beginning of the interview was awkward, the children were generally quite frank. Most were ready to be critical of their teachers or became so with encouragement. ("Which of your teachers do you like least?" "I like all my teachers." "Um. Well, who do you like a little less than the others?" "Well, there's ____, she's. . . .") Some who had no critical comments were apologetic about it, and thus presumably speaking genuinely. These responses of course indicate something about the student culture of these schools where teachers were not believed to be made of radically different stuff than children.

The requirement that I obtain parental permission before interviewing children reflects the uneasy relationship between parents and schools as they share guardianship over the young. In Canton parents were especially vigilant over their children's rights and the principals were not being fanciful in thinking some parents might object. Several were concerned to question me in my follow-up telephone contact. All seemed reassured when I explained the character of the questions and the fact that they dealt only with the child's life in school and with him as an informant about the school rather than about himself.

The principals made it clear in our initial contacts that they would be very uneasy with my questioning children outside the interview. Given my purposes, I did not think it worth the necessary large expenditure of the principals' good will to attempt to re-open this option later. So my observation of children was limited to the classroom and to listening and watching in the halls and cafeterias at those times when adults and children were unselfconsciously present together.

My difficulties in gaining access to the social world of the children reflected an important line of social demarcation between adults and children in the schools. This line was far more permeable at Hamilton than at Chauncey, as discussed in the text. But it was there at all the schools.

Bibliography

Adorno, T. W., et al. *The Authoritarian Personality.* New York: Harper Brothers, 1950.

Anderson, James G. *Bureaucracy in Education.* Baltimore: Johns Hopkins University Press, 1968.

Ashton-Warner, Sylvia. *Teacher.* New York: Bantam Books, 1964.

Barnard, Chester I. *The Functions of the Executive.* Cambridge, Mass.: Harvard University Press, 1962. (First published 1938.)

Becker, Howard. "The Career of the Chicago Public School Teacher." *American Journal of Sociology* 57 (March 1952): 470–77.

———. "The Teacher in the Authority System of the Public Schools." *Journal of Educational Sociology* 27 (November 1953): 128–41.

Bidwell, Charles. "The School as a Formal Organization." In *Handbook of Organizations,* edited by J. March, pp. 972–1022. Chicago: Rand McNally, 1965.

———. "Students and Schools: Some Observations on Client Trust in Client-Serving Institutions." In *Organizations and Clients,* edited by William R. Rosengren and Mark Lefton, pp. 37–70. Columbus, Ohio: Charles E. Merrill Publishing Company, 1970.

Blau, Peter. *The Dynamics of Bureaucracy.* 2d ed. Chicago: University of Chicago Press, 1963.

Boocock, Sarane S. "The School as a Social Environment for Learning." *Sociology of Education* 46 (Winter 1973): 15–50.

Bossert, Steven. "Tasks and Social Relationships in Classrooms." Unpublished doctoral dissertation, University of Chicago, 1975.

Brophy, Jere E., and Good, Thomas L. *Teacher-Student Relationships: Causes and Consequences.* New York: Holt, Rinehart and Winston, 1974.

Carlson, Richard O. "Environmental Constraints and Organizational Consequences: The Public School and its Clients." In *Behavioral Science and Educational Administration Yearbook, Part II,* edited by Daniel Griffiths, pp. 262–76. National Society for the Study of Education, Chicago: University of Chicago Press, 1964.

Cicourel, Aaron, and Kitsuse, John I. *The Educational Decision-Makers.* Indianapolis: The Bobbs Merrill Co., 1963.

Clark, Burton R. *The Open Door College.* New York: McGraw-Hill, 1960.

Coleman, James. *The Adolescent Society.* New York: The Free Press, 1961.

———. *Equality of Educational Opportunity.* Washington, D.C.: U.S. Department of Health, Education, and Welfare, Office of Education, 1966.

Corwin, Ronald G. *Education in Crisis: A Sociological Analysis of Schools and Universities in Transition.* New York: John Wiley, 1974.

———. *Militant Professionalism: A Study of Organizational Conflict in High Schools.* New York: Appleton-Century-Crofts, 1970.

———. *Reform and Organizational Survival: The Teacher Corps as an Instrument of Educational Change.* New York: Wiley-Interscience, 1973.

Cremin, Lawrence. *The Transformation of the School.* New York: Vintage Books, 1964.

Cressey, Donald. "Prison Organizations." In *Handbook of Organizations,* edited by J. March, pp. 1023–70. Chicago: Rand McNally, 1965.

Dennison, George. *The Lives of Children: The Story of the First Street School.* New York: Random House, 1969.

Dreeben, Robert. *On What is Learned in School.* Reading, Mass.: Addison Wesley Press, 1968.

Eddy, Elizabeth M. *Walk the White Line: A Profile of Urban Education.* Garden City, N.Y.: Anchor Books, 1967.

Foster, Herbert. *Ribbin', Jivin', and Playin' the Dozens: The Unrecognized*

Dilemma of Inner City Schools. Cambridge, Mass.: Ballinger Publishing Company, 1974.

Friedenberg, Edgar Z. *Coming of Age in America: Growth and Acquiescence.* New York: Vintage Books, 1967.

Goffman, Erving. *Asylums.* Garden City, N.Y.: Anchor Books, 1961.

————. *Behavior in Public Places: Notes on the Social Organization of Gatherings.* New York: The Free Press, 1963.

Gordon, C. Wayne. *The Social System of the High School.* Glencoe: The Free Press, 1957.

Gouldner, Alvin. *Patterns of Industrial Bureaucracy.* Glencoe: The Free Press, 1954.

Gracey, Harry L. *Curriculum or Craftsmanship: Elementary School Teachers in a Bureaucratic System.* Chicago: The University of Chicago Press, 1972.

Hargreaves, David H. *Social Relations in A Secondary School.* London: Routledge and Kegan Paul, 1967.

Henry, Jules. *Culture Against Man.* New York: Random House, 1963.

Herndon, James. *The Way It Spozed to Be.* New York: Bantam Books, 1969.

Illich, Ivan. *Deschooling Society.* New York: Harper and Row, 1971.

Jackson, Philip. *Life in Classrooms.* New York: Holt, Rinehart and Winston, 1968.

Kohl, Herbert. *36 Children.* New York: The New American Library, 1967.

Kohlberg, Lawrence and Turiel, Elliot. "Moral Development and Moral Education." In *Psychology and Educational Practice,* edited by Gerald S. Lesser, pp. 410–65. Glenview, Ill.: Scott, Foresman and Company, 1971.

Kozol, Jonathan. *Free Schools.* Boston: Houghton Mifflin, 1972.

LaMancusa, Katherine. *We Do Not Throw Rocks at the Teacher!* Scranton, Pa.: International Textbook Co., 1966.

Leacock, Eleanor Burke. *Teaching and Learning in City Schools.* New York: Basic Books, 1969.

Liebow, Elliot. *Tally's Corner.* Boston: Little, Brown, 1967.

Lortie, Dan C. *Schoolteacher: A Sociological Study.* Chicago: University of Chicago Press, 1975.

McCleery, Richard. *Policy Change in Prison Management.* East Lansing: Governmental Research Bureau, Michigan State University, 1957.

McDill, Edward L. and Rigsby, Leo C. *Structure and Process in Secondary Schools: The Academic Impact of Educational Climates.* Baltimore: Johns Hopkins University Press, 1973.

McPherson, Gertrude. *Small Town Teacher.* Cambridge, Mass.: Harvard University Press, 1972.

Metz, Donald L. *New Congregations: Security and Mission in Conflict.* Philadelphia: The Westminster Press, 1967.

Metz, Mary Haywood. "Authority in the Junior High School: A Case Study." Unpublished doctoral dissertation, University of California, Berkeley, 1971.

————. "The Exercise of Control in Two Midwestern Junior High Schools." Final Report to the National Institute of Education, Project No. 4–0661, 1976.

————. "Order in the Secondary School: Strategies for Control and their Consequences." *Sociological Inquiry,* in press.

Neill, A. S. *Summerhill.* New York: Hart Publishing Co., 1960.

Nordstrom, Carl; Friedenberg, Edgar Z.; and Gold, Hilary A. *Society's Children.* New York: Random House, 1967.

Ogbu, John. *The Next Generation: An Ethnography of Education in an Urban Neighborhood.* New York: Academic Press, 1974.

Peabody, Robert. *Organizational Authority.* New York: Atherton Press, 1964.

Perrow, Charles. "Hospitals, Technology, Structure, and Goals." In *Handbook of Organizations,* edited by J. March, pp. 910–71. Chicago: Rand McNally, 1965.

————. "A Framework for the Comparative Analysis of Organizations." *American Sociological Review* 32 (April 1967): 194–208.

Rhea, Buford. "Institutional Paternalism in High School." *The Urban Review* 2 (February 1968): 13–15, 34.

Rist, Ray. "Student Social Class and Teacher Expectations: The Self-Fulfilling Prophecy in Ghetto Education." *Harvard Educational Review* 40 (August 1970): 411–51.

Rosenthal, Robert, and Jacobson, Lenore. *Pygmalion in the Classroom: Teacher Expectation and Pupils' Intellectual Development.* New York: Holt, Rinehart and Winston, 1968.

Schlecty, Phillip. *Teaching and Social Behavior: Toward an Organizational Theory of Instruction.* Boston: Allyn and Bacon, 1976.

Schrag, Peter. *Village School Downtown.* Boston: Beacon Press, 1967.

Seeley, John R.; Sim, R. Alexander; and Loosley, E. W. *Crestwood*

Heights: A Study of the Culture of Suburban Life. New York: Basic Books, 1956.

Selznick, Philip. *TVA and the Grassroots.* Berkeley: University of California Press, 1949.

Sieber, Sam D., and Wilder, David E. "Teaching Styles: Parental Preferences and Professional Role Definitions." *Sociology of Education* 40 (Fall 1967): 302–15.

Silberman, Charles. *Crisis in the Classroom: The Remaking of American Education.* New York: Random House, 1970.

Spady, William, "The Authority System of the School and Student Unrest: A Theoretical Exploration." In *The Seventy-Third Yearbook of the National Society for the Study of Education, Part II,* edited by C. Wayne Gordon, pp. 36–77. Chicago: University of Chicago Press, 1974.

St. John, Nancy. "Thirty-Six Teachers: Their Characteristics and Outcomes for Black and White Pupils." *American Educational Research Journal* 8 (November 1971): 635–48.

Stanton, Alfred H., and Schwartz, Morris S. *The Mental Hospital.* New York: Basic Books, 1954.

Stinchcombe, Arthur. *Rebellion in a High School.* Chicago: Quadrangle Books, 1964.

Swidler, Ann. "Organization Without Authority: A Study of Two Alternative Schools." Unpublished doctoral dissertation, University of California, Berkeley, 1975.

Sykes, Gresham. *The Society of Captives: A Study of a Maximum Security Prison.* Princeton: Princeton University Press, 1958.

Thompson, James. *Organizations in Action.* New York: McGraw-Hill, 1967.

Trow, Martin A. "The Second Transformation of American Secondary Education." *International Journal of Comparative Sociology* 2 (September 1961): 144–66.

Udy, Stanley H., Jr. "The Comparative Analysis of Organizations." In *Handbook of Organizations,* edited by J. March, pp. 678–709. Chicago: Rand McNally, 1965.

———. *Organization of Work.* New Haven: Human Relations Area Files Press, 1959.

Waller, Willard. *The Sociology of Teaching.* New York: John Wiley, 1965. (First published 1932.)

Wax, Murray L.; Wax, Rosalie H.; and Dumont, Robert V., Jr.

"Formal Education in an American Indian Community." An SSSP Monograph. Supplement to *Social Problems,* vol. 11, no. 4 (Spring 1964).

Weber, Max. *From Max Weber: Essays in Sociology.* Translated, edited, and with an introduction by H. H. Gerth and C. Wright Mills. New York: Oxford University Press, 1958.

Werthman, Carl. "Delinquents in Schools: A Test for the Legitimacy of Authority." *Berkeley Journal of Sociology* 8 (1963): 39–60.

White, Ralph K., and Lippitt, Ronald. *Autocracy and Democracy.* New York: Harper and Bros., 1960.

Willower, Donald J., and Jones, Ronald G. "Control in Educational Organizations." In *Studying Teaching,* edited by James Raths, John R. Panella, and James S. Van Ness, pp. 424–28. Englewood Cliffs, N.J.: Prentice-Hall, 1967.

Wittes, Simon. *People and Power: A Study of Crisis in Secondary Schools.* Ann Arbor: Institute for Social Research, The University of Michigan, 1970.

Wolcott, Harry F. *The Man in the Principal's Office: An Ethnography.* New York: Holt, Rinehart and Winston, 1973.

Woodward, Joan. *Industrial Organization.* New York: Oxford University Press, 1965.

Index

Abdication of teaching responsibility, 63–65

Ability groups. *See* Tracks

Accomodation: students' to teachers, 121, 123, 227, 228, 229; teachers' to students, 101–103, 105–116, 119–120, 141–144, 186–187

Administration. *See* Canton school board and administration

Administrators. *See* Dean; Prncipal's role

Adorno, T. W., 248

Age of children, effects of, 51–52, 69–70

Aides, teachers', 49–51, 60

Alienation of students: from pledge of allegiance, 202–203, 206–207; from school, 81, 83, 164, 228–229, 233, 237; strategies for reducing, 113–116, 244–245, 246

Alternative schools, and authority, 249–250

Anderson, James, 23n, 212n

Architecture. *See* Plant

Arrangement of the situation, 98, 101–103, 122, 151–152

Assignments. *See* "Stupid assignment" and other stories of classroom conflict

Attendance, compulsory, 31. *See also* Cutting

Authoritarian teaching style, 36

Authoritarianism, 248–249

Authority, 26–32, 247–254; and classroom interaction, 69–70, 97, 114, 123–126, 141; and conflict in the teacher-student relationship, 122, 123, 126–140, 141–142; defined by students, 73–81, 81, 88, 89–90; defined by teachers, 35–59, 65; and principals, 190–196 *passim*; 199–202 *passim*; and proto-authority, 61, 249

Autonomy. *See* Teachers' autonomy

Bad faith, teachers', 133–136

Barnard, Chester, 29n

Becker, Howard, 112

Behavioral goals, 42–48

Black population of Canton, 7, 9, 10. *See also* Parents

Black students: and adults in the school at large, 212–213, 217; attitudes toward school, 83–84, 85n, 86–88, 104–105, 139, 228–229, 253–254; and crisis, 231, 231–232, 233–237; distribution in tracks, 71–72; and educational goals, 83, 87–88, 252–253; and games of wits, 82, 94–96, 127; number of, 168n; in student social structure, 220–227; and teachers, 94–96, 140, 215, 217. *See also* Low track students; Students' background characteristics

Board of education. *See* Canton school board and administration

Bock, Miss (English teacher), 132–133, 134–136

Bossert, Steven, 67n
Brandt, Mr. (principal of Chauncey),
189–198; choice of goals, 188–191,
211–212; effect on school, 238–239;
and pledge of allegiance, 203–206,
207–209. *See also* Chauncey
Bulletins, school, 193, 217, 234
Bureaucracy. *See* Structure of the schools
Bureaucrat, role of teacher as, 55–56,
76–77, 118, 133, 191

Cafeteria: disorder and, 163, 232, 235;
and faculty relationships, 178, 182
Canton, city of, 6, 7, 9–10
Canton school board and administration:
goals and structure of schools, 25,
143–144, 188–189, 238; and the
problem of order, 25–26, 158–160,
166–167, 238
Canton schools: distinctive characteristics
of, 6, 7–8, 142, 143–144, 237–238
Challenges, students': in the school at
large, 213, 214–215, 240; to teachers
in the classroom, 76–77, 92–97,
126–128, 133–140; variations in
teachers' response to 53, 55–56, 57,
58–59, 62
Character education, 42–48
Chauncey: control of students at, 172–
173, 184–185, 195–198, 208–209,
212–213, 217; and crisis, 230–231,
232–233; faculty culture, 180–186,
212–213, 217; faculty recruitment,
181; history, 9, 174; level of order,
158, 169–171, 184–186; plant, 172;
pledge of allegiance, 203–209; principal, 189–198, 203–209, 211, 238–
239; students' behavior, 183–185,
220–229, 231, 232–233; students'
characteristics, 9, 168, 212–213
Child-centered education. *See* Interests,
students; Non-directive guidance; Progressive education
Child development: teachers' implicit
theories of, 48–53
Children. *See* Students
Classroom activity: in high and low track
classes, 102, 105–107. *See also* High
track classes; Low track classes; Teacher-
student relationship
Classroom management. *See* Control
Coercion: forms of, available in Canton,
61, 100–101; and incompetence,

129–130; and low track students, 108,
131; physical, 61, 66; and proto-
authority, 61
Collective disturbance, 163, 170, 233–
236
College, students' plans toward, 75n, 98
Commitment of students to school goals:
in the classroom, 73–75, 81, 83, 88,
114, 164, 243–245; in the school at
large, 164, 167, 228, 229, 236–237,
244–246
Communication: about disorder, 154,
170–171, 196–197; between principal and teachers, 193, 201; between
students and teachers, 213–214, 216–
218; among teachers at Chauncey, 182,
196–197, 205; among teachers at
Hamilton, 178–180, 209–211
Community. *See* Environment; Parents
Competence. *See* Teachers, competence of
Confidentiality, 170–171, 197, 201
Conflict: and analysis, 12; in the classroom, 66, 107, 121–140; racial, 162–
163, 170, 233–236; among staff members, 21, 66, 192, 198. *See also* Challenges, students'; Disorder; Faculty: factions; Principal-teacher relationship;
Teacher-student relationship
Control: at Chauncey, 172–173, 184–
185, 195–198, 208, 212–213, 217;
in the classroom, 96–97, 105–109,
114; in crisis, 230–232; forms of, 97–
101; in the "good old days," 152–155;
at Hamilton, 152–153, 172–173,
183–184, 214–218; of teachers by
students, 120; of teachers by Mr.
Brandt, 190, 191–195, 197–198,
208, 212–213. *See also* Arrangement of
the situation; Authority; Coercion; Exchange; Influence, personal; Institutionalization of innocence; Myth of coercive
control
Corwin, Ronald G. 15n, 113n, 201n
Creativity. *See* Educational goals; Interests,
students'
Credibility gap, 79, 80
Crisis, 8, 12, 170, 229–237
Cutting, 162; at Hamilton versus Chauncey, 171; and high track students, 75–
76, 164–165, 166–167

Darwin: and crisis, 163, 231n; faculty culture, 110, 180n; history, 9, 154–155,

157, 173; and pledge of allegiance, 203; student characteristics, 9

Dean, 100–101; referral to from classroom, 44–45, 86, 136, 155, 162; referral to, varies with track, race, and sex, 108–109, 162, 256

Defenses, psychological, against failure, 82, 86–88, 103–105, 177, 196–197

Definition of the situation: at Chauncey, 192–195 *passim*, 198, 212–213; in the classroom, 65–66, 120, 123–126, 138–140. *See also* Authority

Department chairmen, 194

Desegregation, 6, 9–11, 173–174, 247. *See also* Racial contact

Detention, 86, 100, 101

Developmental approach: and academic goals, 36–41; and behavioral goals, 42–48; conditions encouraging, 113; in school at large, 163–167, 215–218; and students' role, 48–53; and other teaching philosophies, 65–66; and teachers' role, 53, 56–59. *See also* Developmental teachers

Developmental teachers: in action, 113, 114; and importance of authority, 249; characteristics of, 112, 116–118, 143–144; students' response to, 89–90, 123, 124. *See also* Developmental approach

Discipline. *See* Control; Order

Discretion. *See* Teachers' role

Dismissal, of teacher for physical punishment, 66, 201

Disorder, 121–144 *passim*, 161–162; degree of, 161–162, 169–171; sources of, 148–150, 160–161, 183–185, 196–198, 214–215; visibility of, 170–171, 197, 201. *See also* Challenges, students'; Collective disturbance; Conflict; Order

Dreeben, Robert, 31n

Dumont, Robert V., 105n

Educational goals, 3, 16–17; and authority, 5, 133–140, 249–250; conflict over, 133–140; defined by Mr. Brandt, 190–191; defined by students, 73–76, 84–85, 87, 88, 89; defined by teachers, 36–48, 59–62, 65–66; and desegregation, 6; historical changes in, 3–6; and order in the classroom, 25, 105–110, 141–143; and order in the

school at large, 22–25, 189, 211–212, 237, 238, 243–247. *See also* Order

Environment, 22–26, 158–159, 167, 237–238, 245. *See also* Law; Parents

Etiquette, and institutionalization of innocence, 154

Exchange: as a form of control, 30–31, 98–99, 109, 116–118

Excuse from parents: for political protests, 166; from saying the pledge of allegiance, 208, 209

Expectations. *See* Goals; Students' role; Teachers' role

Expert professional: role of teacher as, 56–57, 76, 118

Expulsion, 101, 155

Extracurricular activities: assignment of teachers to, 191–192

Facilitating leader: role of teacher as, 57–59, 76

Faculty: committees, 192, 194, 203, 206–207; culture, 110, 174–187, 212–218 *passim*; factions, 175–180, 201, 205, 209–211; meetings, 193, 203–205, 209–210; migration, 111–112; socialization, 111–112. *See also* Teachers

Faculty Senate, at Chauncey, 198

Failure, response to: students', 82, 86–88, 103–105; teachers', 104–105, 176–177, 183, 196–197, 212–215; principal and, 195–197, 201

Fairness, 77, 141. *See also* Authority; Legitimacy

Families. *See* Parents

Fights: in the classroom, 46, 162; in the corridors, 158, 162, 163

Flag. *See* Pledge of allegiance

Free schools, 249–250, 253n

Friendliness, teachers', 114; and students' response, 125–126

Future, effects of students' anticipation of, 75, 82, 84–85, 86, 98, 253–254

Games of wits, 82, 94–96, 127

Goals, organizational, 16, 17; conflict among, 18, 24, 25. *See also* Educational goals

Goffman, Erving, 23n, 157n

Gordon, C. Wayne, 120n

Gracey, Harry, 67n

Grade level: studied, 11, 12; effects of, 51–52, 69–70
Grades: as incentives, 31, 98; and high track students, 75, 98

Hamilton: control of students at, 152–153, 172–173, 183–184, 214–218; and crisis, 231–232, 233–237; faculty culture, 111, 175–180, 183–187, 209–211, 214–218; faculty factions, 175, 176–180, 184; faculty recruitment, 174, 175; history, 9, 152–153, 173–174, 176; level of order, 152–153, 169–171, 183–185; plant, 171–172, 178; pledge of allegiance, 209–211; principal, 199–202, 209–211, 216, 238–239; students' behavior, 78, 183–185, 220–229, 231–232, 233–236; students' characteristics, 9, 168
Hargreaves, David, 86n, 111n, 119n
Henley, Mr. (principal of Hamilton), 166, 189, 199–202, 238–239; choice of goals, 189, 199, 212; and crisis, 234, 235; and pledge of allegiance, 209–210. *See also* Hamilton
Herndon, James, 88n, 105n, 149n, 157n
High track classes: challenges to teachers, 76–78, 92, 126–127, 128, 132–136; classroom behavior, 92, 93–94, 96–97, 107, 108; criteria for legitimate classroom authority, 73–81, 126–127, 128, 132–136; teacher-student relationship, 105–108, 123, 125. *See also* High track students; Tracks
High track students: and authority, 249; feelings toward the school, 73–76, 80–81, 83; and research process, 259–261; in the school at large, 220, 227–228. *See also* High track classes
Hiring, 7, 111–112, 174, 181
Historical change. *See* Social change
History of the schools, 9, 152–158 *passim*, 173–174, 176
Hostility, teachers': and students' response, 125–126, 137, 176, 184. *See also* Teacher-student relationship

Incorporative approach: and academic goals, 36–40, and behavioral goals, 42–48; and students' role, 48–53; and teacher's role, 53–57; in relation to other educational philosophies, 65–66. *See also* Incorporative teachers

Incorporative teachers, 111, 143, 163, 175–177; and students' response; 111, 123, 124, 125. *See also* Incorporative approach
Indian students, 105n
Influence, personal, 99, 114, 250
Innovation: and alternative schools, 250–251; and black students, 254; plans for, at Chauncey, 194–195; teachers' desire for, 38
Institutionalization of innocence, 153–154, 156–157, 212–215 *passim.*, 244, 245
Interests, students': black students', 83, 87–88, 252–253; and developmental approach, 36–41, 48–51; 114; and high track students, 73–76, 87–88; and learning, 243–245, 249–252; and traditional education, 3–5, 36–38, 49–51, 74–75, 249–252
Interviews: character of, 12–13, 256–257, 261; in combination with observation, 11, 64–65, 256, 258; discrepancy in teachers' statements during, 179–180; sampling and recruitment for, 11–12, 255–256, 260–261; students' response to, 79n, 228, 260–261; teachers react to students', 213–214. *See also* "Stupid assignment" and other stories of classroom conflict; Wizard's power, interview question granting
IQ: distribution of scores in Canton, 72; and track placement, 70n

King, Martin Luther, assassination of, 163, 170, 229–237

Laissez-faire approach to teaching, 63–65
Law: and cutting, 167; and Mr. Brandt, 193, 203–208 *passim*; and pledge of allegiance, 203–204, 205–206, 207, 208, 210, 211
Leacock, Eleanor Burke, 71n, 106n
Leaders, student, 72–73, 85–86, 220–221, 222–227, 229–237 *passim*
Learning. *See* Commitment of students to educational goals; Educational goals
Legitimacy: of Hamilton faculty, and Black Students Union, 236n; of principal's acts in teachers' eyes, 192–193, 201; of teachers' commands in students' eyes, 126–140, *passim. See also* Author-

ity; Educational goals; Students' role;
Teachers' role

Levels. *See* Tracks

Lewin, Kurt, 119n

Liebow, Elliot, 253n

Lincoln, 9, 110–111, 154–155, 157;
development of faculty culture at, 110–
111; order at, 154–155, 157

Lippitt, Ronald, 119n

Lortie, Dan C., 21n

Lounge: lack of student, 165; teachers'
178, 180n, 182

Low track classes: challenges to teachers
in, 82, 92–93, 127–128, 131–132,
136–137, 137–140; classroom behavior, 93–94, 96–97, 103–105, 108;
criteria for legitimate classroom authority, 81–88, 127–128, 131–132,
136–140; effects of movement of students on, 116; teacher-student relationship in, 102–110; 113–116, 123–
126. *See also* Black students; Low track
students; Tracks

Low track students: defenses from failure,
82, 86–88, 103–104, 105; feelings
toward the school, 81, 83, 228–229;
and research process, 259–261. *See also*
Black students; Low track classes

McCleery, Richard, 23n, 156n

McPherson, Gertrude, 20n

Manipulation, 99–100

Marks, 31, 75, 98

Martin Luther King. *See* King, Martin
Luther

Minority students, 10n, 71, 105n, 168n,
222n. *See also* Black students

Moral order in authority, 26, 27, 28, 35.
See also Educational goals

Myth of coercive control, 155–157,
160–161, 212, 244–245, 247. *See
also* Coercion

Non-directive guidance, 62, 65–66, 67–
68, 118n

Observer effect, 129–131, 213–214,
257–258, 259–260

Ogbu, John, 85n, 111n

Open classrooms, 250–252. *See also* Non-
directive guidance

Order, 17; as a classroom goal, 25, 42,
105–110, 142; versus commitment,

230, 231, 232, 240; and educational
goals, 22–25, 105–107, 109, 189,
190–191, 211–212, 237, 238, 243–
247; effects of students' characteristics
on, 4–5, 6, 173–174, 244–247 (*see
also* High track classes, Low track classes); and faculty culture, 183–187; versus
freedom, 150, 199, 211–212; and principals, 189–190; 211–212, 238–239.
See also Control; Disorder

Oriental population of Canton, 10n

Oriental students, 10n, 71, 168n, 222n

Parent, role of teacher as, 53–54, 76–77,
118, 133–136, 191

Parents: characteristics of, 7, 9, 10; influence on schools, 24–25, 159, 166,
197, 237–238, 261; influence on
students, 75n, 79–81, 260, 261

Peabody, Robert, 28n

Permissive teaching style, 36, 249–250.
See also Non-directive guidance

Philosophy of education. *See* Developmental approach; Incorporative approach; Non-directive guidance; Proto-
authority

Physical punishment, 61, 66, 201

Physical surroundings. *See* Plant

Plant: and faculty culture, 178, 180n,
182; and students, 22, 148–149, 165,
171–172, 246

Pledge of allegiance, 202–211, 216–
217

President of student body, 222–227,
232–236 *passim*

Principal's role, 188–189, 238; defined
by principals, 191–192, 193–194,
199–200; and pledge of allegiance,
205, 208, 210–211. *See also* Brandt,
Mr.; Henley, Mr.

Principal-student relationship, 195–196,
208–209, 212–213, 214, 216

Principal-teacher relationship: at Chauncey, 189, 190–198 *passim*, 203–205,
207–208, 212–213; at Hamilton,
200–201, 209–211, 212

Prisons, compared to schools, 23, 26n,
156n, 157n

Programmed instruction, 124n

Progressive education: and developmental
approach, 37; history of, 4–5. *See also*
Developmental approach; Interests,
students'

Protests. *See* Challenges, students'; Parents: influence on schools
Proto-authority, 59—62; and academic competence, 125; and Canton school district, 67, 143; confused with authority, 248—249; and control in the school at large, 163; students and, 110—111, 123—124, 125; in relation to other teaching philosophies, 65—66
Punishment. *See* Coercion; Myth of coercive control; Rules
Pupils. *See* Students.

Quiet students, 89—90

Racial conflict, 162—163; 170, 233—236
Racial contact: amount of, 8, 71, 162; quality of, 162—163, 220—227 *passim*, 228—229, 230—237 *passim*
Rebellion. *See* Conflict; Disorder
Recruitment of teachers, 7, 111—112, 174—181
Referrals, 12. *See also* Dean
Research: process, 11—14, 255—261; setting, 6—11. *See also* Interviews; Observer effect
Respect, 77, 78
Responsibility: demonstration of, by students, 232, 233—234, 235, 236—237; expectations for, from faculty, 189, 201, 202, 214; expectations for, from students, 164, 167, 202, 215—217; location of, 188—189, 211—212, 214, 238
Retreat, student, 184, 216
Rhea, Buford, 84n
Rist, Ray, 111n
Roles. *See* Principal's role; Students' role; Teachers' role
Rudeness, 78, 227
Rules, 5, 42—48, 151—152

Sampling, 11—13, 255—256, 260
Schedule, 38, 148, 165, 194—195
School board. *See* Canton school board and administration
Schrag, Peter, 84n
Secondary education, contrasted with elementary, 67—68, 250—251
Sergeant, role of teacher as, 61—62, 131
Social change: effect on students, 3—5, 7, 73—74, 79—80, 166—167, 202—203

Social class: in Canton, 10—11; and track placement 71—72
Special classes, 197
Stinchcombe, Arthur, 86n
Strain, 8, 24, 243—247
Structure of the schools, 21—25, 165, 166—167, 211, 244—246
Student body: backgrounds of 7, 168; culture of, 227—229; president, 222—227, 232—236 *passim*; social structure of, 219—227
Students. *See* Alienation of students; Black students; High track students, Interests, students'; Leaders, student; Low track students; Minority students; Quiet students; White students
Students' background characteristics: effects on methods for maintaining order, 153—156, 160; effects on relationships with teachers, 80, 104—105, 212—213; effects on students' attitudes to the school, 83—85, 86—88, 153—156, 253—254; and school goals, 3—5; and tracking, 8—9, 70—73. *See also* Black students; High track students; Low track students; Minority students; White students
Students' role: conflict over, 131—133; defined by principal, 193—197; defined by students, 78—81, 81—83 *passim*, 89; defined by teachers, 48—53, 59—62; effect upon attitude to authority relationships, 30—32; and pledge of allegiance, 202—203, 206—207, 208—209, 209—210; rewards of, 30—32
Student-teacher relationship. *See* Teacher-student relationship
"Stupid assignment" and other stories of classroom conflict: students' responses to 79, 82, 90; teachers' responses to, 54, 55—56, 57, 58
Subject matter, importance of, 37, 40
Subjects, differences among: and high track students' attitudes, 76; and teaching style, 68, 144, 251—252
Subordinate role in authority, 26, 27, 28, 29; Canton students' conception of, 30; special character of public school students', 30—31. *See also* Students' role
Superordinate role in authority, 26, 27, 28. *See also* Principal's role; Teachers role

Supervision outside the classroom, 152, 172–173, 190–191
Suspension, 60, 101, 153
Sykes, Gresham, 23n, 150n

Taylor, Duncan (student body president at Chauncey), 222–225, 226–227
Taylor, Mr. (math teacher), 124, 129–131
Teachers: competence of, 116–120, 125, 126–131; defenses against perceived failure, 104–105, 177, 196–197; philosophy in relation to practice, 49, 179–180, 182, 182–183, 186–187; recruitment of, 7, 111–112, 174, 181; and research process, 129–131, 213–214, 257–259; transfer of, 111–112, 192; union, 200n. *See also* Faculty
Teachers' autonomy, 22, 23; at Hamilton, 199–201, 202, 214, 215
Teachers' role, 22; conflict over, 126–131, 133–140; defined by district administrators, 25–26; defined by principal, 195–196, 199–202 *passim*; defined by students, 76–78, 80, 81–83, 87–88, 89–90; defined by teachers 53–59, 61–62, 65–66. *See also* Bureaucrat; Expert professional; Parent, role of teacher as
Teacher-student relationship, 101–116, 121–140; effect of teacher's personal tone on, 114, 125–126, 131n, 137–140, 176; in high track classes, 74–75, 76–77; in low track classes, 82, 83, 87–88, 104–105; with quiet students, 89
Technology, 18–21, 101–107; and structure of school, 22, 38, 67, 238, 245. *See also* Developmental approach; Incorporative approach; Non-directive guidance; Proto-authority
Theobold, Mrs. (math teacher), 56, 93, 137–140
Therapist, role of teacher as, 62

Tracks: characteristics of students in, 8–9, 70–73; and desegregation, 8, 71; design of, 8, 70; movement between, 116; and participation in student social structure, 220–221, 226–227; students' attitudes towards, 85, 223–226; 233–235; and teachers, 8, 141, 142. *See also* High track classes; Low track classes
Tradition, transmission of, 4, 5, 38, 50
Traditional education, defined by high track students, 74–75
Transfer of teachers, 111–112; compulsory, 192
Trust, 28, 77, 126–127, 250
Truancy. *See* Cutting

Union, teachers', 200n

Values. *See* Educational goals; Interests, students'
Visible students, 72–73, 85–86, 220–221
Volunteer aide: and debate about importance of students' taste, 49–51

Wax, Murray, 105n
Wax, Rosalie, 105n
Weber, Max, 29n
Werthman, Carl, 84n, 88n
White, Ralph K., 119n
White students, 71–72, 94–96, 168n, 220–223. *See also* High track students; Students' background characteristics
Wizard's power, interview question granting: Chauncey versus Hamilton students' responses, 228–229; and low track students, 81–82; and quiet students, 89

Young, Warren (student body president at Hamilton), 223–227, 232, 233, 235, 236n